The Red Sea
Cookbook

Over 100 family recipes and stories from Saudi Arabia

Madeeha Qureshi

Photography Patricia Niven

In loving memory of my late father
and my best friend forever
Gulzar Ahmed Qureshi.
"You will always be in my memories
and I will cherish them,
till we meet again."

THE RED SEA COOKBOOK
Madeeha Qureshi

First published in the UK and USA in 2026 by Nourish, an imprint of Watkins Media Limited
Unit 11, Shepperton House, 83–93 Shepperton Road, London N1 3DF

enquiries@nourishbooks.com

Editorial Director: Ella Chappell
Copy editor: Rebecca Woods
Head of Design & Art Director: Karen Smith
Typesetting: Eleri Stanton
Commissioned Photography: Patricia Niven
Food Stylist: Polly Web Wilson & Bianca Nice
Food Assistant: Susannah Cohen
Photography Assistant: Sam Reeves
Prop Stylist: Julie Patmore
Head of Production: Uzma Taj

A CIP record for this book is available from the British Library
ISBN: 978-1-84899-443-0 (Hardback)
ISBN: 978-1-84899-444-7 (eBook)

10 9 8 7 6 5 4 3 2 1

Typeset in Benguiat Caslon & Cera Pro
Colour reproduction by Rival Colour
Printed in China

The manufacturer's authorised representative in the EU for product safety is:
eucomply OÜ – Pärnu mnt 139b-14, 11317 Tallinn, Estonia, hello@eucompliancepartner.com, www.eucompliancepartner.com

Publisher's note
While every care has been taken in compiling the recipes for this book, Watkins Media Limited, or any other persons who have been involved in working on this publication, cannot accept responsibility for any errors or omissions, inadvertent or not, that may be found in the recipes or text, nor for any problems that may arise as a result of preparing one of these recipes. If you are pregnant or breastfeeding or have any special dietary requirements or medical conditions, it is advisable to consult a medical professional before following any of the recipes contained in this book.

Notes on the recipes
Unless otherwise stated:
Use medium fruit and vegetables
Use medium (US large) organic or free-range eggs
Use fresh herbs, spices and chillies
Use granulated sugar (Americans can use ordinary granulated sugar when caster sugar is specified)
Do not mix metric, imperial and US cup measurements:
1 tsp = 5ml 1 tbsp = 15ml 1 cup = 240ml

nourishbooks.com

Contents

4 Introduction

8 About the Author

11 About the Red Sea

14 Don't Underestimate the Power of the Pantry

22 Small Plates, Big Flavours

68 Salads for Life

90 Reign the Mains

156 Breaking Bread Together

176 A Drizzle of Magic and a Sprinkle of Spice

198 Cakes, Bakes and All Things Great

236 Just in Time for Desserts

268 Cheers to Drinks and All the Hard Work

292 Shukran

295 Index

Introduction

ABOUT THE BOOK

This is my love letter to Saudi Arabia and its people.

The Red Sea Cookbook is driven by commemoration, reconciliation and creativity, tangled with melancholy of the fondest memories and happy times. I have lived through peace, I have lived through war and civil unrest. I have lived through tragedy and happiness, and this book weaves a rich tapestry of stories and recipes celebrating love and life. It is a lifelong ambition reaching its fulfilment. For me, food is a universal language and I have attempted to write this book using it.

This book is a catalogue of a journey that took place through food. It is physical, emotional, nostalgic and, at times, very personal. Events that shaped me into who I am, how I approach food and, most importantly, what I have learned from life through sharing my table and plates of food with others.

Even though this book is written to celebrate life and freedom of spirit through food, there is something far more compelling that has galvanized my inner self to share my love of food and learning, whether growing up in Saudi Arabia (KSA) or travelling across half the world. This is how to have a blissful culinary experience from recipes that took their shape whether in the hour of necessity or crafted out of love and creativity.

The idea behind writing this cookbook is to inspire you to cook different, simple yet luxurious, healthy yet comforting and enjoyable meals from a probably lesser known amalgam of cuisines while being amused and engrossed in little stories from my life. The aim is to encourage you as a reader to go into the kitchen without worry of failure and be proud of what you create using my foolproof recipes, and then share them with your loving families and friends. To me, it is of paramount importance that the recipes and full-on flavours of this book reach the wider world.

So I welcome you to my world of vibrant colours and intensity, condiments and everything thrown in together, totally informal and a complete opposite of any fine-dining experience, a very relaxed approach, something which we all need in life now more than ever. This book is anything but boring. I want you to give these recipes a go and say "OMG, what was that? What did I just taste? Why haven't I had this before? That's some lip-smacking food. Wow, I want more!" Even if you are missing one or two ingredients from a recipe, please don't hesitate to try it.

Come and fall in love with food all over again.

Madeeha xx

کر رہا تھا غم جہاں کا حساب
آج تم یاد بے حساب آئے

I was measuring the pain this world has given me
Today, I longed for you immeasurably

كنت أقيس الألم الذي أعطاني إياه هذا العالم
اليوم، اشتقت إليك بما لا يقاس

Faiz Ahmed Faiz

ABOUT THE AUTHOR

"Study the past, if you would define the future"

Confucius

Let's begin at the beginning then.

In 1981, my family moved to Saudi Arabia when I was a baby. I grew up there, learned a different language – well, quite a few of them to be precise – and made memories for life, which I will carry with me forever, wherever I go.

It all began when my dad went to Saudi Arabia and worked for the Royal Refinery of Yanbu and Jubail in 1978. Later on he joined Aramco briefly. Soon after my birth, we all moved there and for the next 18 years or so, my time spent there defined me as who I am today.

Being the only child of my parents, I had a very lonely childhood, because back then, there were very limited creative activities for girls in a very conservative and patriarchal Arab country, but things changed a lot, and all for good reasons, as I grew up, hence my extraordinary closeness to my dad. He was my best friend for life.

My obsession with food in general, and Saudi ingredients in particular, started early. I precociously started cooking when I was about 8, having a play around with fragrant spices like cardamom and molasses of all sorts, be it pomegranate or dates or grapes. My mother lost count of how many dresses I ruined in order to feed my curiosity.

Baking simple Victoria sponges with passionfruit buttercream was another craze that I had, with passionfruit seeds flying all over the kitchen cabinets. All these influences that came into my very early cooking were from Dad's expat friends, who came from almost every corner of the world to the coastline of the Red Sea, where I witnessed the true meaning of diversity and diffusion of world culinary influences.

As I grew a bit older, the crevasse between the Middle Eastern countries began to emerge, or maybe I started to understand the bitter reality a little bit more. When the Gulf War (1990–1991) broke out, things changed quite dramatically for people living an otherwise very subtle Bedouin lifestyle. From abundance to rationing and back to abundance in a very short time span. There were curfews, and life became dire for the working class in a matter of days. But people across all walks of life came together, opening their hearts and homes to those in need, and the situation started to improve a lot quicker than anticipated.

Once the war was over, there was a sudden surge of American food chains, food products and retail stores. The pace of life changed almost overnight. It was a stamp on life that left its mark. Things were never the same again. Saudi Arabia embraced the change and was on the verge of becoming modernized in line with the rest of the world at lightning speed.

When I came to the UK in 2007, I had to cook for myself as money was tight and I never liked to rely on takeaways anyway. No offence, but I always thought I cooked better than a takeaway. That was the time when all those bitter-sweet memories from my childhood in KSA and travelling abroad came to life again and I started recreating those colourful, bold and punchy flavours with the best of British produce, putting them on a plate for me, my friends and housemates to enjoy. That's why I never felt homesick, because I always carried the fragrant memories of my loved ones with me. I found my new home here.

For me, time and food have one commonality: they are never static. Just like time, food keeps on ever-evolving, firmly holding on to its roots in the distant history while breathing out new hopes of a brighter, more tranquil and fairer future. For me, food is beyond any discrimination of caste, creed, colour and culture. It is irrespective of perceived differences. It has this incredible ability to bring people together from all walks of life.

It was that one immense driving force to display my accumulated knowledge spanning three decades, and the little precious memories attached to them, that compelled me to become part of MasterChef UK and provided me with the confidence to pen down those recipes that have been confined in the four chambers of my heart up till now.

My culinary journey so far has been nothing less than a metamorphosis of cultural integration. The Saudi cuisine I showcased to the world through the camera lens for the very first time holds many untold layers of significance for me.

The inspiration behind this book came from the desire to share the diverse Saudi cuisine as I know and love it, whether inherited or learned first-hand. I am not trying to make my food look like a garden here. My efforts are to present myself and my well-fused cuisine with honour and respect, which I showcased on the TV, even though it was only a glimpse, leaving the audience asking for more. This book is a humble but very proud presentation of the vibrancy, diversity, the depth of what Middle Eastern and Saudi food is to me. It's an attempt to show that food has this incredible power to transport you to places without physically being there, and during these unpredictable times, this is the best we can do.

There is a common misconception about Saudi food for being too meaty, too bland, too beige or boring. In fact it's the polar opposite. It is thriving with life; it's zingy, zesty and offers a riot of flavours in every mouthful. You are about to experience it in this book. I promise.

Lastly, I would like to mention that this book is written in loving memory of my dad, who I refer to as "Aba Jan" in my recipes and background stories, alongside some very generous people from all walks of life in Saudi Arabia. It pays homage to the boundless laughter, floods of tears, the hard times and the good times. To the dreams of my mystic Arab ancestors and to the diverse future that is yet to come.

Me and Aba Jan,
cable car/chair lift ride,
Murree, Pakistan

"What you seek is seeking you"
Rumi

ABOUT THE RED SEA
(Places where I grew up)

Geologically ancient, biblical and strategically located, the Red Sea has been serving as a trade route since the dawn of civilization. Pharaohs once ruled its harbours; prophets crossed its waters; Roman and Ottoman empires traced its coastlines. Saudi Arabia shares the largest Red Sea coastline stretch with a 92-island archipelago in the north and the Farasan islands in the south. Today, freighters, sea surfers and fishing boats share the rides with its enchanting bottlenose dolphins and passing whales.

YANBU

In the swaying breeze of the Red Sea, nestling on Saudi Arabia's western shore lies Yanbu – a suburban town where time seems to ebb and flow with the tide.

To a traveller, Yanbu is a city of paradoxes. It is both ancient and modern, a place where oil refineries look over the old town's coral stone walls that were once sourced from the bed of the Red Sea. The scents of salty air and diesel dance together, a reminder that this city bears the weight of both history and industrialization.

The best meals are served in the most modest of the eateries and shacks with plastic chairs, right on the beachside. The fish is fresh, caught on the day, and the flavours are honest, clean and crisp. You taste the sea itself, and something more: the life around it.

But for me, it is my earliest memories of freshly caught salty water fish and the drama of seeing it prepared there and then in the local fish market. The sound of fishermen auctioning their catch at the highest timbre of their voice, that will live on with me for the rest of my life. Yanbu, I miss you.

My whole universe in 1984, lost now

JEDDAH

I grew up in Jeddah, in the district of Balad and Kandarah (which have now become a UNESCO heritage site). Running alongside children from my neighbourhood, through the old cobbled streets with wooden lattice terrace windows leaning towards each other on both sides of the street, like two elder ladies sharing secrets. Calling out the street hawkers, whom we knew by name, sometimes to buy Baleela or Ta'miyyah, sometimes just the little cuckoo's eggs, and sometimes just to say hello.

The scent of oud and spice in the neighbouring Bab Makkah still lingers around in my senses. Yes, I have a habit of sniffing spices and anything that makes me feel at home.

Bab Makkah, which literally means "door to Makkah" (Mecca) is located at the old sea port in Jeddah. That is why to me Jeddah is not just a port, it is a portal, a gateway to the holy city of Makkah. It is the city of eternal transit. Year-round, pilgrims from all over the world pass through this city on their sacred journeys, but they never forget the warmth and hospitality of its people. The locals regard pilgrims as the guests of Allah.

Then there is Corniche, a ribbon-like stretch along the Red Sea shore, lined with sculpture gardens, cafés, shopping complexes and the restless sparkling deep blue sea. A place where I went every weekend, for a stroll with Aba Jan, for a picnic or just to watch tiny little crabs climbing up the rocks.

In Jeddah, nowadays, with all the development and modernization, a skyscraper might stand beside a crumbling coral wall, and neither feel out of place. Jeddah, you will always live in me.

Beit Al Sharbatly Al-balad

An old plastered wall baring directions to Al Kandarah and Al Balad (the two places where I have fondest memories)

A mosque on Jeddah Corniche sea front

Jeddah sea front, Corniche stretch aka Al Shatti

Aba Jan enjoying cola and mutabbaq at Yanbu sea front sitting on his Mazda 626 bonnet

Me aged 3 on holiday at Farasan Islands

My 4th birthday

JAZAN & THE FARASAN ISLANDS

We will talk about Jazan and its beauty later on in the book.

Just off the beautiful city of Jazan lie the Farasan Islands, the tourist destination of my childhood, when shorelines were fairly concrete-free. Where the sea kissed the sky endlessly as if they were lovers.

Farasan Islands is a sun-drenched island archipelago of Saudi Arabia in the southern Red Sea. The air is thick, warm, balmy and briny. It smells exactly how a sea should smell: crisp, clean and marine.

The sea here is unimaginably clear, of a deep sapphire colour. The water is so clear that bright red and orange-coloured coral reefs can be seen from a distance, as if the divine force of nature has attempted to paint this sea in its brightest tones.

The *Fidjeri*-style folk songs of the pearl divers and fishermen still echo in my ears. These islands are not crowded. Very few people live here. They have been living here for as long as time remembers. Life is very simple, and the locals are very passionate about their culture and fishery.

I still have some sea shells from my childhood breakaways at Farasan Islands, hidden away somewhere in the attic, as a reminder of the majesty of this calm place.

The Holy Ka'aba, Makkah

Spice market, Jeddah

Masjid Shuhada, battlefield of Uhud, Madinah

DON'T UNDERESTIMATE THE POWER OF THE PANTRY

Welcome to the realms of my kitchen Narnia. It is a secret portal to hidden flavours where I keep all of my most valuable belongings – yes, all my preserved potions, herbs, spices and condiments that are very precious to me.

My pantry is a bit of an Alice in Wonderland situation. It is small, tucked away in my cosy garage with a small windowsill wide enough to house my tiny kitchen/herb garden and a small fridge-freezer unit. It houses all the bare essentials and a few staples worth investing in, from flours to canned and jarred condiments. You don't need to be rich or have a lot of space to have a pantry; it exists in the nooks of your kitchen and will keep expanding in your imagination.

My tiny pantry unleashed its powers when we hit the dreaded Covid-19 lockdown and the shelves of supermarkets went bare. I turned to my pantry, which I had kept naturally restocked, an inherent habit that paid off when we were able to enjoy and share warm, hearty and nutritious meals for a good few weeks before things began to normalize. I even prepared my audition dish for MasterChef from the scrapings of my pantry, which allowed me fly through the auditions.

Now, to put your mind to ease, all of the ingredients along with their substitutes (where necessary) in this book are readily available. Most of them can be found in pretty much any grocery store. A few you may have to source from your local Asian/Arab/Turkish/Middle Eastern shops or buy online, but they are well worth the buck.

I recommend, before you go and completely revamp your kitchen pantry, that you take a gradual approach: have a look at the recipes you fancy making and go through the list of ingredients first. See where you can make a start with the ingredients to hand. But if you can't find a particular ingredient, please don't hold yourself back from trying a recipe.

I usually don't create recipes with a laundry list of expensive ingredients because, as a working mother of three, I neither have that much spare time nor the deep pockets to pull off that kind of dish myself!

Listed below are a few staple ingredients, handy pots, pans and condiments which you can find in my kitchen pantry; it doesn't mean that you must have them, it's just a glimpse into what I use often. Please feel free to experiment with unfamiliar flavours.

Bread

First things first, let's talk about bread. I need bread – to mop up stews; and the buttery juices flowing from meat, as a boat to swim through hummus and dips, but also to soak up the tears and sorrows of life, and everything else in between. Bread is basic. Bread is sustenance. Bread is life. Don't run away from it; be friends with it.

"Breaking bread together" is a significant phrase of honour among the Arab Bedouins even to this day. To break bread is an unbreakable bond, so much so that they can't have animosity towards the person with whom they have shared their bread.

No matter what the occasion is, there is always bread on my table. I like to make my own bread from scratch when I have time, whether it's Khobz/Pitta (page 166), Taftaan, Simit, Roti or Naan (page 160) bread, but you can use store-bought as well. There are a few handy bread recipes in this book.

Eggs, mighty eggs

How would I have survived without eggs in my student years? A massive thank you to all those chickens for laying gorgeous bundles of joy for me. Always buy good free-range eggs, because free-range eggs are happy eggs laid by happy and free chickens. Keep them in the fridge if it's warm in your pantry, and please – for the love of God or whoever you believe in – always respect the use-by date.

Milk & yogurt

Always buy full-fat because fat is flavour, my darlings, and a life without flavour is no life. I see no point in a 0% fat Greek yogurt; for me these two things don't exist together, but that's my very personal opinion. (You can substitute dairy products as per your preference for any recipe throughout the book, unless otherwise stated.)

Say cheese!

Things that bring a smile to your face are good (unless you are intolerant to them, in which case, I am sorry.) Comte and Manchego have my heart. Parmesan is just overrated, frankly speaking. Sliced cheddar is my lot's best friend and there is always a pack or two in the fridge. Textured fruity cheeses are for the dinner party cheese board. I use a mix of Turkish, Palestinian and Lebanese cheeses for sweet and savoury fillings, mezzes and salads (feta, akawi, peniyr, kaval twisted or braided cheese.)

Once cheese is opened, make sure you have clean and dry hands when storing them and keep them in a sterilized airtight container in the fridge or somewhere cooler away from sunlight. They have a vampire nature to go bad, but following simple precautions as mentioned above enhances their shelf life.

Butter

Trust me, it's worth buying a really, really good quality butter or – even better – churning your own if you have spare time to hand. I have to confess that I have a lifelong love affair with whipped soft, creamy white butter when it is spread generously on a slice of bread. It makes everything look promising. It gives you hope that everything will be alright and it's not the end of the world yet.

If there is one thing that has been a source of absolute comfort in my life, from little brawls to the darkest of times when I hit the rock bottom of my soul, when everything seemed to be doom and gloom, it is the humble Saudi sandwich, which is made up of a baguette-shaped bread known as *samooli* (a cross between a brioche and a sausage roll) smothered with salted butter and dolloped with a special kind of Watermelon Pith Jam (see page 197). Take a bite into it and, all of a sudden, life becomes worth living.

I survived my student years on this sando, wrapped in paper towel, running from one platform to another on the busy London Underground. Or, as a child, sneaking my hand out of the duvet to grab one that my dad had lovingly left for me next to my bed while we were not on talking terms just because I was mad at him for one thing or another.

Glee of ghee

There is an exultant joy when this liquid gold hits the hot pan along with vibrant spices and herbs. The bags of aroma released are simply unparalleled. Ghee has always been the preferred medium for cooking in the Arabian Peninsula and South Asia. It is considered a symbol of purity and good health. It adds flavour, it adds life. That is why it is considered the food of gods. I won't delve into the scientific nitty gritty of its health benefits. For me, anything made with ghee and love always tastes better. In Arabic it's called *samn*.

Sugar

I do use a wide range of sugar, depending upon my mood and also what the recipe calls for. White granulated sugar is used for most cookies, pavlovas and fancy bakes; brown sugar for cosy loaf cakes; and dark muscovado sugar for that ultimate treacly, almost smoky decadence.

Sea salt

For me it has to be Maldon, end of story. Just look at the giant prism-like crystals, a thing of beauty and a joy forever. I happen to sprinkle it on just about anything I eat. In my recipes, salt is always to taste.

Flour

I think I have lost count of how many kinds of flour I have used in my lifetime. But in my current pantry it is mostly plain flour (Turkish-branded plain flour is the best), refined wheat flour aka Indian maida, white chapatti flour, wholemeal flour, rice flour, chickpea flour/besan for pakora/batter, and cornflour.

Sumac & za'atar

BFFs. These spices are the best things that ever happened to the Arab and Levantine food scene, in my highly opinionated opinion (after olive oil, of course). Za'atar is a flavour bomb exploding with the earthiness of thyme, the citrusy tang of sumac and the warmth of toasted sesame seeds. Sumac is woody, lemony, wild and mouth-puckeringly sour. It brings out the inherent Arab flavours in a way akin to salt. It's a spice and a condiment at the same time. My favourite go-to brands are Zaytoun and Yaffa, both easily available on both sides of the Atlantic.

Olive oil and other oils

I absolutely love the unique peppery taste of Palestinian early-harvest olive oil. Oh, please don't politicize olive oil even though food is and always has been political. The second best for me is Greek olive oil.

I suggest curating your own oil collection. For example, I use early-harvest, cold-pressed olive oil sometimes infused with herbs, garlic and chillies, to generously drizzle on my salads and dips, whereas mild or lightweight olive oil is used for bread-making and cakes.

For deep frying and searing, it has to be refined oil due to its higher smoking point, and it crisps up the batter better than other oils (It is also way cheaper).

Canned or jarred vegetables, fruits, dried grains and beans of all sorts

These are lifesavers in the hour of need and for difficult days. There are good brands available in the market that won't break the bank. Chuck a jar of roasted red peppers and some sun-dried tomatoes with some walnuts and some seasonings in a blender and you have a finger-licking Muhammara dip (page 218) ready in a jiffy if you are too peevish to leave the house.

Tinned tuna, anchovies, mackerel and crab meat

These are little wonders of nature in a tin. There is nothing fishy about tinned fish, just bang-on umami flavour. Great for sandwiches, dressings and quick-fix delicious nutrient-packed salads. When I was a child I was notorious for eating tuna straight out of a tin and then putting the empty tin back in the storecupboard to be found later by my mother.

Chillies of all sorts

Fresh, powdered, pickled or paste, there's an array of chillies that I use in my day-to-day cooking. From fruity, aromatic and bright Aleppo pepper flakes (pul biber) to dark red chilli flakes (gochugaru) for sprinkling/ seasoning breakfasts and dips; to chilli powders of varying strengths for spicing up curries; to biber salcasi (Turkish pepper paste) for marinades and for flavouring gravy bases.

Citrus

Next comes the mighty lemon or lime, or both. I have to admit that I have a crush on lemons, and I do use quite a lot in my recipes, whether fresh, pickled, zested, dried, in curd form, or juiced to the last drop. There is always a lemon or two sitting and slightly going off at the bottom of my fridge. Don't worry, if they become a little rusty or soggy, they should still be fine to use.

Garlic

And then comes the glorious garlic. To be honest, I can't envisage a Mediterranean or Middle Eastern dish without garlic – that's just not natural to me. So buy the fattest bulbs of garlic and don't throw the sprouted ones. Sow them in a pot and leave it on your window sill or in your greenhouse if you have one. Wait a few days and watch the magic.

Fresh ginger

It may sound rude, but I just can't understand the logic behind vigorously rubbing the back of a spoon against a piece of ginger to peel it, all while pulling all sorts of weird faces. The scene is an eyesore to me.

To peel a piece of ginger, take a paring knife (or a butter knife if you are too scared) and gently scrape the skin of the ginger; it peels off right away. No need to be violent. It is just a piece of ginger for God's sake. Catharsis done, rant over.

On another note, ginger is one of the must-have ingredients that lives happily in my fridge. I use it throughout the day, from my glass of morning hot water to the garnishing of my meals. It's woody, fiery, zingy and earthy, just like me.

Onions

One ingredient that I would suggest not to be rushed while cooking is onions. If a recipe requires the browning of onions, do it on a slow to medium flame. It will take 15–20 minutes to brown properly, but it's extremely crucial not to rush it at this initial stage, because this will build up the base of flavour. Brown onions are for cooking, green or spring onions/scallions for stir fries, red onions/shallots for pickling and salads.

Rice

A versatile grain that lives in my pantry.

Basmati rice, where would I be without you? I can't emphasize enough the importance of the quality and aging of basmati rice, but equally the right technique to cook basmati rice is also crucial for the fluffy end result.

Basmati rice is divided into two main types. The first is aged long-grain basmati rice commonly used as plain boiled rice or pulao/pilav. The second one is **sella basmati rice** aka golden par-boiled basmati rice, which sometimes has a specific identification code (1121) on its packaging. Basically, this is an extra-long hybrid variety of basmati rice that has been treated, par-boiled while still in its husk, and then milled for a sturdier structure and enhanced taste. Due to this toughening process, sella basmati is the go-to choice for biryani, Lahm al Mandi, Saudi Kabsa, my Carrot Rice and my all-time favourite Jewelled Rice (see pages 104, 124, 168 and 169).

To make a perfect batch of fluffy sella basmati rice, wash the rice at least 3–4 times until the water runs clear and then let it soak for at least 45 minutes in tepid water. Season boiling water with plenty of salt and add a couple of teaspoons of white vinegar before adding the rice. Once the rice is in the boiling water, cook for around ten minutes on high heat. Keep checking the grains and when they reach al dente stage (90% cooked), the rice is ready to drain and use as per the recipe. You will end up with the fluffiest rice of your dreams.

Risotto rice is not only used for risotto in my home but also for rice puddings, kheer, kedgeree and as stuffing for dolma, aka Kubiybat al Ha'il (page 106), courgettes, peppers, etc.

Frozen vegetables

The best plan B. If you see a real bargain or a reduction on fresh fruits and vegetables, grab them. Chop them up or purée them – whatever you like – and freeze them for unexpected times ahead.

Hummus, which literally means chickpeas in Arabic

This one deserves a whole chapter to be written in its honour and that's exactly what I have done (see pages 46–53)

Honey

I love you.

Dates

It seems unfair not to showcase dates in a separate section when this book is about the world's largest date palm producer. So you will find a few date recipes in this book.

Pomegranates

This fruit exists in my earliest memories. I have ruined countless dresses, along with my mother's white marble worktops, feeding my curiosity to discover how many seeds there are in a pomegranate! I have grown old and have become a mother but still haven't found the answer to my burning question. Nevertheless, I generously load my food with these sparkling rubies. They make anything look pretty on a plate.

**"Guarded treasure,
honeycomb partitions,
richness of flavour,
pentagonal architecture.
The rind splits: the seeds fall –
Crimson seeds in azure bowls..."**

ANDRÉ GIDE, "THE LAY OF THE POMEGRANATE", *FRUITS OF THE EARTH*

Molasses: date, pomegranate, grape & carob

Each to their own, but I love all of them. They make boring salads and bland meals edible. Just use the right one at the right place at the right time and you will be in culinary heaven. They also last for ages as long as they are kept away from direct sunlight, just like olive oil and vampires.

Saffron

The symbol of culinary luxury. Take good care of it and keep it somewhere safe. Use it when you want to create some magic and wow factor. It's worth more than its weight in gold – though I only buy saffron and not gold (unless it's in edible form!). Please don't buy cheap saffron; it's not saffron and it doesn't taste of anything other than a cheap food dye.

Nigella seeds or black cumin

There is a sense of beauty and spirituality to nigella seeds. They are called *Habat al Baraka* in Arabic, which translates to "Blessed seeds". They are highly regarded in prophetic medicine and very generously used in both savoury and sweet dishes, pickles and breads across Arab and South Asian countries.

Spices

Apart from the above, I have a very few basic day-to-day spices in my kitchen cupboard. I don't have any fancy racks, just small jars that usually fit in about 100–150g/3½–4oz of ground spice. I usually buy my spices in large bags from Asian grocery stores, an absolute bargain. Then I transfer them into these tiny little jars so they are handy to use in my kitchen without spilling. Any leftover spices go in a zip-lock bag and into the darkest, deepest pit of my pantry to retain their freshness.

**"Concerning the spices of Arabia
let no more be said.
The whole country is scented with them,
and exhales an odour marvellously sweet"**

HERODOTUS

I mostly use **Kashmiri chilli powder** for colour, as it's very mild, **red chilli** powder for more Asian-style curries and marinades, sweet and smoky **paprika** for Arab and North African cuisine, and **pul biber** aka Aleppo pepper for more Middle Eastern and Turkish dishes.

Turmeric, the gold dust – where possible I try to source organic. Once you get your hands on it, you will see the difference. It not only adds a glow to your dishes but it is also a powerful anti-inflammatory natural healer. So it's a must-have in my kitchen and first-aid box. A heat patch made with equal amounts of turmeric powder and coarse salt instantly levels out any bumps, brings down a swelling and soothes the affected area. Very handy when you have football- and rugby-crazy kids who come home with these frequently.

Cumin and coriander, partners in (flavour) crime. How can my bipolar Arab/Asian personality even think of cooking without these two? One is naughty and nutty and the other is grounded with its earthy notes. Cumin is versatile and pungent; if there is one spice I toast religiously, it's cumin. Roasting draws out the nutty flavour. I could easily rename this book *Just Add Cumin*. When in doubt, sprinkle some cumin. Coriander was once a prized commodity in Ancient Egypt. So much so it was found in Tutankhamun's tomb. Fresh coriander leaves taste greener, grassier than the seeds, the latter with a nuttier flavour. If using fresh coriander, aka cilantro, save the stalks! The main flavour is locked there.

Cardamom, a quintessential part of our Silk Route DNA. Green cardamom is held in the same reverence, if not more, in Arab/Asian cuisine as vanilla pods are in French cooking. It is used in both savoury and sweet concoctions.

Always buy whole cardamom pods as green as possible and grind them fresh when needed, to get as much flavour as possible. Keep them in an airtight jar in a dark and cold place.

Cinnamon, the aromatic, sweet, enchanting stick. I can't leave it out of my meals. I'm not sure who is the best contender for the first position in spices when it comes to Saudi food. Is it cardamom or is it cinnamon? I leave it down to you.

Bay leaves, floral, subtle, leathery, woody and considered to be divine. Bay leaves are also known as laurel leaves, an honour leading to their use in laurel wreaths once worn by the Roman gods and emperors. So please do give them the respect they deserve. I have a tiny bay tree in a clay pot that sits majestically in a corner of my garden.

Lavender, I have 5 little bushes of them: floral, minty, woody and ethereal.

Rose water, delicate, musky, perfumed – and no it doesn't smell like grandma's bathroom if used properly. There are no substitutes for rose water; it is a very definitive flavour.

Loomi, the dried lemon, star of Arab cooking if I say so myself. Dried and wizened, the size of a walnut, hiding a world of complex, bitter, musky and citrusy flavours. In order to extract maximum flavour out of this ping pong-sized ball, pierce it with a sharp paring knife or a skewer to release the flavours. These can easily be ground in a spice grinder or pestle and mortar.

Black pepper, always whole peppercorns, crushed as and when needed.

Tamarind, another diverse ingredient that integrated into every single country it touched on the Silk Route of trade. Its role in Saudi cuisine is no different. A much-loved potent, sour, fruity, sweet, tart and fudgy date-like flavour genie. I suggest buying a block of tamarind pulp and making your own tamarind paste rather than using store-bought as it's laden with salt.

Herbs, nuts, seeds, dried fruits and all other important things

that I use are grouped in this section. To be honest, I could write an entire book on just the ingredients in my pantry and why they are important to me, but I don't want you to get intimidated, so here is a list of other ingredients that I will be frequently using in this book.

I use both fresh and dried herbs on a daily basis. Keep fresh herbs wrapped in a paper bag and they will last a fortnight easily.

Always respect the expiration dates for nuts, buy them in small amounts and keep them in airtight containers, as they have a tendency to go rancid quickly, especially in humid conditions.

- Mint
- Parsley
- Basil
- Chives
- Dill
- Almonds
- Cashews
- Wild rocket/arugula
- Walnuts
- Pistachios
- Pecans
- Garlic granules
- Dried onion
- Jumbo raisins
- Dried apricots
- Shredded coconut
- Vanilla bean paste
- Mixed seeds/char maghaz
- Bicarbonate of soda/baking soda
- Baking powder
- Dried lemon and lime
- Tahini (both OG and black)
- Gum arabic/goondh kathira
- Kewra (kadi/screwpine) water
- Dried cherries and cranberries
- Pakistani pine nuts (long ones look pretty)
- Instant coffee and unroasted coffee beans
- Sesame seeds, both white roasted and black
- Vinegar: white, apple, balsamic and Moroccan
- Homemade shatta (Middle Eastern hot sauce) and amba sauce
- Middle Eastern and Pakistani pickles (cucumber, turnips, carrots, mango etc.)

Pots, pans and everything in between

I won't say you must have all of these to start cooking my recipes but I will just share a list of the fiddly things and gadgets I had when I started living on my own in a tiny studio in London. I had:

- A big knife (cleaver style)
- A small paring knife
- A chunky chopping board
- A couple of pots of different sizes with lids
- A large frying pan that worked as a wok as well
- A roasting tin
- A cake tin
- A silicone spatula
- Scales
- A couple of bowls, big and small
- A pestle and mortar
- Nylon sieves
- A hand blender (life saver)
- Tongs
- A few napkins
- Measuring spoons and cups
- A peeler
- A juicer

Small plates, big flavours

There are so many topics in this book that I could absolutely write a whole book about: all-day breakfasts are one of them. I will keep it short and sweet for now. The title of this chapter says it all. In Saudi Arabia and much of the Arab world, we don't do starters as such. We make pretty little plates of flavourful food, lots of them, and mop up the delicious detritus with warm, toasty pitta.

You can either make my pitta bread recipe (page 166) or buy thin Lebanese khobz/pitta bread. The rest of the thick, slabby pittas are, as I class them, an abominable grief.

We eat these all-day starters at any time of the day. No rules, as and when your heart desires. The recipes in this section are plentiful, as this is what I cook day in day out. Or when I don't want to cook, this is what I cook. They are very close to my heart, and they are cherished and loved by my friends and family. The British audience fell in love with Mutabbaq (page 38) when I made it on MasterChef UK. That immense love and appreciation led me to write this book.

Then there is Baleela (page 34), simple but punchy. Baleela consists of warm chickpeas floating in a pool of ruby-red, tangy and spicy aquafaba, topped with a freshly made cucumber and beetroot pickle and dusted with ground cumin, sumac and a touch of hot shatta (a Middle Eastern hot sauce).

In recent years, musabaha has become known as the rough-sleeping cousin of the sophisticated hummus to help the western world understand what it is all about. But I categorize Musabaha (page 37) as the grandad of dips, because I think it is where hummus might have originated.

Hummus and Ta'miyyah (pages 46–53 and 58) deserve a whole chapter to themselves, and you will know why once you read it.

There are a couple of soul-warming traditional soups in this chapter. Shorba Adas (page 33) is a classic lentil soup enjoyed throughout the Middle East and central Asia. Every country and every family has their own version. It is a flavoursome meat-free, quick and easy winter warmer for those long dark chilly evenings, often enjoyed with a piece of toasted bread or pitta croutons or simply on its own. A soup for me is a little bowl of calm. I season my soups as the mood takes me.

Then there is something for a quick BBQ nibble, which can be done on the stovetop: the Dirty BBQ Corn with loads of dukkah (page 29) and Kammouneh-infused Grilled Chicken Livers (page 41). Madinian Buffs (page 26) are little morsels of love. And the list goes on.

Please make them, all of them, for yourself and your loved ones.

MADINIAN BUFFS
(*Buff* is an Arabic corruption of the English word puff)

These firm family favourites are bite-sized savoury parcels with crinkly edges that are usually a centrepiece at the Saudi Iftar table during Ramadan. As the buff fries, it balloons up and looks like a fluffy pillow with a crispy exterior and a steamy, slightly stretchy thin pastry inside, and a filling that rattles around.

Madinian Buffs were originally made using a rich beef and egg filling but, as time evolved, fillings have changed and diversified. These days beef can be substituted with chicken, lamb, just eggs or even feta. As always, these little crispy puffy yum-yums are served with the classic three supporting condiments: jajeek, shatta and daqqus. Simply make a little hole in the puff and tip in your choice of sauce. I dare you to resist the temptation of putting the whole thing in your mouth in one go. That's what I do; not really sophisticated but, hey, it doesn't has to be if it brings joy to your life.

INGREDIENTS:

- 500g (1lb 2oz/3¾ cups) plain (all-purpose) flour, plus extra for dusting
- 20g (¾oz) salt
- 2 tbsp melted ghee
- ¼ tsp baking powder
- 275ml (9½fl oz/scant 1¼ cups) tepid water
- 1 large egg, beaten
- Sunflower or vegetable oil, for greasing the bowl and deep frying
- Shatta (see page 195) and/or Zhoug (see page 192), to serve

For the filling:

- 2 tbsp neutral cooking oil
- 300g (10½oz) lean minced (ground) beef
- 1 onion, very finely chopped
- ½ tsp Baharat spice mix or ground allspice
- A pinch of roasted ground cumin
- 1 tsp onion powder
- 20g (¾oz) flat leaf parsley, finely chopped
- 10g (⅓oz) coriander (cilantro) leaves, finely chopped
- 10g (⅓oz) chives, finely chopped
- 2 hard-boiled eggs, roughly mashed or grated
- Salt and freshly ground black pepper

Makes 48

Start with the dough. Into the bowl of a stand mixer or a mixing bowl, tip the flour, followed by salt, ghee, baking powder, water and egg. Using the hook attachment, knead it for about 6–8 minutes, or knead by hand in the mixing bowl for 10–12 minutes, until the dough starts to come together.

Transfer the dough to a greased bowl, cover with cling film (plastic wrap) and leave to rest for 1 hour.

While the dough rests, prepare the filling. In a frying pan on a medium–high heat, heat the oil, then add the beef and cook for about 5–7 minutes, or until the meat browns and there is no liquid left in the pan.

Add the onion and sauté for 1–2 minutes, then add the Baharat spice mix, cumin and onion powder, season with salt and pepper, and sauté for further minute.

Once it's all fragrant, add all of the herbs and the grated eggs. Mix well off the heat and let it cool down completely.

Tip the dough onto a floured work surface and divide it into four equal-sized balls. Cover them and let them rest for another 10 minutes.

One by one, roll out each ball into a sheet that is thin enough for you to see your hand beneath it – about 2mm (1/16 inch) thick. Trim the irregular edges so that you can have a neat square or a rectangle (no need to be too precise).

Now, using a measuring ½ tablespoon as a guide, place small mounds of filling over half of the sheet, leaving equal gaps between them and with enough space around the filling to be able to cut 5cm (2-inch) square parcels, like ravioli.

Wet your fingers with water and gently dab the dough around the filling – this will help seal the parcels.

Now cover the filling mounds with the other half of the dough sheet and press gently between each mound of filling to seal. Using a pinwheel pastry or pizza cutter (the one with crinkle effect is a must for this recipe to give it the exact traditional look) cut 5 × 5cm (2 × 2-inch) squares. Repeat to use up all the filling and pastry – you should get about 48 pastries. (The buffs can be frozen at this stage for up to 2 months.)

For frying, fill a deep saucepan or deep-fat fryer around halfway up with oil and heat to around 170–180°C (325–350°F). Check if the oil is hot enough by adding a small piece of dough – if it rises to the surface immediately, we are good to go with the frying.

Working in batches of 3–4 at a time, place the buff parcels into the oil and press them down gently for 30 seconds with a slotted spoon – don't let them float at this stage or they will not puff up and create that little dome we are after. Once puffed up, turn them over and fry until golden. This whole process should take 2 minutes.

Scoop them out onto paper towels and let any excess oil drain while you cook the remaining buffs.

Plate up and serve with your favourite condiments.

DIRTY BBQ CORN WITH LOOMI AND MADINIAN DUKKAH

I love a fresh whole corn on the cob charred over an open fire pit with the sweet milky juices spitting out of the kernels as they come in contact with flames. But I don't just stop there with a simple butter lamination – I always wanted more. More flavour – the messier, the tastier – and I absolutely can't live without Madinian Dukkah. I literally sprinkle it on anything and everything, so I thought why not combine my beloved items together? I don't even want to *try* having a corn on the cob any other way.

Try it for yourself and let me know what you think!

INGREDIENTS:

- 1 whole black loomi (dried lime)
- 4 corn on the cobs, husks removed if using fresh
- 4 tsp unsalted butter, softened

For the dirty dredge:

- 1½–2 tbsp mayonnaise
- 2 tbsp spreadable cream cheese (I use Primula Original)
- 1 fat clove of garlic, crushed
- 1 spring onion (scallion), very finely chopped
- A sprinkle of fine sea salt and black pepper

For topping:

- 2 tbsp Madinian Dukkah (see page 187)
- ½ tsp pul biber (Aleppo pepper flakes) or normal chilli flakes
- 1 tbsp chopped chives (or the green part of spring onions/scallions)

Serves 4

★V

Start by preparing the dirty dredge. In a bowl, mix together all of the dredge ingredients, then set aside.

Now crush the black loomi with the palm of your hand on a work surface; it will break open easily. Remove any seeds, then pound the rest into powder using a pestle and mortar, or put the bits in a strong bag and bash it with a rolling pin to get the desired result.

If you are using fresh corn cobs, they may come with the husks still attached, so tear off the outer husk and silky hair/threads with your hands. Don't worry if a few hairs are left behind – they will get burnt as they cook, and contribute to the smoky flavour.

Preheat a griddle pan over a medium-high heat (or get a barbecue/outside grill ready) Place the cobs straight onto the griddle pan (or hot barbecue) and grill them for 10 minutes, turning them over occasionally, until they are nicely charred and oozing on all sides. Transfer them onto a tray and brush liberally with the butter, then dust with the powdered loomi and let it seep in for 30 seconds.

Apply the dirty dredge mixture generously all over the corn cobs, then sprinkle them with the dukkah, pul biber and chopped chives. Serve straight away, on their own or as part of a barbecue party.

AL ULAWI SOUP

Al Ulawi soup has been a part of my existence since I was little, as far as my memory goes back. The first time we visited Madinah during Ramadan, we had it at our host's house as a pre-starter, served in traditional decorative silver bowls. Warm, aromatic and comforting to such an extent that my weary little soul fell asleep straight away after having it. (We had had a very long and tiring journey to Madinah from Jeddah.)

Since then, this soup has been a permanent guest appearing every Ramadan on our table and during the very cold and wet British winters as well. I often get requests from my circle of friends and family to make it and I think it's the perfect time for me to share it with you.

This is a native dish from Al Ula, an oasis city (located in Madinah province) steeped in biblical history and an archaeological site twinning it with the temples of Petra, Jordan. This soup is traditionally made with freekeh-style Ulawi wheat known as *gasia*, but I use Scottish rolled jumbo oats, which are easier to cook and cuts preparation time in half. My British side kicks in here.

There is a folklore poem about this traditional soup, written by a locally renowned poet and writer Mohammad Abdullah Al-Qadi, where he praises its historic and religious importance and summarizes what this soup means to Saudi culture:

O, this soup, exuding a fragrant aroma

Reminding us of the delicious food with its goodness

The wheat in it comes from ancient cultivation

It fills dining tables with wafting scents

It has existed since olden times

Those who have savoured its aroma never forget it

Its soup is in demand in beautiful times

And blessed Ramadan is the time for it.

INGREDIENTS:

- 2 tbsp olive oil or vegetable oil
- 1 large onion, finely chopped
- 2 fat cloves of garlic, minced
- 500g (1lb 2oz) lamb on the bone, cut into 5cm (2-inch) chunks (lamb shoulder is ideal for this soup), or chicken can be used as an alternative
- 1 tsp tomato purée (paste)
- 3 large tomatoes, skin removed and finely chopped
- 2 black loomi (dried limes), pierced in a couple of places
- 2.5cm (1-inch) piece of fresh galangal or dried (optional but highly recommended)
- 1 × 5cm (2-inch) cinnamon stick
- 1 tsp whole black peppercorns
- 1 tsp Baharat spice mix or ground allspice
- 1 tsp roasted ground cumin
- 2 green cardamom pods
- 250g (9oz) jumbo rolled oats or freekeh

To serve:

- Natural yogurt, whipped
- Extra virgin olive oil

Serves 4

Heat the oil in a heavy-based pan on a high heat, add the chopped onion and sauté for 4–5 minutes until translucent. Add the minced garlic and sauté for 30 seconds, then add the lamb and sauté for 3–4 minutes

Now add the tomato purée and chopped tomatoes and sauté for 1–2 minutes, then add all the remaining ingredients except the freekeh or oats. Add 1.5 litres (50¾fl oz/6 cups) water, cover and let it cook on a low–medium heat until the lamb falls off the bone – this will take about 45 minutes. (You can also use a pressure cooker for this if you prefer.)

Now, the next step is not very traditional. At this stage I remove the meat into a bowl, set aside and strain the stock to remove any whole spices and bits. Squeeze the juice out of the loomi into the strained stock – that's the essence of this soup. Transfer the stock and meat back to the cooking pot, return to the heat and add the jumbo rolled oats. Cook for further 15 minutes, stirring every now and then so that the oats don't stick to the bottom of the pan. Once the oats are super soft, we are ready to serve up the soup.

Ladle the soup into serving bowls and drizzle with whipped yogurt and extra virgin olive oil.

SHORBA ADAS (SOUP) WITH CHILLI-CHEDDAR CRISP

This soup has been my silent beloved companion of financially tough times during my student years and has nourished me like a mother. Over the years I have made it with all sorts of lentils, different vegetables and sometimes spiced it up a little, but this version is my favourite. With the addition of a glamorous umami chilli-Cheddar crisp on top it is elevated to a whole new fine-dining level.

INGREDIENTS:

- 1 tbsp olive oil
- 1 large onion, medium diced
- 1 floury potato, peeled and diced small
- 2 medium carrots, shredded
- 1 tsp roasted ground cumin
- 2 tsp paprika
- 1 tsp fine sea salt
- 200g (7oz/heaped 1 cup) red lentils
- 1 litre (35fl oz/4¼ cups) chicken or vegetable stock
- Juice of 1 large lemon

For the chilli-Cheddar crisps:

- 250g (9oz) Cheddar cheese, grated
- 4 tbsp grated Parmesan
- 1 tbsp pul biber (Aleppo pepper flakes)
- 1 tbsp black sesame seeds

To serve:

- Lemon wedges
- Thin pitta breads

Serves 4

★V★GF

Heat the olive oil in a heavy-based pan on a medium-high heat. Add the onion and sauté for 2–3 minutes until translucent. Add the potato, carrots, cumin, paprika and salt. Cook for 10 minutes, stirring every now and then.

Add the lentils and the stock. Stir well, bring to a boil and then turn the heat down to low, partially cover the pan and let it simmer for 30 minutes, or until the lentils are mushy.

Blend the mix until smooth using a stick blender (or transfer to a jug blender to purée, then return to the pan). Bring it to a boil, then turn off the heat, cover and set aside.

Now prepare the chilli-Cheddar crisps. Heat a non-stick frying pan. Mix the two cheeses, then divide the mixture into four portions. Place one portion at a time into the middle of the hot pan and spread it out with your hand or a spoon into a thin circular disc with as few gaps as possible. As soon as the cheese starts to melt, sprinkle with the pul biber and black sesame seeds. Cook until the edges start to brown – this can take up to 7 minutes.

Flip the crisp over carefully with a large pallet knife or flat spatula and cook for a further 10 seconds. Flip it onto a wire rack to crisp up and cool down completely while you repeat to cook the remaining three crisps.

To serve, warm up the soup and add the lemon juice. Ladle it into serving bowls. Top each bowl with a chilli-Cheddar crisp so that it covers the bowl without touching the soup. Serve with lemon wedges and thin pitta bread on the side and enjoy!

BALEELA
(A lip-smacking, slurpy Saudi street food)

This is a Saudi street food so popular that you will find it at every street corner, in every souk, all along the coastline of the Red Sea (Jeddah), outside schools and almost everywhere. Vendors selling it – along with other sweet treats – in their portable insulated vessels are truly a sight to witness when school finishes and children gang up around them.

As a teen experiencing the hormonal surge, baleela was my go-to snack on my way back home from school after a stressful day. I would slurp the warm, nutty liquid, making a few splatters here and there on my white and green uniform: crucial evidence for my mum to figure out the reason for my sore throat and lost voice (due to that spicy, tangy liquid). Nevertheless, I had my share of soul comfort and now I can deal with her motherly disappointments in me!

I have shortened tremendously the time it takes to make this recipe by using canned chickpeas and ready-pickled beetroot for a quick fix.

INGREDIENTS:

- 2 × 400g (14oz) cans of chickpeas (or use 200g (7oz) dried chickpeas; see tip overleaf)
- ½ tsp bicarbonate of soda (baking soda)

For the pickle:

- 2 pickled beetroots, chopped into small cubes
- 2 small cucumbers (ideally the ones from Arab shops), chopped into small cubes
- 50ml (1¾fl oz/3½ tbsp) grape vinegar or apple cider vinegar
- 1 tsp salt
- 1 tsp ground cumin, plus extra to garnish
- ½ tsp sweet paprika
- 45ml (1½fl oz/3 tbsp) hot sauce (I use Crystal brand), plus extra to garnish
- Pinch of sumac (optional), plus extra to garnish

For the drizzling vinegar:

- 50ml (1¾fl oz/3½ tbsp) grape vinegar
- Pinch of salt

Serves 4–6

★V★DF★GF

To make the pickle, put the chopped beetroots and cucumbers in an airtight container or a preserving jar. Pour in the vinegar and add about 150ml (5fl oz/scant ⅔ cup) water (or enough to cover the veg), the salt, ground cumin, paprika, hot sauce and sumac, if using. Put the lid on and give it a good shake. This pickle can be prepared a day ahead and can live in the fridge for up to 3 days.

Empty the cans of chickpeas into a saucepan (including the liquid), add the bicarbonate of soda and simmer for 30 minutes.

Meanwhile, mix the ingredients for the vinegar blend in a squirty bottle or any pourable vessel; it is ready to be used.

To assemble, transfer the warm chickpeas, along with a cup of the cooking liquid, to a serving bowl. Squirt in some of the vinegar blend and give it a good mix.

Drain the pickling liquid from the pickle and pour it over the chickpeas. Top the chickpeas with the pickled beets and cucumber. Sprinkle with ground cumin, salt and sumac and serve with extra hot sauce and the remaining vinegar in the squirty bottle

TIP: If you choose to go down the traditional route, soak the dried chickpeas overnight. The next day, put the soaked chickpeas in a pan with about 2 litres (2 quarts) of water and the bicarbonate of soda (baking soda). Bring them to a boil on a high heat, remove the scum and then let them cook on a low-medium heat for about 45 minutes until tender. Then continue following the recipe as above.

MUSABAHA
(Chickpeas swimming in a pool of tahini: that's what musabaha means)

If you get a chance to walk the alleys of the Arab world during mid-morning breakfast or brunch, you can witness café and restaurant staff munching on musabaha with freshly baked pitta breads to fuel them up for a busy day ahead.

I like to run a tablespoon of zhoug through my musabaha, top it with a dollop of preserved shatta, drizzle with tangy fruity amba sauce and enjoy with freshly baked pitta bread. (You can easily find mini pitta breads from the supermarket; toast them in the toaster for 30 seconds and you have a very cute fresh accompaniment!)

INGREDIENTS:

- 200g (7oz) dried chickpeas, cooked as per the instructions on page 36
- 2–3 tbsp tahini (as per your preference), plus 1 tbsp to serve
- 1 clove of garlic, minced
- 1 tsp roasted ground cumin
- 1 heaped tbsp yogurt (optional)
- Juice of ½ lemon
- 1 tbsp Zhoug (see page 192)
- Salt

To serve:

- 1 tbsp red Shatta (see page 195, or easily available at most Asian and Arab grocery stores)
- Amba Sauce (see page 182)
- Extra virgin olive oil

Serves 4–6

★V★DF★GF

Cook the chickpeas according to the method on page 36. Once drained, transfer half of the warm cooked chickpeas to a bowl and add the tahini, garlic, cumin, yogurt (if using), lemon juice and a splash of cooking liquid from the chickpeas. (Adjust the consistency as per your liking.) Season to taste with salt.

Gently crush the mixture with a spoon or pestle until the chickpeas are lightly smashed. Add the remaining chickpeas and zhoug and gently fold them in.

Plate up the musabaha, and top it with the tablespoon of tahini and the shatta, some amba sauce and olive oil.

MUTABBAQ
(The iconic Saudi street food)

This street food has won the hearts of millions. Now I am sharing it straight from my heart to yours. This is the iconic mutabbaq: soft and crunchy, mouthwateringly fresh and delicately spiced, it makes a perfect snack at any time of the day. Traditionally it's served with Shatta (an Arab hot sauce, see page 195) and Zhoug (a Yemenite Jewish dip, see page 192) and a wedge of lemon.

For me, street food is the index of a nation's soul: it gives you a snapshot of that particular country, its food, people, diversity and culture. And mutabbaq ticks all of those boxes. It is a warm hug that comforts your soul, and this is how the Saudis are in general: simple, warm, embracing, hospitable and welcoming.

Mutabbaq is something I profoundly associate with my childhood in KSA. It dwells deeply in very loving memories with my Aba Jan (Dad). In the early eighties when Aba Jan was working for the Royal Refinery of Yanbu and Jubail, we lived in Yanbu, a sleepy coastal town steeped in history, at the edge of the Red Sea, that has the most beautiful, rustic, untouched beaches I have ever seen: clear, deep blue sea with red coral visible from a distance and warm sandy beaches to walk on, with not a single man-made structure in sight.

We went to the beach very often to spend hot summer evenings there. I usually sat on the car bonnet with Aba Jan standing next to me, watching the beautiful sunset far away where the sky meets the dancing sea. As we chatted away all the worries in life, we munched on these warm, decadent, crispy morsels, all scoffed down with a can of fizzy pop.

When I came to the UK in 2007 as a student, just before the great stock market crash, money was tight, as is so often the case. So, I started revisiting my foodie memories and spoke with Aba Jan over the phone about our food adventures. These conversations would often remind me of great meals we had shared together, and this was the very first one that came to mind. It is super quick, lip-smacking delicious and packed with nutrients without breaking the bank. Mutabbaq and its memories of Aba Jan still brings a tear of joy to my eyes when I make it for my clan.

I had the privilege to make this humble yet very delicious dish as a starter on MasterChef UK 2021. It won the love of judges and past winners because it came from deep within. Here, I have simplified the recipe to make it even more user-friendly.

INGREDIENTS:

For the chicken filling:

- 1 tbsp vegetable oil
- 125g (4½oz) minced (ground) chicken thigh
- ¼ tsp roasted ground cumin, plus an extra pinch
- 25g (1oz) coriander (cilantro), chopped
- 25g (1oz) flat leaf parsley, chopped
- Small bunch of spring onions (scallions), finely chopped (try to get the onions with longer green parts)
- Handful of chives, finely chopped
- 1 red chilli (or as per your preferred level of spiciness), finely sliced
- 1 firm tomato, deseeded and diced into small cubes
- 1 large egg, lightly beaten
- Salt and freshly ground black pepper

For the pastry parcels:

- Sunflower oil (or any neutral oil), for shallow frying
- 4 large spring roll pastry sheets

To serve:

- Zhoug (see page 192), Shatta (see page 195), Jajeek (see page 190) or any sauce of your choice
- A green chilli (optional but traditional)
- A wedge of lemon

Makes 16

★**DF**

Heat the oil in a frying pan on a high heat. Add the chicken mince and sauté until it is cooked through. Add the pinch of ground cumin and cook until all the liquid in the pan has gone. This will take about 4–5 minutes. Season with salt and black pepper and set aside to cool down.

Mix the coriander, parsley, spring onions, chives, chilli and tomato in a bowl and add the cooked and cooled chicken mince to it. Add the rest of the ground cumin, season to taste, and mix well.

Now add about two-thirds of the beaten egg and give it a mix. If it seems too dry, add the rest of the egg and stir. The filling is now ready for stuffing into the spring roll pastry.

Pour enough oil into a frying pan to shallow fry and place it on a low-medium heat.

Put a couple of tablespoons of the filling mixture in the centre of a pastry sheet, forming a square shape, then fold the edges of the pastry over the filling to form a parcel or envelope. Seal the parcel by dipping your fingers in some water and wetting the edges. Immediately place the parcel in the frying pan. Fry for 1–2 minutes on each side. (I usually fry one at a time in a small pan, but if you are using a wider pan you can fry two at a time without overcrowding the pan.) Once you get a nice golden brown colour all over, take it out and place on a piece of paper towel to drain the excess oil. Repeat with all the parcels.

Cut each parcel into four pieces with a pizza cutter and serve hot with zhoug, shatta, jajeek, tzatziki or any sauce of your choice, a green chilli, if using, and a wedge of lemon.

TIP: This recipe is so forgiving and versatile that you can go completely vegan by replacing the meat and eggs with soya mince and a small boiled and grated potato.

KAMMOUNEH-INFUSED GRILLED CHICKEN LIVERS

(AKA Kibbdeh, a meal on its own as well as a great sandwich filler)

In my early teens I started to bottle up newly found feelings, feelings that confused me at times and that I couldn't share with anyone, lost for words. If I was ever feeling this way or was cross with my Aba Jan, this was one of the tricks up his sleeve: I would open up my heart to him over a bowl of grilled chicken livers, because I have a deep and undivided love for chicken livers. Aba Jan made the best succulent and juicy chicken livers with an ever-so-slightly citric tang. This is his recipe.

Surely, Aba Jan knew how to talk me around.

Whenever I am in my melancholic zone or miss his bodily existence in life, whenever I just want to talk to him about my dilemmas that I don't want to share with anyone in this world, I make these, often on my own, take a moment to let reality sink in that his warm embrace is not around me anymore, and mop up the last bits of lightly caramelized scratchings from the pan with a piece of bread while wiping off tears that have reached my chin by now. This is how a hug in a bowl feels; it allows me to have a silent vent and feel lighter, ready to face life's daily chaos.

Kibbdeh sandwiches are a bit of an icon in the gulf region. This dish works really well in a toasted sausage roll bun as well.

Above: Scared 9-month-old me holding Aba Jan's earlobe
Left: Us three (Aba Jan, Mama and me aged 13)

INGREDIENTS:

- 3 tbsp olive oil or any neutral oil
- 1 tbsp unsalted butter
- 1 small onion, finely chopped
- 6 cloves of garlic, finely chopped or minced
- 1 green chilli, finely chopped or minced
- 400g (14oz) chicken livers
- ½ tsp freshly ground black pepper
- 1 tsp pul biber (Aleppo pepper flakes, optional)
- 1 tsp Kammouneh (see page 196)
- ½ tsp ground coriander
- Juice and zest of 1 lemon
- Fine sea salt, to taste
- 2 tbsp chopped coriander (cilantro) or flat leaf parsley
- 1 mild red chilli, sliced diagonally, to garnish
- Warm Pitta Bread (see page 166), to serve

Serves 4 as a side or 2 as a main

★GF

In a shallow non-stick frying pan, heat the olive oil and butter together until the butter has just melted. Add the chopped onion and sauté on a medium heat until fragrant – about a minute or so. Add the garlic and green chilli and sauté until fragrant.

Tip in the chicken livers, turn the heat to medium-high, and cook until just browned on all sides – this usually takes 5–6 minutes.

Add the black pepper, pul biber, kammouneh, ground coriander, lemon juice and half of the lemon zest. Season to taste with salt. Mix well, then take off the heat and stir through half of the chopped coriander or parsley.

Dish out onto a serving plate and garnish with the sliced red chilli and the rest of the lemon zest and chopped herbs.

Serve with warm pitta breads.

MADINIAN DUKKAH & HOT HONEY BAKED FIGS WITH GOAT'S CHEESE

These baked figs can be served as part of a mezze or with thin toasted sourdough slices. You can also feel free to use feta instead of goat's cheese if you like.

INGREDIENTS:

- 1½ tbsp extra virgin olive oil
- 1½ tbsp Hot Harissa Honey (see page 191)
- 6 large figs, washed and patted dry
- 1 × 150g (5½oz) goat's cheese log
- 8 walnut halves: 6 whole and 2 broken into smaller pieces
- 2–3 small sprigs of fresh thyme or a sprinkle of za'atar

To serve:

- ½ tsp Madinian Dukkah (see page 187)
- Sea salt and fresh ground pepper
- A pinch of pul biber (Aleppo pepper flakes)

Serves 4–6

★V★DF★GF

Preheat the oven to 180°C (350°F), gas 4.

Drizzle half of the olive oil and half of the hot honey into a small baking dish which can easily accommodate all the figs.

Score a deep cross into each fig, cutting three-quarters of the way to the bottom, but making sure you don't cut all the way through. Place the figs in the dish on top of the hot honey and olive oil.

Divide the goat's cheese log into six equal pieces and place a piece into each fig, pressing it down gently.

Press a whole walnut half onto each fig, then drizzle with the rest of the olive oil and sprinkle the thyme (or za'atar) on top.

Bake in the preheated oven for 20–25 minutes, or until the figs are soft and jammy and the cheese is all melted and gooey and slightly browning on the top.

Drizzle with the rest of the hot honey and sprinkle with sea salt, black pepper, Madinian Dukkah, pul biber and the walnut pieces. Serve warm.

THE HUMBLE HUMMUS 5 WAYS
(The creamiest, most blissfully smooth, indulgent hummus ever)

I reverently refer to hummus as "the food that may have salvaged my life and immortalized the love of food in me". This is the food I come back to, that I craft with my hands and pour my heart and soul into. When my brain is exhausted and my soul battered after countless sleepless, stressful nights, this is the food that liberates me. I don't just *make* hummus; it is a ritual.

There have been quite a few rough patches in life when I have found myself not wanting to cook, eat or even think about food, even though I consider myself inextricable from it. Not because I couldn't cook, but because my whole being was bruised, either spiritually, mentally or bodily. Whether pregnancies exhausted me or postnatal depression took its toll, or when my father passing away pushed me into the darkest place of grief, when I couldn't express myself, there have always been little solitary moments in my life where I found myself standing alone in the kitchen in the middle of the night – my mind switched off and my heart drifting away – instructing my hands to make what they knew my soul longed for.

I have made hummus from scratch since a very early age. It's one of the first meals that I learned from my Aba Jan, as I vividly remember him whipping it in a bowl on a weekend morning, long before it shot to fame in the West. I have made hummus in every possible way: in a food processor, smoothie maker, smashed with a can, with a wooden pestle and mortar, even with the help of two empty Kilner jars. And I have eaten it with everything: homemade pitta or lavash bread, with crackers, with eggs, with salad, with countless variations of toppings, ground meat, merguez (Middle Eastern sausage) nuts or herbs, and even fried Padrón peppers.

In times of utter desperation, melancholy and joyous moments alike, I have made it and eaten it – still warm – with a spoon, from a boat made out of paratha or just with my fingers, straight from the mixing bowl. The best way to eat hummus is at room temperature. The flavourless commercialized thing that sits in supermarket chilled aisles is light years away from nutty, creamy and dreamy homemade hummus. Supermarket hummus is still a mystery to me, and to many who have actually eaten hummus in the Mediterranean and Middle Eastern regions.

There is abominable grief in the world right now. There are many things in the world that cannot be fixed for reasons beyond human understanding and control, but there are very few that can't be alleviated, at least momentarily, with a generous spoonful of the smoothest hummus... If Mary Poppins had been of Middle Eastern descent, I'm sure she would agree with me.

INGREDIENTS:

OG Hummus (aka Hummus Bi Tahina)

- 250g (8¾oz) dried chickpeas
- 1½ tsp bicarbonate of soda (baking soda)
- 1 tsp kosher salt/sea salt (or to taste)
- 2–3 ice cubes, for grinding
- 6 tbsp tahini paste (or to taste)
- 4 tbsp freshly squeezed lemon juice (about 2 lemons)
- 2 small cloves of garlic, peeled, halved, the germinating sprout removed, and minced

To serve:

- Chopped parsley or tiny dill sprigs (optional)
- Sumac and/or roasted ground cumin (optional)
- 75–100ml (2½–3¼fl oz/5–6 tbsp) good-quality extra virgin olive oil

All hummus recipes serve 4 generously (although I wouldn't share them with anybody!)
★V★DF★GF

TIP: Always adjust salt and tahini to your taste. If you have ample time to hand, leave the hummus 1–2 hours before consuming to let the flavours develop and do their magic. But if you are as impatient as I am, it's okay to dive in straight away.

Put the chickpeas in a bowl, and add about 1.5 litres (50¾fl oz/6 cups) of water and ½ teaspoon of the bicarbonate of soda. Cover the bowl and leave to soak overnight if possible or for at least 16 hours (the bicarb will soften the skins and make them easier to remove).

Once soaked, drain and rinse the chickpeas. Put them in a saucepan with enough water to cover the chickpeas by at least 10cm (4 inches) and add the remaining 1 teaspoon of bicarbonate of soda. Bring the water to a boil, and skim off the thick white foam that forms on top. Let it boil for 3–4 minutes, then turn the heat down and let the chickpeas simmer for 30–40 minutes on a low heat, until the chickpeas are soft and are easily mushed with the back of a spoon without meeting any resistance. Sprinkle in some salt towards the end of cooking to develop the flavour.

Drain the chickpeas, reserving the liquid. The loose skin will come to the top of the chickpeas and make it easy to pick out – remove as much skin as you can, then slightly rinse the chickpeas under tap water to bring any remaining loose skin to the top. It's absolutely essential to remove the chickpea skins in order to get that ultra-smooth, whipped-cream-like texture.

Add the still-warm chickpeas to the food processor and blend for 1 minute until the mixture reaches a coarse consistency. If the mixture is too thick, add a tablespoon or two of the reserved cooking liquid to thin it out.

Add an ice cube to the blender and pulse in, then add the tahini and pulse again. Repeat, adding another ice cube and pulsing, then add half the lemon juice. Add one more ice cube and then the garlic cloves, then grind continuously for 7–8 minutes, until smooth. Taste and add salt and the remaining lemon juice to your liking.

Transfer the hummus to a serving bowl and, with the back of a spoon, create a small pool or a crater. At this stage, I let loose the Cypriot genie in me and sprinkle generously with chopped parsley, ground cumin and sumac, then drizzle lavishly with extra virgin olive oil, even dirtying up the edges of the plate. Get creative!

HUMMUS BIL FUL

Hummus with a generous topping of hot fava beans is quite a popular version in Egypt and Palestine and loved all over the Middle East. I make this whenever I have leftover ful (see page 134) followed by a chef's kiss. It's damn good.

INGREDIENTS:

- 1 × 400g (14oz) can whole fava beans (aka ful)
- Olive oil, to drizzle generously
- ½ tsp roasted ground cumin
- 1 quantity of OG Hummus (see page 47)
- Salt

To serve:

- Lemon juice, to squeeze on top
- Za'atar
- 1 tbsp Shatta (see page 195, optional)
- Warm bread, to serve

Serves 4 generously

★V★DF★GF

Warm the fava beans in a pan with a little olive oil. Sprinkle in the ground cumin and salt to taste.

Spread the prepared hummus on a plate or dish of your choice. Make a well and top up with the warm fava beans.

Drizzle with olive oil and a squeeze of lemon and sprinkle with za'atar. Top it up with shatta and serve with warm bread.

ROASTED RED PEPPER HUMMUS

I started whipping this version up when I had enough of that abominable store-bought dodgy stuff, unjustly sold under the name of humble hummus. It is way cheaper and healthier without any unnecessary additives that do not belong in our diet.

INGREDIENTS:

- Ingredients for ½ quantity of OG Hummus (see page 47) using 1½ tbsp tahini instead of 3
- 1 × 450g (1lb) jar of roasted red peppers, drained
- Roasted pine nuts, dukkah and fried mint leaves, to garnish

Serves 4 generously

★V★DF★GF

To make the hummus, follow the first four steps of the OG hummus recipe.

Add the still-warm chickpeas to the food processor along with the drained roasted peppers and blend it for 1 minute until it reaches a coarse consistency.

Add an ice cube to the blender and pulse in, then add the tahini and pulse again. Repeat, adding another ice cube and pulsing, then adding half the lemon juice. Add one more ice cube and then the garlic cloves, then grind continuously for 7–8 minutes, until smooth. Taste and add salt and the remaining lemon juice to your liking.

Transfer the hummus to a serving bowl, drizzle generously with olive oil and garnish with pine nuts, dukkah and fried mint leaves.

TANDOORI CHICKEN TENDERS WITH HUMMUS

What a crowd-pleaser this is, packed full of protein and loaded with fusion flavours. A winner for any meal at any time of the day. This can be served as a main or as part of a mezze spread. It is where East meets Middle East.

INGREDIENTS:

- 2 tbsp tandoori masala
- 1 tsp crushed green chilli
- 1 tsp grated ginger
- 1 tbsp lemon juice
- 3 tbsp olive oil
- 1 tbsp natural yogurt
- Salt
- 450g (1lb) chicken tenders
- 1 tbsp butter
- 1 quantity of OG hummus (see page 47)
- Warm bread (ideally mini pitta bread or parathas), to serve
- Lemon wedges, to garnish

Serves 4 generously

*GF

In a bowl, combine the tandoori masala, green chilli, ginger, lemon juice, 1 tablespoon of the olive oil, the natural yogurt and salt to taste. Add the chicken tenders, stir to coat and allow to marinate for 30 minutes.

In a pan, melt the butter along with the remaining 2 tablespoons of olive oil. Sear the marinated chicken over a high heat, turning during cooking, until browned all over. Once browned, add a sprinkle of water, then cover the pan and let it cook on a low heat for about 5–7 minutes until cooked through.

Spread the hummus on a plate, place the chicken tenders on top and spoon over any juices and flavoured oil left in the pan.

Serve with warm bread, and lemon wedges for squeezing over.

FUNKY PINKY BEETROOT HUMMUS

I was making this beautiful dip a long time before it shot to fame on social media and I have a secret to share here... I use pickled beets (the freshly pickled, vacuum-packed ones sitting in the chilled aisles of supermarkets) to whizz up this gorgeousness!

INGREDIENTS:

- 300g (10½oz) OG Hummus (see page 47)
- 300g (10½oz) pickled beetroot
- ¼ tsp roasted ground cumin
- Salt, to taste

To serve:

- Olive oil, to drizzle generously
- Za'atar, to sprinkle
- ½ tbsp toasted pine nuts or almonds
- Feta cheese, to garnish (optional, but adds a distinctive lactic tang)
- 3–4 mint or dill leaves, finely chopped (optional)

Serves 4 generously

★V★DF★GF

Follow the first four steps of the OG hummus recipe.

Add the still-warm chickpeas to the food processor along with the pickled beetroots and ground cumin and blend it for 30 seconds to 1 minute until it reaches a coarse consistency.

Now start pulse grinding for a minute by adding 1 ice cube, then add the tahini and garlic cloves, grind continuously for 4–5 minutes and keep on adding the remaining ice cubes one at a time after every two minutes.

Transfer the freshly whipped hummus to a bowl and drizzle with olive oil. Garnish with a sprinkle of za'atar, pine nuts or almonds, and crumbled feta and mint or dill leaves (if using).

TIP: Form this into a yin-yang shape with the black hummus opposite for the ultimate wow factor.

PITCH BLACK HUMMUS

This deep black hummus holds a constellation of starry flavours and deserves a place on the table with its strikingly pink counterpart (the beetroot hummus opposite). I often serve these together in a yin-yang design. It is a majestic showstopper that packs a punch.

INGREDIENTS:

- 1 quantity of OG Hummus (see page 47), replacing the classic tahini with black tahini (the blackest you can find – Biona is good)

To serve:

- Roasted or fried pine nuts
- White and black sesame seeds
- Warm toasted bread
- Vegetable crudités

Serves 4 generously

★V★DF★GF

Follow the steps for the OG hummus, replacing the classic tahini with black tahini. (A word of caution: black tahini varies in taste and strength, so please begin with a tablespoon at a time, tasting to your preference.)

Spoon it into a serving dish and decorate the way you like with the pine nuts and sesame seeds. Serve with warm toasted bread, vegetables or whatever you fancy.

STUFFED AUBERGINE ROLL MOPS WITH GARLICKY LABNEH
(My take on a classic aubergine fatteh)

This dish evolved in an hour of need. I had some unexpected guests on a meat-free diet visit during my student years, so I had to create something delicious and vegetarian on the spot. We are still friends after all those years, so I think I probably did a good job!

INGREDIENTS:

- 1 large fat aubergine (eggplant), sliced lengthways into 5mm (¼-inch) slices
- Olive oil, for brushing and drizzling
- Leftover Muhammara (see page 218) or red pesto (store-bought will do)
- 2 tbsp crushed walnuts, plus a few to sprinkle

For the labneh spread:

- 350g (12¾oz/1½ cups) Greek yogurt or labneh
- 2 small cloves of garlic, minced
- 1 tbsp lemon juice
- Salt

For the chilli-garlic oil:

- 3 tbsp olive oil
- 3–4 cloves of garlic, sliced
- ½ tsp pul biber (Aleppo pepper flakes)

To serve:

- Pomegranate seeds
- Fried fresh curry leaves or mint leaves
- Pomegranate molasses
- Pitta croutons

Makes 16

★V

Lightly brush the aubergine slices with olive oil and place them on a hot griddle pan over a high heat. Flip them over once you get nice charring marks on one side and repeat until you have cooked all the slices. Take them off the heat and let them cool slightly.

One slice at a time, spread a thin layer of muhammara, ajvar or red pesto (whichever you are using) over the aubergine slices. Sprinkle with crushed walnuts, then roll each slice up.

In a bowl, whip up the labneh spread by mixing together the Greek yogurt or labneh, the minced garlic and lemon juice and season with salt. Spread the garlicky labneh onto a serving plate, creating a well in the middle. Place all of the aubergine rolls in the centre.

For the chilli-garlic oil, heat the olive oil in a small pan and add the sliced garlic. Sauté until the garlic starts turning golden in colour. Add the pul biber flakes and swirl the pan to incorporate them, then pour over the aubergine rolls and labneh.

Sprinkle over pomegranate seeds and fried mint or curry leaves. Drizzle with pomegranate molasses and olive oil. Serve with fried pitta croutons. You can share this as a mezze dish, or enjoy as a main

WHIPPED FETA DIP WITH PICKLED BEETROOT, DILL AND PISTACHIOS

After a long playful afternoon, I would return home with red stains all over my clothes and my mama would get mad at me because I had completely ruined my dress. One of the main culprits was the humble pickled beetroot. This dip is a simple spin on mama's historic disappointments in my ruined dresses and Aba Jan's pickled beet and cucumber salad. Serve it with barbecued meats and vegetables at any time of the day, incorporating all those bold flavours straight from the old souks of Jeddah, with love.

INGREDIENTS:

For dressing the beetroot:

- 500g (1lb 2oz) malt-vinegar pickled beetroot, diced into 1cm (½-inch) cubes or grated on the largest side of a box grater
- 2 baby cucumbers, finely diced
- 3 tbsp full-fat natural yogurt
- 1 tbsp tahini
- 1 tsp sumac
- 1 tbsp roughly chopped dill
- 1 tsp pomegranate molasses
- 1 clove of garlic, crushed
- ½ tbsp extra virgin olive oil
- Juice and zest of ½ lemon
- Fine sea salt, to taste

For the whipped feta base:

- 200ml (7fl oz/scant 1 cup) whipping cream
- 200g (7oz) feta

To serve:

- Handful of the greenest pistachios you can find, roughly chopped
- 1 tbsp chopped fresh dill
- Extra virgin olive oil, to drizzle
- Warm toasted pitta bread (optional)

Serves 4–6

★V★GF

Start by dressing the beets with all of the dressing ingredients except the lemon zest, mixing everything in a bowl. Season with salt and set aside.

Prepare the whipped feta base by combining the whipping cream and feta in a bowl. Using an electric hand whisk, whip air into the mixture until smooth and at stiff-peaks stage. Set aside in the fridge for, ideally, 1 hour.

Swirl the chilled whipped feta onto a serving plate, using the back of a spoon to create a deep crater in the centre. Pile the dressed beetroot mixture into the middle.

Sprinkle with chopped pistachios, the remaining lemon zest and the chopped dill leaves and add a generous drizzle of olive oil. Serve as a side or on its own with warm pitta bread.

EGYPTIAN TA'MIYYAH AKA FALAFEL'S BIG DADDY
(A delicacy as old and exotic as Egypt itself)

An absolute delight when consumed freshly made, Egyptian ta'miyyah are the authentic ancestors of present-day falafels, made from a mixture of chickpeas and fava beans since the beginning of recorded Egyptian history.

For me, ta'miyyah sandwiches are reminiscent of my early years spent playing with other children from the neighbourhood on the old streets and souks of Jeddah. I vividly remember that the other children and I used to get 5–10 Saudi riyals as weekly pocket money, and the street vendors were our ultimate go-to for fresh sesame-encrusted ta'miyyah. Fresh out of the hot oil, they were crushed and squished into warm pitta bread (aka *khobz*), smothered in *tahiniya* sauce, potato chips and fresh minty salad, dusted with tangy sumac and finished with a splash of amba sauce, all ready to be devoured straight away. The captivating aroma still lingers in my mind. We were very loyal little customers of this street vendor, named Matheen if memory serves me right, and he actually used to reserve some for us every day. Life was very beautiful and carefree then.

INGREDIENTS:

For the ta'miyyah:

- 100g (3½oz) split dried skinless fava beans, soaked in water overnight
- 100g (3½oz) dried chickpeas, soaked in water overnight
- 1 banana shallot, peeled and chopped
- Small bunch of coriander (cilantro), roughly chopped
- Small bunch of flat leaf parsley, roughly chopped
- 1 spring onion (scallion)
- 2 tbsp chopped chives
- 1 tbsp chopped dill
- 2–3 fat cloves of garlic
- 1 tbsp gram flour
- 1 tsp ground coriander
- 1 tsp ground cumin
- ½ tsp Baharat spice mix
- ½ tsp red chilli powder (optional)
- ½ tsp ground black pepper
- 1 tsp salt (or to taste)
- 1 tsp bicarbonate of soda (baking soda)
- Oil, for deep frying
- sesame seeds, to coat

Suggestions to serve:

- Fresh Pitta Bread (see page 166) or tortilla wraps
- Tahiniya (see page 184)
- Amba sauce (see page 182)
- Salad (see Tip, overleaf)

Makes 30

★V★DF★GF

Drain the fava beans and chickpeas and coarsely grind them in a food processor. Add the rest of the ingredients, except the bicarbonate of soda, sesame seeds and oil, and pulse until all combined, making sure you keep some texture in the mixture. Transfer the mixture to a bowl, cover and let it rest for at least 30 minutes in the fridge before frying.

When you are ready to fry, take the mixture out of the fridge, add the bicarbonate of soda and mix through lightly.

Heat the oil to 190°C (375°F), ideally in a shallow wok or a deep frying pan. To check whether the oil is hot enough to fry, drop a tiny amount of the mixture into the oil – it's hot enough if it sizzles and floats.

There are couple of ways to shape these: you can either use a falafel tool, or use two spoons to shape them into a quenelle.

Once shaped, dip one side of the ta'miyyah into the sesame seeds and slide them into the hot oil. Cook them in batches, frying for a couple of minutes, until one side turns golden brown, and then flip them over to brown the other side. Once nicely browned all over, take them out of the oil with the help of a slotted spoon and drain on paper towel. Repeat to cook the remaining ta'miyyah.

Serve them hot, either smashed into the pitta bread pockets as sandwiches, with tahini and amba sauce and salad, or just on their own with your choice of accompanying condiments. Ta'miyyah is messy and that's the way it's meant to be – no fine dining here, just finger-licking goodness to be enjoyed from the comfort of your home.

TIP: You can make this recipe with 50/50 chickpeas and fava beans as above, or make it with all chickpeas, or all fava beans, if you prefer.

To serve, I like to make a salad of sliced tomatoes, onion rings dusted with a pinch of sumac, gherkins, lettuce, pickled turnips, olives, fresh parsley and mint.

SWEET POTATO BATATA HARRA
(A healthier, more convenient option)

Batata harra is a much-loved spud side, snack, a munch bowl – or call it whatever you like! It can be a bit time-consuming. But I have a trick up my sleeve – instead of using diced potatoes, my hack is to use frozen sweet potato fries. If you decide to peel and make sweet potato fries from scratch – be my guest. But trust me, using store-bought fries gives it better crunch and the *harra* sauce holds on to the fries well without making the sweet spud soggy.

The word *harra* means "hot", so the sauce is bound to be spicy with a citric tang, but you can adjust the level of heat to your taste. I served this starter to my husband on our very first date, and, yes, I did the cooking!

INGREDIENTS:

- 500g (1lb 2oz) frozen sweet potato fries
- 3 tbsp olive oil
- 2 cloves of garlic, crushed or finely chopped
- ½ tsp Kammouneh (see page 197)
- 1 tsp Turkish red pepper paste (biber salcasi)
- 1 tsp tomato purée (paste), ideally Turkish as it has more flavour
- Juice of 1 lemon
- A small handful of coriander (cilantro), finely chopped, plus extra to garnish
- Sea salt

To garnish:

- 1 sweet red chilli, sliced into rings
- Zhoug (see page 192)
- Store-bought pickled red onions
- Aioli (optional)

Serves 4–6

★V★DF★GF

Cook the sweet potato fries as per the packet instructions. You can oven bake, air fry or deep fry them – your call.

Meanwhile, prepare the sauce. In a frying pan, heat the oil on a medium heat and tip in the crushed garlic. Sauté until it's fragrant – about 30 seconds to 1 minute.

Now add the kammouneh and the pepper and tomato pastes and sauté for another minute. Add the lemon juice and give it a good mix. Throw in the chopped coriander, season with salt, mix well and set aside.

Once the sweet potato fries are cooked and nicely crisped up, throw them in a large mixing bowl and add the prepared hot sauce. Toss until every nook and corner of the fries has been coated.

Plate up the batata harra on a serving dish and sprinkle with sliced red chilli and more chopped coriander leaves. Drizzle some zhoug over and garnish with pickled red onions to your liking. Serve it on its own or with aioli.

YEMENI LAHSA

If you like Turkish shakshuka, this might get you in trouble. It's that addictive.

The Arab alternative to scrambled eggs, only way more flavourful, this dish lives up truly to the term "all day starters" as it really is one. Lahsa can be eaten at any time of the day, literally, as a hearty wholesome breakfast or lively brunch or a very comforting supper. Its classic accompaniments are fresh green chillies and freshly made Mlawa (page 165) or Pitta Bread (page 166), although you can have it with a side of salad greens and olives as well.

Enjoy accompanied by Arab coffee and dates.

INGREDIENTS:

- 2–3 tbsp olive oil
- 1 onion, finely chopped
- 2 large ripe tomatoes, chopped
- ½ tsp freshly ground black pepper
- 4–5 spicy green chillies, roughly chopped (as per your taste), plus extra to serve
- 1 tsp roasted ground cumin
- 1 tsp ground coriander
- 1 tsp paprika
- 1 tbsp tomato purée (paste)
- 4 large eggs
- 140g (5oz) spreadable cheese (I use Primula; Puck is another alternative)
- Sea salt

To serve:

- Coriander (cilantro) or parsley leaves, chopped
- Fresh wild rocket (arugula) leaves

Serves 4–6

★V★GF

Start by heating the oil in a non-stick frying pan and sautéing the chopped onion. Once the onion begins to show signs of slight caramelization, add the chopped tomatoes. Sauté until the tomatoes start to break down into a chunky sauce-like consistency.

Season with salt to taste and add the ground black pepper, green chilli, ground cumin, ground coriander, paprika and tomato purée. Cook on a low heat until a homogenous paste is formed.

Turn off the heat, crack the eggs into the hot mixture and mix it thoroughly. Turn the heat back on at the lowest setting and spread the cheese on top. Cover the pan and let it cook for 4–5 minutes until the cheese is bubbling.

Garnish with fresh coriander or parsley. Serve with wild rocket leaves, warm thin pitta (or any bread) and enjoy.

SASSY COCONUT PRAWNS
(Prawns of my cherished memories)

This is perhaps one of the shining stars of this book. It is a glamorous little plate with big bang flavours. And the best part is that it can be air fried as well.

INGREDIENTS:

- 5 large giant tiger prawns (shrimps)
- 1½ tsp sesame oil
- A fat pinch of salt
- A fat pinch of ground black pepper
- ¼ tsp chilli powder
- ¼ tsp garlic granules
- ¼ tsp onion powder
- ¼ tsp ground ginger
- Vegetable oil, for deep frying

For the coating:

- 60g (2oz/scant ½ cup) plain (all-purpose) flour
- 2 tbsp sparkling water, chilled
- 1 egg, lightly beaten
- Shredded coconut, for coating

For the dipping sauce:

- 2 tbsp Humr sauce (see page 188) or ketchup
- 1 tsp orange marmalade
- 1 tbsp mayonnaise
- 1 tsp lemon juice
- 1 tsp gochujang
- ½ tsp palm sugar or soft brown sugar
- 1 clove of garlic, minced

To serve:

- Micro coriander (cilantro) leaves
- A mild red chilli, sliced
- A few wedges of lemon

Serves 1

★**DF**

Prepare the prawns (shrimps) first. Remove and discard the heads and shells, leaving the tails attached. Devein the prawns by lying each one flat on a cutting board and gently running a paring knife down the back to cut it open slightly, making the vein visible. Pull it out.

Turn the prawns over and make 4–5 cuts on the underside of each one – this will help the prawns stay flat and not curl up while cooking

Sprinkle the prepared prawns with the sesame oil, salt, black pepper, chilli powder, garlic granules, onion powder and ginger powder. Set aside while you prepare the batter for coating.

Put the flour in a bowl, add the sparkling water and egg and mix well. Set aside.

Now, here is how to make as little mess as possible while coating the prawns: Lay a sheet of cling film (plastic wrap) on the work surface and place a handful of shredded coconut in the centre. Dip a marinated prawn in the batter, letting any excess batter drop back into the bowl, then place it on top of the shredded coconut. Now lift the side of the cling film closest to you and roll it away from you, so that the coconut covers the battered prawn. Repeat the process with the rest of the prawns.

Heat the oil for deep frying to 190°C (375°F) and fry the prawns until crispy and golden in colour – this will take 4–5 minutes. You may have to cook them in two batches if you have a small pan.

For the dipping sauce, combine all the ingredients in a bowl and you are done.

TAAWA AKA MANDAZI AKA BAKHUMRI
(There are so many names for it)

My childhood is made up of these pillowy bakhumri dreams dotted with nigella seeds. My mum would buy me this slightly sweet treat from a tiny hole-in-the-wall shop for our tea on our way home from a shopping spree at the local souks in Al Kandrah district of Jeddah, along with beef Buffs (see page 26) and Mutabbaq (see page 38). I often ended up devouring them even before reaching home.

Bakhumri is usually served with traditional *shai* (a minty version of Turkish tea), Karak chai or Saudi coffee, along with white cheese (The Laughing Cow triangles or cream cheese) and date molasses or honey. (These are a must combo with bakhumri.)

INGREDIENTS:

- 220g (7¾oz/1⅔ cups) plain (all-purpose) flour
- 30g (1oz) whole milk powder
- 40g (1½oz/3¼ tbsp) caster (granulated) sugar
- A pinch of salt
- 1 tsp nigella seeds
- ½–1 tsp ground green cardamom
- 1 tbsp baking powder
- 1 large egg, lightly beaten
- 2 tbsp vegetable oil or ghee
- Vegetable oil, for deep frying
- Icing (confectioners') sugar, for dusting

Makes 8–10

★V

To prepare the dough, mix together all of the dry ingredients in a mixing bowl, then add the egg and oil or ghee and massage well. You can also do it in a stand mixer, but I usually knead it by hand.

A little at a time, add 125ml (4fl oz/½ cup) water and bring the dough together. If the dough is a bit stiff, add a little more water. Knead it for 1–2 minutes until smooth, then bring it together into a ball. Cover with cling film (plastic wrap) or a damp cloth and let it rest for 10 minutes.

After 10 minutes, lightly knock out a little air from the dough and make 8–10 small round balls, about the size of a ping pong (table tennis) ball. Dust the work surface with flour. Flatten a ball into a round disc with your hand or a rolling pin until it is 5mm (¼ inch) thick and 7–8cm (3 inches) in diameter. Repeat to shape all the dough pieces into discs.

Heat enough vegetable oil for deep frying to about 180°C (350°F) in a deep pan or fryer. Drop two to three discs at a time into the pan, spooning hot oil over these quickly so that they start to balloon up. Turn over and fry until a rich brown colour is achieved on both sides – this will take around 3–4 minutes. Dust with icing sugar and serve them hot, with accompaniments or on their own.

Salads are for life

They are your best friends when you need something light and fresh, to wake your taste buds up. In times of immense work overload, when too many tasks demand my limited span of attention, I make myself a bowl of salad. In fact, I have lived on it while writing this book.

A Saudi feast is just incomplete without its vibrant varieties of salads and condiments. The more traditional ones, like the Baladi salad (page 89) and heritage tomato and olive salad (page 72) are fairly easy to put together. Then there are a few that are my take on classics – e.g. Tuna and Butter Bean Salad (page 85) and Salata Jazar Mushakil (page 75), which make perfect sides for a BBQ or a light working lunch on a hot afternoon. There is something for everyone.

Tabouleh (page 84) is a perfect example of diversity through food. In Saudi Arabia, Lebanese food is highly regarded and much loved – so much so that it has integrated with Saudi traditional cooking and became an inseparable part of day-to-day consumption. The addition of cinnamon is the Beiruti touch. You will find this power punch at almost every single eatery in KSA. From weddings to casual dine-outs, there is tabouleh on the menu. Tabouleh is a labour of love, but it is well worth it. It's also high in antioxidants because of the copious amount of parsley.

A salad has to be exciting, and there are 8 exciting salad recipes brimming with flavour in this section. From summer fresh salads to much heartier autumnal ones, I have tried my best to give you as much as I can in this compact section, from very traditional sides to salads that can easily become a main meal.

SALATA TAMATIM WA ZYTOUN
(Heritage tomato and olive salad)

This recipe is a display of my colourful personality, if I say so myself! Salata tamatim is a very humble salad that celebrates the freshness of local tomatoes. It is traditionally made with a gorgeous beef tomato variety grown in the agricultural plateaus surrounding the Red Sea coastline and olives from a Palestinian grove, and it is sweet, tangy and fragrant, to say the least. A match made in heaven, just like me and my dad.

I fell in love with British heritage tomatoes at first sight when I visited the Isle of Wight, and this salad does justice to the colourful bounty that British summer offers. Of course, you can make this recipe with any other kind of salad tomatoes.

INGREDIENTS:

- 500g (1lb 2oz) heritage tomatoes (or any other tomato that you like), small ones halved, large ones quartered
- 150g (5½oz) mixed pitted olives
- 1 small red onion, sliced
- 10 basil leaves, chopped
- 2 sprigs of flat leaf parsley, chopped
- A handful of mint leaves, chopped
- 2 cloves of garlic, minced with a few drops of lemon juice
- ¼ tsp za'atar
- 2–3 tbsp extra virgin olive oil, plus extra to drizzle
- 1 tbsp pomegranate molasses
- Salt and freshly ground black pepper
- Croutons, to serve (optional)
- Feta cheese, to serve (optional)

Serves 4 generously

★V★DF★GF

Chuck everything in a bowl and give it a good mix. Season well with salt and pepper.

Plate up and drizzle with some more olive oil.

Serve the salad with your choice of croutons and a sprinkle of feta cheese, if you like.

SALATA JAZAR MUSHAKIL
(Heritage carrot salad)

This minty and aromatic salad is my take on a more traditional carrot salad. It came into existence when I set my eyes on heritage carrots, particularly the purple ones available in the UK. To make it even more visually appealing, I occasionally add cucumbers or baby courgettes if they are available at the market. Serve this salad ever so slightly warm as a bright accompaniment to your barbecues and roasts.

INGREDIENTS:

- 500g (1lb 2oz) heritage carrots
- 1 medium cucumber (the ones you get at Arab grocery stores) or 2 small courgettes (zucchini)
- 1 small mooli (daikon) radish (optional)
- Juice and grated zest of 1 medium orange
- 2 large cloves of garlic, minced
- 10 mint leaves, finely chopped
- 2 tbsp extra virgin olive oil
- Sea salt

Serves 4

★V★DF★GF

Wash and scrape the carrots gently, then, with the help of a potato peeler or a mandoline (if you are comfortable with it), pare them lengthways so that you end up with a medley of long, colourful strips.

Repeat the same slicing process for the cucumber or courgettes and the mooli, if using.

Prepare the dressing by mixing together the orange juice and zest, garlic, mint leaves and olive oil in a large bowl. Season well with salt.

Lightly salt a large saucepan of water and bring it to a boil. Add the carrot slices and blanch for 30 seconds, then strain. Transfer the warm carrots straight into the dressing bowl, along with the cucumber and mooli.

Give it a good mix and serve straight away.

UMI QAMAR'S GADO-GADO SALAD
(Fun to say, delicious to eat)

Food has the remarkable ability to transport you to different places, even if you can't physically go there, and gado-gado is a perfect example of this, taking you to the streets of Jakarta, Indonesia. This is the most famous street food of Indonesia and, as I always say, street foods are the index to a nation's soul.

Gado-gado means "mix mix", which is justified; indeed it is a mix of as many vegetables as you like. Surprisingly, they all work together extraordinarily well, all married with a vibrant and spicy peanut sauce – a perfect example of unity in diversity.

I was first introduced to this lip-smacking salad by my beautiful Saudi–Indonesian land lady, Umi (*umi* means "mother") Qamar, who is of Betawi decent. We used to go together to afternoon tea gatherings in the Indonesian quarter of Jeddah. These gatherings, known as *asariya*, were usually hosted by one of the neighbours on a kind of a rotation. They were as diverse as could be; I can't even begin to think how many different cultures and cuisines I have seen during those years, coming together in perfect harmony.

There was another Indonesian lady called Nadia, who often hosted these gatherings, and this salad was at the top of her menu list. Widowed at a very young age, to feed her family she started to cook and sell her food to the locals and cater on a small scale. I clearly remember gado-gado was 5 riyals per plate and I was happy enough to save some of my pocket money to go and have this once or twice a month with Qamar.

I was so in love with this dish that I requested Umi Qamar show me how to make it, which she lovingly agreed to. I am so grateful and indebted to her for demonstrating to me how to make the iconic gado-gado crunchy peanut sauce on her tiny stone grinder.

This recipe is as close to the original one as I can possibly get here in the UK. I have mentioned a few alternatives, but you can pick and choose the veggies and other ingredients as you like. Feel free to experiment. Gado-gado is a complete meal in its own right and can be made easily vegetarian by leaving out the tiny amount of shrimp paste used in the peanut dressing, and made vegan by also omitting the eggs.

INGREDIENTS:

- 4 large eggs
- A splash of vinegar
- 80g (2¾oz/1 cup) yard long beans or green beans, trimmed
- 100g (3½oz) rice vermicelli
- 2 potatoes (optional), cubed
- A small bag (about 80g/2¾oz) of baby spinach leaves
- 300g (10½oz) beansprouts
- ½ small white or red cabbage, finely shredded
- 3 tbsp groundnut oil
- 200g (7oz) extra-firm tofu or ready-to-eat tempeh, cubed
- 1 lettuce head, shredded
- 2 medium carrots, julienned
- ½ cucumber, cut into thin strips
- 200g (7oz) Indonesian rice cakes (lontong/ketupat), cubed (optional but highly recommended – they come ready to serve in packets available in oriental food markets
- Crispy fried onions (homemade or store-bought, optional)
- 1 red chilli, sliced
- Prawn crackers
- A few coriander (cilantro) sprigs, roughly chopped

For the peanut sauce:

- 200g (7oz) roasted unsalted peanuts
- 4 red bird's eye chillies (or to taste)
- 1 tbsp tamarind paste
- 3 tbsp palm sugar (or soft dark brown sugar)
- ½ tsp salt (or to taste)
- 1 tsp Indonesian dry shrimp paste (if shrimp paste is not available, replace it with 1 tbsp fish sauce or vegan fish sauce)
- 5 tbsp crunchy peanut butter
- 2 tbsp lime juice
- 250ml (9fl oz/1 cup) coconut milk
- 3 tbsp kecap manis (or equal parts honey and soy sauce)

Serves 4–6

★**DF**

First, make the sauce. Using a pestle and mortar, grind the peanuts with the chillies, tamarind paste, sugar, salt, and shrimp paste (if using) until the nuts become as smooth as possible. You can also do it in a food processor by pulse blitzing it.

Add the peanut butter and the lime juice, then add the coconut milk little by little as you mix it. You don't want the sauce to become watery and diluted in taste so you may not need to add it all. Add the kecap manis and stir in. The sauce consistency should be that of salad cream. (This can be made ahead of time and will live happily in the fridge for up to a week.)

Moving on to the salad, start by boiling the eggs: bring a medium saucepan of water to the boil and add a fat pinch of salt and the splash of vinegar (this helps the skin come off very easily). Gently place the eggs in the water one by one with a slotted spoon. Let them boil over a medium heat for exactly 7 minutes for soft and gooey but not runny yolks. Once the eggs are boiled, plunge them immediately into ice-cold water to stop the cooking process, then peel the eggs, cover and set aside.

Next, trim the ends of the long beans and blanch them in salted boiling water on a medium heat for 4–5 minutes, until they are al dente. Drain and place in ice-cold water for 5 minutes to retain the green colour and stop cooking, then drain and set aside.

Soak the rice vermicelli in hot water for about 5–7 minutes, until they are soft, then drain and set aside.

If you decide to add potatoes, peel and cut them into 2½cm (1-inch) cubes. Bring a large saucepan of water to a boil, salt it generously and add the potato cubes. Boil for 10–15 minutes until tender. To check for doneness, insert a knife or fork into a potato; it should slide in easily when cooked. Once done, drain the potatoes, cover and set aside.

Thoroughly wash the spinach leaves and let the water drain out completely. If you wish, you can slightly blanch the leaves in boiling water for a minute, then drain and set aside.

Soak the beansprouts in boiling water for about a minute, ensuring that they don't lose their crunch. Drain and set aside.

Blanch the cabbage for about 2–3 minutes until al dente. Drain and set aside.

Heat the groundnut oil in a frying pan, add the tofu or tempeh and shallow fry for about 3–5 minutes, turning over during cooking, until golden all over.

To assemble the salad, start by placing the spinach leaves and the rice noodles at the bottom and then layer up the lettuce, carrots, potatoes, beans, beansprouts, cabbage and cucumber however you like. Top the salad with the fried tofu, boiled halved eggs and the rice cakes if using, then pour the peanut sauce generously over the salad. Sprinkle with some fried onions, red chilli slices, prawn crackers and coriander.

PAN-FRIED RADICCHIO AND DATE SALAD WITH TAHINI AND HAWAIJ CRUNCHY NUTS

This is a salad in which past meets present and the two live happily ever after. Another one of my nostalgic creations, where I have rocked my Arab roots, playing with familiar flavours while adding ingredients I was not familiar with. During my early student years in the UK, I saw red radicchio at my local grocery store. Wondering if it tasted like gem lettuce, I brought it home and stared at it for a good half hour before wrestling out this salad. The rest is history: because I still love it, I am sharing it with you. The moral of the story? Don't be afraid of trying unknown flavours – you may fall in love with them.

INGREDIENTS:

- 15g (½oz/1 tbsp) butter
- 6 medjool dates, each pitted and cut lengthways into 6 strips.
- 2 heads of red radicchio (or use red gem lettuce), halved lengthways
- Olive oil, for drizzling
- Handful of wild rocket (arugula) leaves
- Date syrup, to drizzle
- ½ recipe quantity (or as much as you like) Hawaij Spiced Crunchy Nuts (see page 186)
- Sea salt

For the shatta-tahini dressing:

- Juice of 1 lime
- 2 tbsp tahini paste
- 2 tbsp maple syrup
- 1 tsp Shatta (see page 195)
- Pinch of cayenne pepper (optional)
- 1 tbsp Greek yogurt
- Sea salt

Serves 2

★V★GF

Start by preparing the dressing. Add all of the ingredients to a blender and blend until smooth (or just stir them together in a bowl). Season with sea salt and set aside.

Put the butter and dates in a saucepan, and sauté over a medium heat for a minute or so until the dates are soft. Sprinkle with some sea salt and set aside.

Now heat a griddle pan (which gives nice charred lines) or a regular frying pan over a high heat. Drizzle the radicchio halves with olive oil and place them in the pan, cut sides down. Cook for a couple of minutes, keeping an eye on them, and as soon as the cut sides start to caramelize, flip them over and cook for a further 30 seconds, then take them off the heat.

To assemble, first spoon the dressing into a serving plate and top with the pan-fried radicchio, charred sides up. Dot the buttery medjool date strips over the top and scatter some wild rocket leaves over. Drizzle lightly with date syrup and top the salad up with Hawaij crunchy nuts mix. Serve this salad warm.

TABOULEH WITH A BEIRUTI TOUCH

Traditionally, the elderly lady of a household, who is usually in charge of overlooking the prep of a feast and making tabouleh, would always bring her hands together and say "Bismillah" (in the name of Allah) first, then the youngest in the kitchen would pour in the olive oil followed by the lemon juice over the prepared salad veggies, mixing love, care and blessings into salad with her wrinkly hands.

There is an Arab saying that "The secret to the best tabouleh is the best intentions, because you can taste someone's intention through their food."

To make tabouleh the authentic way, always use flat leaf parsley, picked and washed well and sliced very finely, not chopped as it will ruin the flavour, nutritional value and texture of the herb.

Ideally serve the tabouleh salad with ice-cold cabbage leaves or Iceberg lettuce to scoop up the citrusy juices in the bowl, which are destined to run down your chin and elbows. Perfect as a light lunch on a hot summer day or as an accompaniment to a Lahm Al Mandi (page 104) and other rice dishes.

INGREDIENTS:

- 2 tbsp fine bulghur wheat
- Juice and grated zest of 2 lemons
- 2 tomatoes, deseeded and diced into small cubes (reserve the tomato juices)
- A pinch of sweet cinnamon
- 1 small white onion (or small bunch of green onions), finely chopped
- 2 bunches of flat leaf parsley, very finely sliced
- 1 bunch of fresh mint, very finely sliced
- 120ml (4fl oz/½ cup) extra virgin olive oil
- Sea salt and freshly ground black pepper
- Lettuce leaves, to serve

Serves 4

★V★DF

Put the bulghur wheat in a bowl and add the lemon juice and any juice that may have escaped from the tomatoes as you chopped them. Leave to soak for about 5 minutes or so until softened.

In the meantime, prepare the rest of the ingredients. Sprinkle the cinnamon and some salt and pepper on the chopped onion – go heavy on the pepper as it is a key flavour in this salad. The seasoning will soften the onion a little and take on the seasoning flavour.

In a bowl, combine all the soaked bulghur with the onion, tomatoes, lemon zest and herbs. Mix well, then drizzle with the olive oil.

Enjoy with any kind of lettuce leaves.

TUNA AND BUTTER BEAN SALAD

To this day I vividly remember when the first branch of Pizza Hut opened its doors to the public in Jeddah – it was in 1987, if memory serves me correctly. It immediately became fashionable and a status symbol for the middle- and upper-middle-class families to dine out at Pizza Hut at the weekend. Back then, it was a thing we kids boasted about. It was our very first taste of American fast food, with all of the glitz and glam.

Pizza Hut used to have a loaded salad bar with a drool-worthy selection. I remember they had an "eat as much as you like" deal, limited only by the size of the plates. I have witnessed hilarious scenes of people loading their plates like there was no tomorrow. I have even heard techniques to pile on as much salad as possible being discussed during pizza parties.

Things have dramatically changed since then, but the memories remain fresh – as does this tuna and butter bean salad, which was my personal favourite on the salad bar and still is. Everyone could discuss the pineapple on pizza conundrum until the cows came home as far as I was concerned; all I cared was how much of this I could scoff.

INGREDIENTS:

- 2 × 125g (4½oz) cans tuna in brine, drained
- 1 small red onion, very finely diced
- ½ red (bell) pepper, deseeded and finely diced
- 1 × 400g (14oz) can butter (lima) beans, drained
- 50g (1¾oz) spring onions (scallions), finely chopped
- 25g (1oz) chives, finely chopped (optional)
- 1 × 195g (7oz) can sweetcorn, drained
- 2–3 hot green chillies
- 125g (4½oz/½ cup) mayonnaise
- 1 tsp American-style yellow mustard
- 1 tbsp soy sauce
- 1 tsp icing (confectioners') sugar
- 1 tsp freshly ground black pepper (or to taste)
- Sea salt

Serves 4–6

★DF★GF

Mix everything in a bowl and serve.

This can stay in the fridge for up to 2–3 days.

TIP: This salad works brilliantly as a deli filler for sandwiches, toasties and jacket potatoes loaded with cheese. I make it all the time and it's a family favourite – it costs a fraction of the amount we pay for tuna melt toasties at eateries and is way more flavourful.

3H BAKED AUBERGINE, FIG AND FETA SALAD WITH ORANGE-TAHINI DRESSING

(The 3H is for Hot Harissa Honey not 3 hours!)

The 3H abbreviation was coined by my 7-year-old son when he had just started school. He loves aubergines and I love the funny words he comes up with, so I named this salad after his playful spin on an otherwise mouthful of a name.

If you love aubergine, this salad might get you in trouble, because anyone who tries it is hooked for good – it is highly addictive. This one humble salad has the ability to convert the most stubborn aubergine haters. It's meaty, soft, zingy with lactic tang, rich, earthy and sweet all at the same time.

INGREDIENTS:

For the aubergines:

- 5 tbsp Hot Harissa Honey (see page 191)
- 2 tbsp light olive oil
- 2 tbsp sesame oil
- 3 aubergines (eggplants) stems trimmed and each cut lengthways into 6 wedges
- 1 tbsp toasted sesame seeds

For the orange-tahini dressing:

- Juice and zest of 1 small orange
- 80g (2¾oz/⅓ cup) Greek yogurt
- Pinch of cayenne pepper
- Pinch of lemon salt (citric acid)
- 2 tbsp tahini paste
- 1 tbsp extra virgin olive oil, plus extra to drizzle
- Sea salt

For the salad:

- A handful (about 20g/¾oz) of wild rocket (arugula)
- A handful (about 20g/¾oz) of watercress
- 200g (7oz) feta or any white salad cheese
- 6 semi-dried or fresh figs, quartered
- About 25g (1oz) toasted pine nuts or chopped toasted almonds (or a mixture of both)
- Za'atar, to sprinkle
- Pomegranate molasses or balsamic vinegar, to drizzle

Serves 4–6

★V★GF

Preheat the oven to 180°C (350°F), gas 4.

In a small bowl, combine the hot harissa honey, olive oil and sesame oil to form a paste.

Brush the paste onto the cut sides of the aubergines, then sprinkle with the sesame seeds. Transfer them to a baking sheet and bake for about 25–30 minutes until the aubergines are cooked through and offer little resistance when squeezed with your fingers.

Meanwhile, prepare the dressing by blending together all of the dressing ingredients. Season to taste with salt and set aside.

Assemble the salad on a serving plate: place the greens on first, then crumble over the feta, breaking it into bite-sized chunks as you go. Place the quartered figs and roasted aubergine wedges on top and sprinkle with the toasted nuts and za'atar. Drizzle with pomegranate molasses or balsamic vinegar and more olive oil, then serve warm.

SALATA KHADRA
(AKA baladi salad with a twist)

A salad where simplicity reigns. Chunky, crunchy cuts of cucumber, tomatoes, capsicum and onion dressed up in a very basic vinaigrette is a colourful sight that pleases both the eye and the palate. Daqqus and salata khadra are the Laurel and Hardy of a typical Saudi spread. You can add or remove the veggies and adjust their quantities as per your liking. The following works well for me.

INGREDIENTS:

- 1 medium tomato, deseeded and diced (don't discard the seedy bits, we will use them in the dressing – remember, no waste!)
- 2 medium Arab cucumbers or 1 English cucumber, diced into chunky bite-sized cubes
- ¼ head of Iceberg lettuce, sliced
- 1 banana shallot or 1 small red onion, diced
- 1 yellow pepper (or any colour), diced
- Handful of pitted black olives, halved (optional)
- 2 tbsp finely chopped parsley
- 100g (3½oz) feta or salad cheese, crumbled

For the vinaigrette dressing:

- 3 tbsp extra virgin olive oil, plus extra to drizzle
- Juice and zest of ½ lemon
- 2 tsp honey
- Sea salt and freshly ground black pepper

Serves 4–6

★V★GF

Make the dressing first by stirring together all the ingredients. Strain the seedy centres of the tomatoes you have reserved and add the tomato juice to the dressing. Season with salt and a fat pinch of black pepper. The dressing can be stored in the fridge for up to 3 days.

For the salad, mix together all the vegetables, olives and parsley in a bowl. Pour over the dressing and toss well.

Transfer the salad to a serving plate or bowl.

Sprinkle with the crumbled feta or salad cheese, drizzle with olive oil and serve.

Reign the mains

The mains scene is quite unique in Saudi Arabia, in a sense that each province has its proud main dish which is consumed throughout the kingdom but always associated with the region it came from, its origin remaining highly regarded.

From Harees to Saleeq, from Lahm Al Mandi to Marqooq, and from galette-like, herby Aish Abou Lahm to Kawareh Wa Kubeibat, there is a world of hidden gems that we are about to explore in this chapter.

How dare I not mention Saudi Kabsa when writing about Saudi food? It has to be the crowning glory of the mains, but at the same time, there is much more to Saudi cuisine than just kabsa.

But first, let's talk about the kabsa. It is more than just a dish. It is a story told in steam, spice and all things nice – a national culinary anthem that echoes through the tiled kitchens of metropolitan Riyadh to deep within the wind-swept Bedouin desert of *Rub Al Khali* (the Empty Quarter). It arrives not quietly but with the regal etiquettes and a drum roll of tradition, its fragrance bold enough to summon distant memories and appetites alike.

The rice used in this dish should be of the best-quality basmati that one can source. The rice absorbs not only the stock in which it simmers, but also the history of the hands that cook it. Saffron lends its golden hush, while black lime mimics the majestic black mountains of the Najd region[1] and sun-dried bitterness, like the hot desert breathing through the pot. The meat can be lamb, chicken, sometimes even camel, and it is not merely cooked, but honoured, roasted and stewed to perfection, ready to yield its fragrant and spicy secrets to tingle your taste buds and say "Hello, dinner is served."

Then come the garnishes, which are mandatory, crowning the kabsa with toasted almonds, plump jumbo raisins and caramelized carrots. These are not mere decorations but punctuation marks in this savoury sentence. Kabsa is often presented on a communal platter that invites not only hands but also stories, laughter and shared silences all at the same time.

To taste kabsa is to sit at the very heart of Saudi Arabian cuisine – to know its warmth, complexity, hospitality and the pride it carries in every single morsel.

[1] *central province of KSA and the Royal seat*

Mandi is the second most popular main and more often consumed. Pair Lahm Al Mandi with my loaded Jewelled Rice (page 168) and you are in for a treat. This is one undisputed versatile main that always dawns on my Eid dinner table every year. You've got to try it to appreciate the countless layers of flavour.

Not to miss out on Saleeq, a rich, creamy rice dish with a rotisserie-style chicken on top. This is a much-loved main dish originating from the Holy city of Makkah Al Mukarramah (Mecca, Hijaz, western province). The Word *saleeq* literally means "white-faced" in Arabic. No racism involved here; in fact this dish was named by the people of the Makkah and Taif region due to its milky white risotto-like appearance as it does not contain any hot spices.

And then comes a giant whole fried fish, Shaoor Maghli. A feast for your eyes and tongue. We are talking about the Red Sea, so fish, of course, is part of the main course section here. It's all in the names: Emperor Fish and Leopard and Coral grouper. The crowning glories of the Red Sea. This book would have been incomplete without mentioning these two Red Sea royals. These species are native to the Red Sea and roam freely across its length and breadth.

The way these fish are prepared and fried is very unique to the Saudi coastal towns of the Red Sea. Freshly caught fish are descaled and gutted at one of the old Balad (historic city centre and UNESCO Heritage site in Jeddah) souk shops with an outer carved wooden hatch. They are dusted with local coarse salt, and then washed off and pushed into a wide, slightly tilted skillet filled with bubbling oil to deep fry. Once the skin has crisped up and the exposed nuggets of flesh turn brown, the fish is taken out and given a heavy dusting of a zingy spice blend.

As much as I like making a feast out of my mains, I have to admit that I am a huge admirer of one-pot wholesome cooking. It saves time, energy and a lot of washing up. These one-pot wonders fill you up, and also fill your fridge if you cook mammoth portions like me.

Marqooq is one such wonder I had the privilege to enjoy growing up in Saudi Arabia, often during school breaks and visiting Aba Jan's friends in their Bedouin tents. Marqooq, Matazeez and Thareed are all very similar, with their origin going back to Prophetic times of Muhammad (peace be upon Him).

In recent years, I have longed for this piping hot bowl of deep amber-coloured broth with lamb bits falling of the bones and vegetables so tender that they don't even bother resisting when touched. All of the goodness cuddled up in plump wholewheat discs mimicking a wholewheat pasta but way better as those little morsels have soaked up the broth flavours. I just couldn't find time to recreate it; life just got in the way.

And then magic happened. A couple of years ago, a young lad named Aymen from Saudi Arabia, who came to London for higher studies in culinary arts, opened up the first-ever Saudi restaurant, Hijazi Corner, which sits between Old Marylebone Road and the city's very hustling and bustling mini Middle East (Edgware Road). He got in touch with me after my MasterChef UK appearance, invited me to his restaurant and served me a steamy hot bowl of Marqooq on a very cold and wet November evening. I took a sip of this deep, decadent broth, and in that moment of time we became friends for life. The rest is history.

To my vegetarian and vegan readers, I haven't left you out. There are a handful of main recipes that are naturally vegan or can easily be made vegan by substituting with plant-based ingredients. There is a much-loved Tahini, Aubergine and Cauliflower Tray Bake, Ful Two Ways, Makarona bil Laban, Halloumi Cheese with Madinian Dukkah Oil – all meat-free – and Marqooq and A Very Relaxed Aubergine Fatteh, which can easily be made vegan.

And that's not the end of the story for mains. I have also lined up for you the simplest and juiciest of Mabshoor kababs, which I absolutely adore. And a zingy, smoky, gnarly stickiest-wings-of-your-dreams dish to ace your mains game.

There is a recipe for anyone and everyone in this book.

AISH ABOU LAHEM
(Spiced lamb galette)

A delicious cross between a bready deep-dish pizza and a galette, this herbaceous and fragrant protein-packed pie hails from the Holy region of Makkah. It is a Ramadan staple in every household and loved by the locals so much that it has attained a proverbial status. There is a very well-known saying about aish abou lahem that, literally translated, means "bread with meat", which indicates the homeliness of the dish: "Whatever a man [guest] brings is a blessing, even if it is just aish abou lahem." This recipe is very forgiving and can be made with soya mince for a vegan option, plenty of fresh dill and baby leeks or spring onions. The meat filling on its own is so addictive that it'll be hard to resist the temptation to faceplant the filling bowl. Aish can be eaten hot or cold and is perfect for picnics and packed lunches as well. For picnics, I usually make small individual pies, which are really handy.

INGREDIENTS:

For the dough:

- 2 tbsp chana dal (split chickpea lentils)
- 350g (12½oz/2⅔ cups) plain (all-purpose) flour
- 1 tbsp sugar
- 7g (¼oz) fast-action dried yeast
- 1 tsp salt
- 1 tsp ground mahlep (or a couple of drops of almond extract)
- 1 tsp nigella seeds
- 1 tsp coarsely ground fennel seeds
- ½ tsp ground allspice or Baharat spice mix
- 60ml (2fl oz/¼ cup) melted ghee or olive oil
- Olive oil, to grease your hands and spread the dough

For the filling:

- 2 tbsp butter or olive oil
- 1 medium onion or 150g (5¼oz) spring onions (scallions), finely chopped
- 2 cloves of garlic, minced
- 450g (1lb) lean minced (ground) lamb or beef, or soya mince
- 1½ tsp Baharat spice mix
- 1 tsp freshly ground black pepper
- 400g (14oz) baby leeks or spring onions (the green part), very finely chopped
- 100g (3½oz) dill, finely chopped (or you can substitute with parsley)
- 30g (1oz) flat leaf parsley, chopped
- 1 small tomato, deseeded and finely diced
- Sea salt

For the tahini sauce:

- 175g (6oz) tahini
- 1 tbsp white vinegar
- 1 tbsp grape vinegar or balsamic vinegar

To assemble:

- Handful of grated Manchego cheese (optional; I know it's Spanish but I love its nutty pairing with the dish)
- 1 plum tomato, sliced (optional)
- 1 egg yolk, mixed with a few drops of milk, for egg wash (skip if making a vegan option)
- A sprinkle of za'atar and sesame seeds

Serves 4–6

★V★DF

Wash the lentils, then soak them in cold water for 30 minutes at least. Drain the lentils, put them in a small saucepan and cover with 300ml (10½fl oz/1¼ cups) of water. Cover the pan and cook over a medium heat for 5–7 minutes until the lentils are soft but hold their shape. Strain and reserve the liquid for the dough – you will need 250ml (9fl oz/1 cup) of the leftover, warm cooking liquid.

To make the dough, combine all the dry ingredients in a bowl, then rub in the melted ghee or olive oil until you have a very fine crumb.

Add the tepid lentil liquid, little by little, and knead gently until it comes together into a soft dough ball. The dough will be loose and slightly sticky but that is fine; don't be tempted to add more flour. Add the lentils at the end and fold them in, then bring it all together with a scraper. Drizzle with a little oil, cover and let the dough rest for at least an hour in a warm place until it almost doubles in size.

In the meantime, prepare the filling. Put the butter or oil in a frying pan on a medium heat and sauté the chopped onion until translucent. Add the garlic and sauté for 30 seconds until fragrant.

Add the mince and sauté on a high heat until the meat browns – about 5 minutes, then add the Baharat spice and black pepper and season with salt to taste. Sauté for another couple of minutes, then turn off the heat and set aside to cool slightly.

Meanwhile, whip up the sauce: add the tahini, both vinegars and 175ml (6fl oz) tepid water to a bowl and mix well.

Preheat your oven to 180°C (350°F), gas 4.

Now, to the cooled-down filling, add the leeks or spring onions, chopped dill and parsley, chopped tomato and the tahini sauce. Mix well, then taste and adjust any seasoning to your taste.

Brush a 24cm (9½-inch) round dish or mould generously with oil and spread the proven dough out gently to a roughly 2cm (¾-inch) thickness, covering the sides of the dish. Let the dough go slightly over the rim of your dish.

Tip in the filling, pressing it down gently to even it out. Pull the overhanging dough inwards to cover the edges of the pie like a galette.

Sprinkle your grated cheese over and arrange the sliced tomatoes on top, if using. Brush the top of the pie with egg wash, then sprinkle with za'atar and sesame seeds.

Bake in the oven for 25–30 minutes, or until evenly browned. I recommend placing the dish on a rack set just lower than the middle (but not on the bottom of the oven).

Let the pie cool down for 15–20 minutes before diving in. Serve with a side of fresh salad and chunky chips (fries).

MARQOOQ
(A very traditional recipe dedicated to the first Saudi restaurant in England)

This is Chef Aymen's recipe that he lovingly shared for my debut cookbook.

Marqooq is named after the special wholemeal dough that is hand pulled and stretched until thin, cut into discs and traditionally cooked in a very fragrant meaty broth with lots of autumnal vegetables, marking the change of seasons as it starts to get a bit cooler.

Marqooq is a well-known dish, eaten especially during Ramadan due to its comforting and soul-warming nature, just the kind of meal you would want to have after a long day without food and water. It is the iconic representation of an authentic Saudi table.

INGREDIENTS:

For the dough:

- 300g (10½oz/2¼ cups) wholemeal flour, plus extra for dusting
- 75g (2½oz/heaped ½ cup) plain (all-purpose) flour
- ½ tsp salt
- 100ml (3½fl oz/scant ½ cup) warm water

For the stew:

- 2 tbsp vegetable oil
- 1 large onion, finely chopped
- 2 cloves of garlic, minced
- 750g (1lb 10oz) lamb shoulder, preferably on the bone, cut into 5cm (2-inch) pieces (ask your butcher to do this)
- 2 tomatoes, finely chopped
- 1 tbsp tomato purée (paste)
- 1 tsp ground coriander
- 1 tsp ground cumin
- 1 tsp Baharat spice mix
- ½ tsp black pepper
- ½ tsp ground turmeric
- 1 litre (35fl oz/4¼ cups) hot water
- 2 dried black limes (loomi)
- 2 Arab (light coloured and known as khusa) courgettes (zucchini), or normal ones if you can't find, cut into 5cm (2-inch) rounds
- 2 carrots, cut into 5cm (2-inch) chunks
- 1 small pumpkin, cut into 5cm (2-inch) chunks
- Sea salt

To serve:

- 2 tbsp chopped coriander (cilantro)
- Mild green chillies, sliced (optional)

Serves 4–6

★DF

First, prepare the dough. In a bowl, mix the wholemeal flour, plain flour and salt. Gradually add the warm water while kneading until you get a soft and smooth dough. Cover the dough and let it rest for 30 minutes.

Divide the dough into six small balls and roll each one out on a floured surface until very thin – about the thickness of a pound coin.

For the stew, heat the oil in a deep pan over a medium heat. Add the onion and sauté until soft, about 3–5 minutes. Add the garlic and lamb and cook until the meat is slightly browned – about 5 minutes. Add the chopped tomatoes, tomato purée and spices, and season with salt. Cook, stirring, for about 5 minutes to combine the flavours.

Pour in the hot water, then add the dried limes and let the stew simmer for 40–50 minutes until the meat is fork tender.

Once the lamb is tender, add the chopped vegetables to the pan and let them cook for a further 10 minutes.

Add the rolled-out dough pieces to the stew one at a time, stirring gently to prevent them from sticking together. Let the marqooq simmer on a low heat for 15–20 minutes, until the dough is fully cooked and absorbs the flavours.

Serve the marqooq hot in a deep serving dish, garnished with fresh coriander and sliced chillies, if desired.

LAHM AL MANDI
(Roasted lamb with fragrant jewelled rice)

Deeply rooted in Yemen, this dish has travelled the length and breadth of the Silk Route, loved by Saudis and anyone who tries it. No celebration or wedding is complete without this showstopper. Saudis take pride in displaying the best version possible. Traditionally this recipe involves a whole lamb or goat, roasted with its head still on, served on a mound of smoky and fluffy aromatic jewelled basmati rice, loaded with fried nuts, lemon wedges and served with a bowl of fragrant meaty broth, all arranged on a gigantic silver platter. I have reduced the recipe to cater generously for four to six people, but with the same wow factor. Serve this dish with daqqus (Saudi salsa), shatta, and Sidr honey or date molasses for each diner to drizzle on their lamb individually.

INGREDIENTS:

For the lamb mandi:

- 1 medium onion, thickly sliced
- 6–7 whole cloves of garlic
- 1 tbsp salt (or to taste)
- 5cm (2-inch) piece of fresh galangal (or use dried – widely available in Asian supermarkets)
- 2 bay leaves
- 10–12 cloves
- 10–12 whole green cardamom pods
- 4 dried black lemons (loomi)
- 1½ tsp whole allspice berries (pimento)
- 1 tsp ground black pepper
- ½ tsp ground turmeric
- 1 whole lamb shoulder on the bone, fat on, or large lamb chunks with fat on (about 1.25kg/2¾lb)
- 2 tbsp ghee
- ½ tsp saffron, ground, or yellow food colouring

For the jewelled rice:

- 1 tbsp white vinegar
- 5–6 green cardamom pods, lightly crushed
- 750g (26½oz) easy cook (sella) basmati rice, soaked in warm water for 1 hour
- 3 tbsp neutral oil, such as vegetable
- 2 tbsp ghee (or 1 tbsp olive oil and 1 tbsp unsalted butter)
- 75g (2½oz/½ cup) blanched almonds
- 75g (2½oz/½ cup) cashews
- A handful of pine nuts
- 75g (2½oz/½ cup) mixed raisins and dried cranberries
- 1 small onion, finely chopped
- 2–3 jalapeño peppers (optional)
- 1 tsp Baharat spice mix
- A few strands of saffron soaked in 2 tbsp kewra (screwpine) water (or use rose water, but please ensure that it's not rose essence – you don't want the rice to smell like grandma's bathroom)
- Sea salt

To serve:

- A few pomegranate seeds
- A handful of slivered pistachios
- Daqqus (see page 183)
- Shatta (see page 195),
- Sidr honey or date molasses, for drizzling
- Fresh salad of your choice (I serve it with the tomato and olive salad on page 72)
- Tabouleh (see page 84)
- Jajeek (see page 190)

Serves 4–6

★GF

To a large pot which can fit in all the lamb, add all of the lamb mandi ingredients except the lamb, ghee, saffron and turmeric. Place the lamb on top of these spices and herbs. Add 500–750ml (17–26fl oz) of hot water, making sure that the water is not covering the lamb completely; it should be below the meat. (You could also use a wire rack of some sort to place the meat on.) Cover the lamb with a cartouche (a circle of baking paper) and cover the pot with a tight lid.

Cook on a high heat for at least 10 minutes, or until steam starts coming out. Turn the heat down to the lowest setting and let the lamb cook in its own steam for 3 hours, or until it is falling off the bone. (Alternatively, pressure cook for 1 hour without using the paper cartouche.) Once cooked to perfection, strain to remove any liquid. Set the liquid aside and cover the lamb with baking paper and then a layer of foil so that it stays warm and moist.

In the meantime, prepare the rice. Pour plenty of boiling water into a large, wide pot, and season it well with salt and the vinegar. Add the green cardamom pods. Tip in the soaked rice and let it cook on medium heat for about 5–7 minutes until 80 per cent done (it will be cooked but still have a slight bite to it – see page 18). Drain the rice and set aside.

In the same wide pot, heat the neutral oil and ghee together on a medium heat, then fry the almonds, cashews, pine nuts and mixed raisins and cranberries for 3–4 minutes. Take them out and leave to drain on a piece of paper towel.

In the same oil, on a medium heat, sauté the onion until soft, then add the jalapeño peppers, if using.

Pour in about 250ml (9fl oz/1 cup) of the reserved liquid from the lamb, and add the Baharat spice mix. Taste and adjust for salt if required. Give it a stir, then tip in the boiled rice and fried nuts and fruit, reserving a few for garnish. Gently mix everything together in a folding motion. You can add the saffron-water mix in a swirling motion at this stage if using.

Let the rice cook on a very low heat until all of the liquid has been absorbed and the rice grains have fluffed up. This will take about 7–10 minutes.

Meanwhile, combine the ghee, turmeric and saffron (or food colouring) in a bowl. While the rice is in the final stages of cooking, remove the lamb from the foil and brush it with the ghee mixture.

Either grill (broil) the lamb under a very hot grill until the fat bubbles up and gets crispy with a nice golden colour, or pan fry it to give it a nice colour. (I grill it for 10 minutes approximately, but keep watching like a hawk so it doesn't burn!)

To plate up, get a wide serving dish or a large platter, fluff the rice up and spread it out on the platter. Place the lamb on top and garnish your heart out with pomegranate seeds and pistachios and the reserved fried nuts/fruit.

To give it a proper authentic touch, place a small heatproof bowl on the platter. Heat a small piece of barbecue charcoal on the hob until it becomes ashy. Place the charcoal (in the bowl) on the platter and drizzle a few drops of oil or ghee onto it. Cover the platter and leave for 2–3 minutes to give the dish a delicate charcoal smoke. Discard the coal before serving.

Serve with fresh salads and accompaniments of your choice.

KAWAREH WA KUBEIBAT
(Stuffed vine leaves cooked in beef trotter broth, a very Egyptian dish)

This is a two-in-one recipe; it is an amalgam of Egyptian and Saudi cooking – the beef trotter part is Egyptian, while the stuffed vine leaves are a Saudi variation known as Kubiybat al Ha'il. When cooked together, the results are sublime. If you like stuffed vine leaves, you will fall in love with this recipe. It is way more simple to prepare than the traditional Lebanese method of meticulously wrapping vine leaves tightly into the shape of a cigar. In the Ha'il region, where it's known just as kubeibat, they use more of a freestyle wrapping, then pack the parcels into a baking dish to be topped up with falling-off-the-bone-tender beef trotter tendons and their fragrant citrusy broth.

It took me almost two decades to find the same nostalgic taste in London (my love at first sight) in a very Traditional Egyptian restaurant Al-Basha in Knightsbridge. This recipe is loosely based on their take on this decadent dish. Enjoy!

INGREDIENTS:

For the kawareh (beef trotter):
- 1 large beef trotter, cut into 5cm (2-inch) rounds (ask your butcher to do this)
- 2 lemons, quartered
- 2 oranges, quartered
- 2 large tomatoes, quartered
- 2 large white onions, quartered
- 2 large carrots, peeled and cut into chunks
- 100g (3½oz) fresh ginger, cut into 1cm (½-inch) chunks
- 1 bulb of garlic, cut horizontally in half
- 4–5 bay leaves
- 2 cinnamon sticks
- 1 tbsp whole green cardamom pods
- 1 tbsp black peppercorns
- Sea salt

For the stuffed vine leaves:
- 750g (1lb 10oz) Egyptian rice or Arborio rice
- 2 medium tomatoes, quartered
- 2 medium onions, quartered
- 1 tsp Baharat spice mix
- 1 tsp ground turmeric
- 1 tsp roasted cumin
- 1–2 tbsp Shatta, depending on your heat tolerance (see page 195)
- 1 tsp freshly ground black pepper
- 30g (1oz) spring onions (scallions), finely chopped
- 40ml (1¼fl oz/2½ tbsp) olive oil
- 1kg (2lb 4oz) grape vine leaves in brine (there will be about 170–180 leaves)
- 2 large potatoes, peeled and sliced into rounds 5mm (¼ inch) thick
- Sea salt

To serve:
- Pomegranate seeds
- Yogurt, Tahiniya (see page 184) and Shatta

Serves 6 generously

★GF

Clean the beef trotter to ensure there are no hairs, although usually they come already cleaned (if not, see tip opposite). Put the trotter pieces in a large pot and add enough water to cover them by around 5cm (2 inches). Bring the water to a rolling boil over a medium heat and cook for 20–30 minutes until all of the unwanted fat and dirty foam rises to the top; skim the top completely.

Now add rest of the karaweh ingredients and season generously with salt. Bring to the boil, then reduce the heat so that the liquid is simmering, cover and leave to simmer gently for 6–7 hours, until the tendons are fork tender (literally falling off the bone), then turn the heat off.

While the meat is still warm but is cool enough to handle, separate the bones and gelatinous tendons from each other, making sure the tendons are clean of any veins and bone. Cover and set aside. Discard the bones.

Sieve the stock while it is also still warm and set the liquid aside for later use.

To prepare the stuffed vine leaves, start with the filling. Wash and soak the rice for about 2 hours, then drain well and set aside.

In a food processor, blend the tomatoes, onions, Baharat spice mix, turmeric, cumin, shatta, black pepper and some salt with 2 tablespoons of water into a coarse paste.

Now, tip the tomato mixture over the rice and mix well, then add the chopped spring onions along with the olive oil. Mix again and set aside.

Fill a large heavy-based pan three-quarters of the way full with water, place over a medium heat and let the water come to a boil. Carefully unroll the vine leaves from their packaging and discard any brine solution. Slightly loosen the leaves without any forceful separation.

Turn the heat under the boiling water to very low and add the vine leaves. Cover and let them steep for 3–5 minutes.

Remove the leaves from the pot into a sieve or a rice strainer, and rinse under cold water to stop the cooking process. Transfer to a bowl, cover them and leave aside for 10–15 minutes. Once completely cooled down, spread them out on a tea towel loosely and cover them with another tea towel so that they don't dry out.

Using a knife, cut out any hard centre stems from the vine leaves.

Now to fill the vine leaves, which is the fun part. You don't really have to make a cigar shape as Lebanese counterparts do; the Saudi way of rolling the vine leaves is very relaxed and freestyle. First, separate a leaf gently from the pile and place it, shiny side down, on the work surface. Add a teaspoon of the rice filling to the centre of the leaf, then bring the edges of the leaf towards the centre, covering the filling completely and firmly and overlapping each other, so that it becomes a little sealed square-ish parcel. Do not wrap it too tight as the rice will expand while cooking. Repeat the process until all leaves are filled and rolled up.

Preheat the oven to 170°C (325°F), gas 5.

Now place the potato rounds at the bottom of a deep pot (ideally a terracotta pot), or a baking dish. Season with salt and freshly ground black pepper.

Layer the stuffed vine leaves into the dish, packing them close to each other with seam sides facing downwards so that they don't open during cooking.

Now, place the gelatinous part (the tendons) of the kawareh on top of the vine leaves, packing them in tightly.

Place a heavy heatproof plate, inverted, on top of the kawareh to weigh it down while cooking. Pour over the stock from the kawareh so it trickles down the sides of the inverted plate until you can see the liquid coming right up to the plate. Cover the dish completely with foil.

Place the dish in the oven and let it bake for approximately 2 hours, checking halfway through. If the liquid has completely dried up, top it up with a little more stock or water so that it doesn't burn. Cook until the vine leaves are completely tender but still holding their shape.

Take the pot out of the oven and remove the inverted plate – please be very careful as it will be very hot.

You can flip the pot over onto a serving platter, or serve as it is in the baking pot as I do. Scatter some pomegranate seeds on top and serve hot with yogurt, tahiniya and shatta.

TIP: If there are hairs on the trotters, char each piece lightly all over with a blowtorch or by holding them over a gas hob until the hairs are burnt. Scrape them away with a paring knife under running water.

TAAWA KEEMA
(Lamb, chicken or beef mince cooked on a large traditional hot plate)

This is a much-loved easy-to-put-together main that is adored by every household in KSA. The word "keema" derives its origin from the Turkish for ground meat. It wouldn't be an exaggeration to class keema as one of the great culinary wonders of the Silk Route, as wherever the traders from Arabia and central Asia went, they took such recipes with them, only to return with countless flavourful versions of this recipe.

This particular version of keema is very popular as a humble homemade supper kind of dish, where often tired mums after day-long chores would rustle up frozen minced meat with some whole spices – whatever they could find in the cupboards – often cooking the mince on a large hot plate called a tawa (which is also used to make rotis and bread) and serving it with warm naan bread or run through some yogurt pasta, aka Makarona bil Laban, and that used to be a treat on its own.

This is my mum's recipe from her fading memories, which she taught to anyone who asked.

Surprisingly, this main can be made vegan just by replacing the animal protein with plant-based protein. It is perfect paired with the Makarona bil Laban on page 127.

Me and Mama, selfie-mode at Knightsbridge station

INGREDIENTS:

- 125ml (4fl oz/½ cup) neutral cooking oil
- 500g (1lb 2oz) lean minced (ground) lamb or beef, or soya mince
- 3 fat cloves of garlic, minced
- 2 large tomatoes, chopped
- 40g (2½oz) fresh ginger, peeled and julienned
- ¼ tsp ground turmeric
- ½ tsp ground coriander
- 1 tsp red chilli powder
- 2 brown onions, finely sliced
- Sea salt

For the whole spices:

- 1 tbsp whole coriander seeds
- 2–3 whole dried red Kashmiri chillies
- 6 cloves
- 6 black peppercorns
- 1 tsp roasted cumin seeds
- 2 black cardamom pods

To serve:

- 1 tsp garam masala
- 50g (1¾oz) coriander (cilantro), chopped
- Mlawa (see page 165) or garlic naan
- Jajeek (see page 190)

Serves 4

★**GF**

In a wide wok or a large shallow frying pan, heat the cooking oil over medium heat and add all of the whole spices. Let them swell up and crackle for 1–2 minutes.

Now add the mince and the garlic, and sauté for about 5 minutes or until the mince is browned.

Add the chopped tomatoes, ginger, ground turmeric, ground coriander and chilli powder, then season with salt and continue frying for another minute or so. Add 250ml (9fl oz/1 cup) water, cover the pan with a lid and let it cook for 10–15 minutes, or until the water has fully evaporated.

Now remove the lid, and stir the mince, then add the sliced onions and mix well gently. Cover with the lid again and let it sit on the lowest-possible heat for 10 minutes until the sliced onions are softened.

Once ready, transfer it to a serving dish (or serve in the same pan) and garnish with the garam masala and chopped coriander. Serve with mlawa or garlic naan and jajeek.

MOROCCAN HARISSA CHICKEN WITH BURGHUL PILLAV
(A no-fuss take on a North African dish)

This is a true one-pot wonder. It's the perfect choice when I haven't got a clue what to rustle up for a mid-week meal and I'm running short on time with five hungry bellies to feed.

This is a quick-fix version of a classic harissa chicken that hails from North Africa but is equally loved throughout the Middle East, and is now my family's fave recipe. It takes minimal effort and suits a tight budget since it uses all storecupboard ingredients. Ideal for meal preps and packed lunches, it is loved by all. I like to serve it with Jajeek (also known as *cacik*, aka Arab tzatziki – see page 190) and pickles.

INGREDIENTS:

- 6 chicken thighs (preferably with skin and on the bone for extra flavour but skinless and boneless will do as well)
- 3–4 tbsp oil, for searing the chicken
- Jajeek (page 190) and pickles, to serve

For the harissa marinade:

- Drizzle of olive oil
- Juice of ½ lemon
- ¼ tsp ground turmeric
- ½ tsp sumac
- ½ tsp paprika
- ½ tsp ground cumin
- Sea salt, to taste
- 1 tsp garlic powder
- 1 tsp onion powder
- 1 tsp black pepper
- ½ tsp chilli powder
- 1 tsp ground coriander
- 1½ tsp freshly minced garlic or garlic paste
- 1½ tbsp harissa spice mix
- 25g (1oz/2 tbsp) butter

For the burghul pillav:

- 1 tbsp butter
- 1 small onion, diced
- 2 tbsp tomato purée (paste)
- 1 tbsp Turkish red pepper paste (biber salcasi), or 1½ tsp sweet paprika mixed with 1 tsp water
- 2 tomatoes, chopped
- ½ tsp ground cumin
- ¼ tsp Baharat spice mix
- 1 tsp chicken seasoning powder (such as Aromat)
- 300g (10½oz) burghul (cracked) wheat, washed
- Sea salt

Serves 4, with leftovers

Combine all of the harissa marinade ingredients. Add the chicken and coat well, then leave for 30 minutes if possible – or you can start cooking straight away if you're short on time.

In a wide frying pan, heat the oil on a medium heat. Sear the chicken thighs for 2–3 minutes on each side. Once the thighs are nicely coloured, take them out of the pan and set aside.

Use the same pan to make the pillav. De-glaze the pan by adding the butter. Once melted, add the onion and fry until translucent. Then add the tomato purée and Turkish red pepper paste, and sauté for a minute.

Add the chopped tomatoes, sauté for a minute and cover. Let it cook for 5 minutes on a medium heat or until the tomatoes have started to break down into a chunky sauce.

Add the spices and chicken powder and season with salt, if needed. Sauté for another 30 seconds before adding the washed burghul wheat. Mix thoroughly.

Add 325ml (11fl oz/1⅓ cups) water to the pan and mix well, then lay the seared chicken on top of the burghul. Cover and let it simmer on a low heat for 10–15 minutes, until the burghul is tender and the chicken thighs are cooked through.

Serve with Jajeek and pickles of your choice.

SALEEQ
(Saudi risotto with roast chicken)

Despite its simple ingredients, the elegance of saleeq lies in the way it is presented. This is a very low maintenance but attractive-looking main, especially when showered with some shaved or thinly sliced truffles and dressed with truffle oil instead of glistening ghee (which is my spin on this Saudi classic) all around the edges of the dish, giving it *Lord of the Rings* vibes.

It is rich, creamy, flavoursome, with the melt-in-your-mouth texture of juicy rotisserie-style roasted chicken. One bite and I am rolling in food heaven.

INGREDIENTS:

- 2 tbsp ghee or butter, plus extra for brushing the chicken
- 1 large onion, finely chopped
- 1 white loomi (dried lemon), pierced
- 2 bay leaves
- 1 stick of cinnamon
- 5 green cardamom pods
- 1 medium whole skin-on chicken, cut in half, lengthways, or 4 chicken legs
- 350g (12oz/1¾ cups) risotto rice
- 100g (3½oz) clotted cream, thick cream or ashta (sterilized cream)
- 1–1.25 litres (35–44fl oz/4¼–5½ cups) whole milk
- Salt and freshly ground black pepper

To serve:

- 2 tbsp ghee
- 1 tbsp truffle shavings (I use a mandoline to shave, optional but highly recommended)
- Daqqus (see page 183)

Serves 4

★GF

Melt the ghee over a medium heat in a pan that is large enough to eventually accommodate all of the ingredients. Add the onion, loomi, bay leaves, cinnamon stick and cardamom pods and sauté for 30 seconds. Add the chicken and sear it on a high heat until it's golden on all sides – the deeper the colour on the chicken, the better the flavour.

Add 1.25 litres (44fl oz/5½ cups) water and season with sea salt. Partially cover the pot and boil for about 30 minutes, or until the chicken is super tender.

Preheat the grill (broiler) function of the oven to 180°C (350°F).

Remove the chicken from the pot and place it on a wire rack set in a baking tray. Brush with some ghee and grill (broil) it in the oven for about 5–7 minutes, or until nice and crispy. Keep an eye on it so that it doesn't burn on the top. Take it out and cover with foil until ready to serve.

Wash the rice, then drain and add it to the stock in the pan. Let it come to a boil over a high heat, then drop the heat so the liquid is simmering and let the rice cook and absorb all the stock – this can take about 12–15 minutes.

Once the liquid in the pan has almost gone, add the clotted cream (or whichever option you choose) and 1 litre (35fl oz/4¼ cups) of the milk. The milk should be at least 2cm (¾ inch, or half an index finger) above the rice, so add more milk if needed.

Season with salt and pepper to taste, and keep stirring the rice over a medium heat so that the rice starts to break down a little bit and release some of its starch. It will take around 10 minutes for the rice to start soaking up the milk.

If you see the mixture is thickening and the rice is still not completely soft, add the rest of the milk. The rice grains should be super soft and tender with almost no resistance when pressed between your fingertips. The mixture should still be a tiny bit loose as it will thicken when it begins to cool on the plate.

Transfer the rice to a flat serving plate and top with the chicken.

Melt the ghee to serve in a small frying pan and add the truffle shavings. Swirl it around for 10–15 seconds, then spoon the truffle shavings on top of the chicken pieces and pour the ghee all over the dish. Serve it with a generous helping of daqqus and enjoy!

QAHWA (SAUDI COFFEE) & HAWAIJ STICKY CHICKEN WINGS WITH POMEGRANATE BBQ SAUCE

(For the love of chicken wings)

Anyone who knows me from my teen years knows well enough of my chicken-wing addiction. I am a diehard admirer and a self-proclaimed authority in my household on where to get the best chicken wings. Be it deep-fried, breaded, grilled, baked, crispy or sticky, smothered in a nice buffalo sauce, I love them in all forms. I think they are the best bits a chicken has to offer us humans. My love (and craze) for sticky, glazed and grilled wings knows no boundaries, so much so I won many wing-eating street and school competitions in my wild teen years, with a jaw dropping technique of putting the whole wing in my mouth from one side and spitting the squeaky clean bones out from the other side.

This is my much-loved recipe, which is just perfect for any season.

INGREDIENTS:

- 1kg (2lb 4oz) skin-on chicken wings

For the rub:

- 1 tbsp Hawaij Spice Mix (see page 186)
- 1 tbsp ground Saudi coffee, or the mildest roasted coffee you can find
- ¼ tsp ground cardamom
- 1 tsp brown sugar

For the marinade:

- 60ml (2fl oz/¼ cup) pomegranate molasses
- 2 fat cloves of garlic, minced
- 45g (1½oz) ginger, finely grated or minced
- 1 tsp paprika
- ½ tsp chilli flakes
- 2 tbsp ketchup
- 2 tbsp barbecue sauce
- 20g (¾oz/2 tbsp) brown sugar
- ½ tsp fine sea salt
- 1 tsp olive oil

To serve:

- Lime wedges
- Mlawa (see page 165, optional)
- Autumnal Maftoul (see page 173)

Serves 4

★DF

Preheat the oven to 180ºC (350ºF), gas 4, and line a large baking tray with baking paper.

Put the chicken wings in a wide bowl along with all the rub ingredients and rub them well together, massaging every nook and cranny of the wings. Cover with a tea towel and set them aside for 15 minutes at least. This step can be done a day ahead – let the chicken marinate in the fridge.

Mix all of the marinade ingredients together in a large mixing bowl. Add the rub-coated chicken wings and turn them around until well coated in the marinade.

Shake off any excess marinade and reserve it for later use. Lay the marinated wings, skin side up, on the lined baking tray and bake for 25 minutes. These can also be cooked on the barbecue or air fried.

Remove the tray from the oven and smother the wings generously with the remaining marinade, then roast for another 35–40 minutes until rich brown in colour and cooked through. Serve straight away with lime wedges and with mlawa bread and/or vegetable maftoul, if you like.

MABSHOOR
(Saudi lamb kababs over charcoal)

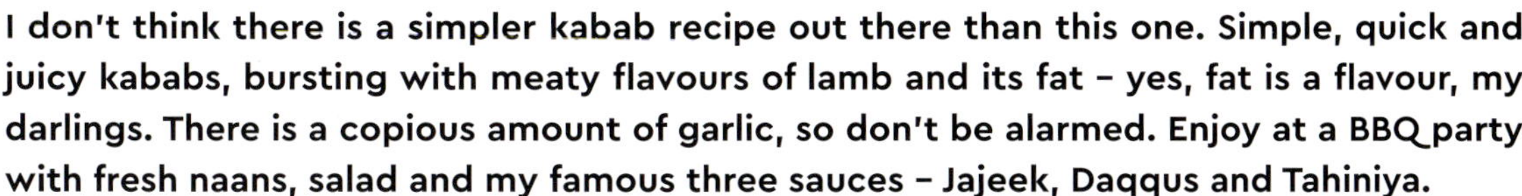

I don't think there is a simpler kabab recipe out there than this one. Simple, quick and juicy kababs, bursting with meaty flavours of lamb and its fat – yes, fat is a flavour, my darlings. There is a copious amount of garlic, so don't be alarmed. Enjoy at a BBQ party with fresh naans, salad and my famous three sauces – Jajeek, Daqqus and Tahiniya.

INGREDIENTS:

- 500g (1lb 2oz) minced (ground) lamb (at least 30% fat)
- Cloves from 1 bulb of garlic (about 30g/1oz), crushed
- 1 tsp salt
- 1½ tsp freshly ground black pepper
- A fat pinch of roasted ground cumin (optional)

For the yogurt:

- 250g (9oz/1 cup) Greek yogurt
- 2 cloves of garlic, minced
- Sea salt

To serve:

- Naan or pitta bread (optional)
- Fresh parsley, chopped
- Toasted pine nuts or almonds
- Shatta (see page 195), Jajeek (see page 190) and/or Tahiniya (see page 184)
- Tabouleh (optional; see page 84)

Serves 4 generously

★GF

In a large bowl with a flat base, combine the mince, garlic, salt, black pepper and cumin (if using). Mix well, then rub it with the palm of your hand against the vessel to smooth it out, about 2–3 minutes.

Cover the mince mixture and refrigerate for 30 minutes; this will help the mince and fat to mingle and bind well.

Now prepare the yogurt base by mixing together the Greek yogurt and garlic, then seasoning to taste with salt. Set aside.

Light the barbecue and wait for the charcoal to go ashy before starting to cook.

While the charcoal is getting ready, take the lamb mixture out of the fridge and form it into walnut-sized balls (a measuring tablespoon can be used as a rough guide for size – you should get 16–20 balls). Place four or five of them onto each of four metal skewers.

Place the skewers onto the charcoal grill and cook for about 7 minutes, turning every 2–3 minutes, until the Mabshoor is cooked through. Once nicely browned all over and dripping with fatty juices, remove from the barbecue.

Spread the garlicky yogurt over the naan breads or pitta, place the skewers on top and sprinkle with some chopped parsley and pine nuts or almonds on top. Serve along with the three saucy musketeers – shatta, daqqus and tahiniya – and tabouleh salad.

SAUDI KABSA
(The national dish of Saudi Arabia)

No celebration is complete without this centrepiece. It is a one-pot wonder.

If you love a pulao or pilav, this dish might hook you up for the rest of your eating existence. The best rice dish to ever exist is a Saudi kabsa, in my humble opinion.

INGREDIENTS:

- 500g (1lb 2oz) basmati rice
- 40g (1½oz) ghee or vegetable oil
- 1 large onion, very finely chopped
- 2 sticks of cinnamon
- 6 cardamom pods
- 3 black cloves
- 2 whole black loomi (dried lime)
- 3 bay leaves
- 3–4 cloves of garlic, minced
- ½ tbsp freshly grated ginger
- 1 medium chicken, cut in half lengthways or quartered
- 1 tbsp double-concentrate tomato purée (paste)
- 1 × 400g (14oz) can of chopped tomatoes (fresh chopped tomatoes can be used as well)
- 1 chicken stock cube (Maggi is the best choice as it is used in every single household in KSA)
- Zest of 1 orange
- Sea salt

For the aromatic kabsa spice mix:

- 6 strands of saffron
- 1 tsp black pepper
- 1 tsp red chilli powder
- 1 tsp ground coriander
- 1 tsp ground nutmeg
- 1 tsp ground cinnamon
- 1 tsp ground cardamom
- ½ tsp ground cumin
- ½ tsp ground turmeric
- ½ tsp powdered loomi (dried black lemon)

To garnish:

- 2 tbsp ghee or vegetable oil
- 70g (2½oz) blanched and halved almonds
- 150g (5½oz) carrots, grated on the large holes of a box grater
- 50g (1¾oz) jumbo raisins, soaked in hot water for 10 minutes and drained (if you can't find them, just replace them with normal raisins)
- 50g (1¾oz) sultanas (golden raisins), soaked in hot water for 10 minutes and drained
- 2 hard-boiled eggs, shelled and halved
- Whole red and green chillies
- Wedges of lemon
- A sprinkle of coriander (cilantro) or parsley
- Handful of crispy fried onions (homemade or store-bought)
- Salata Khadra (see page 89)
- Yogurt, sprinkled with Madinian Dukkah (see page 187)
- Daqqus (see page 183)

Serves 4 generously

★DF

Start by washing the rice at least twice to remove extra starch, then soak it in a bowl of water for 30–45 minutes.

In the meantime, put the ghee or vegetable oil in a heavy-based pot that is large enough to eventually accommodate everything. Place on a medium-high heat and add the chopped onion along with all the whole spices and the bay leaves. Sauté for 3–5 minutes until the onion becomes translucent. Add the garlic and ginger and sauté for another minute until fragrant.

Place the chicken pieces, skin side down first, in the pan and sear for 4–5 minutes on each side until a nice golden colour is achieved, then remove from the pot and set aside on a plate.

Now, add the tomato purée, chopped tomatoes, chicken stock cube and orange zest, and season with salt. Sauté for 2–3 minutes until well combined, then add all the aromatic kabsa spices and mix well. Add 1 litre (35fl oz/4¼ cups) of boiling water to de-glaze the pan and make a stock.

Put the seared chicken pieces back in the pan, cover and let it simmer for 20 minutes on a medium-low heat, until the chicken is completely cooked through and the stock is slightly reduced.

Preheat the grill (broiler) function of your oven to 180°C (350°F) and line a baking tray with foil. Once the chicken is cooked, remove it from the stock and place it on the lined baking tray. Brush the chicken pieces with any oil that has risen to the surface of the stock, then grill (broil) for 10–15 minutes, until it is a nice golden brown colour.

Meanwhile, strain the stock by passing it through a sieve (strainer) set over a bowl, squeezing all of the liquid out in the sieve.

Pour the stock back into the pan, bring it to a gentle boil on a medium-high heat, then add the soaked and drained rice. Top it up with more water if needed to cover the rice – the water level should be about 1cm (½ inch) above the rice for it to be cooked to perfection and be fluffy.

Keep the heat at medium-high, Once the rice starts to absorb the stock and small craters start to appear, place a sheet of baking paper on top of the pot and place the lid on tightly so that the paper works as a sealant (cartouche). Turn the heat up to high for 1 minute, then down to the lowest heat and let the rice cook for 15 minutes, moving the pan around every 5 minutes for equal distribution of heat. Turn off the heat and let the rice sit for another 10 minutes, undisturbed.

Meanwhile prepare the garnishes. Heat the ghee or vegetable oil in a frying pan and fry the almonds until golden, then remove to a plate lined with paper towels.

Now add the grated carrots, jumbo raisins and sultanas, and sauté for 2–4 minutes until the raisins are nicely puffed up. Turn the heat off and remove from the pan. Set aside along with the almonds.

Remove the lid from the rice pan and gently fluff up the rice. Dish out onto a large serving platter or a traditional round dish and place the grilled chicken pieces on top. Garnish with the egg halves, whole chillies and wedges of lemon, then sprinkle with the fresh coriander or parsley, fried almonds, raisins and carrots, followed by the fried onions.

Serve with salata khadra, yogurt sprinkled with madinian dukkah to your liking, and a generous amount of daqqus.

MAKARONA BIL LABAN

This is pasta like you have never seen it before. My heartfelt apologies to my Italian counterparts – you may find this recipe blasphemous to traditional Italian pasta dishes, but it's very popular in the Middle East and now it's time for the West to open up their minds and taste buds to this much-loved take on pasta.

This original version of this dish is vegetarian and served in a variety of ways. Enjoy on its own with a tempering of pine nuts in olive oil, a bit of sumac and fresh chopped parsley sprinkled on the top, or along with my Taawa Keema recipe (see page 110); both versions are very popular across the Middle East, with every household having their own variations on it. This can be served warm or cold and is perfect for packed lunches.

INGREDIENTS:

- 500g (1lb 2oz) dried pasta (most common are elbow/macaroni pasta or shell pasta)
- 4 tbsp olive oil, plus extra to drizzle
- 500g (1lb 2oz/2¼ cups) thick Greek yogurt (the best you can get your hands on)
- ½–1 tsp ground allspice (adjust according to your preference)
- 2 cloves of garlic, crushed
- ½ tsp freshly ground black pepper
- 1 tsp dried mint or dried dill
- 2 tbsp pine nuts (ideally long Pakistani pine nuts)
- Sumac or pul biber (Aleppo pepper flakes), to sprinkle (your call – both work well)
- Chopped parsley and/or pomegranate seeds, to garnish
- Salt

Serves 4

★V

Fill a large heavy-based pot with plenty of water, salt it generously (like the salty water of the Red Sea) and bring to a rolling boil. Cook the pasta per the packet instructions.

Once pasta is cooked, reserve 125ml (4fl oz/½ cup) of the cooking water and strain the pasta in a colander. Drizzle generously with olive oil and toss through the boiled pasta so that it is well coated and doesn't stick together. Let the pasta cool down to room temperature.

In the meantime, prepare the yogurt sauce. In a bowl that is large enough to eventually accommodate the boiled pasta, combine the yogurt, allspice, crushed garlic, black pepper and dried mint or dill, and mix well until it is smooth. Add the reserved pasta water to loosen the yogurt to a thick sauce consistency.

Once cooled, add the pasta to the bowl and mix well.

In a small frying pan, heat the 4 tablespoons of olive oil on a medium heat and add the pine nuts. Fry until they are golden brown (which will be a minute or so), then remove them from the pan with a slotted spoon and sprinkle them on the pasta dish.

Sprinkle the sumac or pul biber into the remaining olive oil in the pan, give it a swirl, then drizzle it on top of the pasta. Sprinkle with the freshly chopped parsley and/or pomegranate seeds and serve.

MY SILK ROUTE HAREES
(AKA Jareesh, Hareesh, Hareesa, Bokoboko, Arizah, Kashkeg)

If there is one dish that ultimately defines the diverse influences and regional flavours of the old Silk Route integrated into food, it's got to be harees.

Harees is one of the main dishes of Saudi identity. It has recently made its mark on the UNESCO Representative List of the Intangible Cultural Heritage of Humanity. It is the very heart of Najdi cuisine (a central region of Saudi Arabia).

Hisham Baeshen, a local food content creator and a friend of mine, very fondly narrated the cultural value of harees, particularly in the rural areas of Riyadh.

According to Hisham, Bedouin mothers would teach their daughters the techniques of how to make the smoothest harees from a very early age, in order to find the best suitor for them when they came of age. A harees cooking competition would take place and the girl who made the best harees was to be betrothed to the heir apparent of the tribal chief. Very interesting!

INGREDIENTS:

- 200g (7oz) long-grain or basmati rice
- 500g (1lb 2oz) cracked wheat or freekeh
- 2 heaped tbsp ghee (or 4 tbsp vegetable oil)
- 1 medium onion, sliced
- ½ bulb of garlic, cloves peeled and sliced
- 1.25–1.5kg (2¾–3¼lb) lamb shoulder or leg, cut into 4–5 big chunks (ask your butcher to cut these up for you; chicken can be substituted)
- 8–10 green cardamom pods
- 4 whole white loomi (dried lemons)
- 2 bay leaves
- ½ tbsp black peppercorns
- 3 litres (105fl oz/13¼ cups) hot water plus more if needed to thin out to a desired consistency
- Sea salt

For the Kashna (traditional tempering):

- 250g (9oz/1 cup) ghee (yes this much as it is the star of the show)
- 1 medium onion, finely chopped
- 3 cloves of garlic, finely sliced
- 2 medium tomatoes, chopped
- 5–6 green chillies, slit in half lengthways
- 1 heaped tsp ground loomi (preferably white)
- 5–6 strands of saffron
- ½ tbsp ground coriander
- 1 heaped tsp ground green cardamom

To serve:

- A small handful of chopped coriander (cilantro)
- 1 tbsp toasted pine nuts
- Mabshoor (see page 123; optional, but this gives a very Kashmiri touch and completes my Silk Route Harees)

Serves 10 generously

Wash the rice and cracked wheat, then soak them together in a bowl of water for at least 4 hours or overnight until the grains are soft and plumped up. Drain and set aside.

In a heavy-based pan that is large enough to eventually accommodate the rest of the ingredients, heat the ghee on a medium-high heat. Add the sliced onion and garlic, and sauté for about 2–3 minutes until fragrant.

Tip in the meat and sear until golden in colour. Add the cardamom pods, loomi, bay leaves and peppercorns and sauté for 1 minute.

Add the hot water and bring it to a boil. Let it boil for 5 minutes, skimming off any dirt or foam forming on the top. Season with salt, tightly cover the pot with a lid and lower the heat. Let it simmer for 2 hours on a low heat, until the meat is fork tender and falls off the bone.

Remove the cooked meat, loomi and bay leaves from the stock. Discard the bay leaves and, once the loomi have cooled down enough to handle, squeeze any juices from them back into the pan, then discard the rest. Place the meat in a bowl and with the help of a fork and spoon, separate the bones and any sinew from the meat and shred it roughly. Discard the bones and any sinew and return the shredded meat to the stock.

Now, add the soaked and drained grains to the meat stock pot and give it a good mix, then cover the pot and let it cook on a low heat for another 2 hours.

Once the wheat grain is so super soft that it doesn't resist when squished between thumb and finger, use a potato masher to mash the grains to a very thick porridge-like consistency; keep the pot on the heat while doing this step, although be very careful not to ignite your clothes. An immersion blender can be used to make the process quicker and easier.

Once the desired consistency is achieved, turn the heat off and set aside while you prepare the kashna tempering.

For the kashna traditional tempering, heat the ghee in a frying pan on a medium heat and add the finely chopped onion. Fry until it just starts to take on colour – about 3–4 minutes.

Add the garlic to the frying pan and sauté for about 1 minute until fragrant.

Tip in the chopped tomatoes and the rest of the ingredients, and season with salt. Still on a medium heat, sauté until the tomatoes just start to soften up – another 2–3 minutes – then turn the heat off.

To serve, pour the desired amount of harees into a serving bowl, make a small shallow dip in the middle of the harees and pour the desired amount of piping-hot kashna in the middle, then drizzle any leftover ghee all over the harees.

Garnish with chopped coriander, toasted pine nuts and kababs if using.

Serve and enjoy a soul-comforting bowl of goodness.

HALLOUMI CHEESE WITH MADINIAN DUKKAH OIL AND MINT CRISPS

(A cheese, onion and pickle kinda dish)

A perfect light lunch or dinner on its own or part of an elaborate brunch, this is a flavour bomb of a recipe, bursting with the minty freshness of Madinian Dukkah. This recipe can easily be made vegan by substituting extra-firm tofu in place of the halloumi.

INGREDIENTS:

- 2 × 225g (8oz) blocks of halloumi
- 2 tbsp extra virgin olive oil
- ½ tbsp runny honey (or maple syrup for a vegan option)

For the Madinian dukkah oil:

- 4 tbsp olive oil
- 1 tbsp Madinian Dukkah (or to taste, see page 187)
- 1 tsp pul biber (Aleppo pepper flakes)
- 1 tsp rose harissa paste
- 1 tsp brown sugar
- Juice and zest of 1 lemon
- Juice and zest of 1 small clementine
- 80g (2¾oz) sun-dried tomatoes, very finely chopped
- 50g (1¾oz) roasted cashews or peanuts (or a combination of both), halved
- 50g (1¾oz) gherkins, roughly chopped
- 1 tbsp parsley, finely chopped
- 1 tbsp dill, finely chopped

For garnish:

- handful of fresh mint leaves
- 2 cloves of garlic, crushed
- handful of pomegranate seeds
- pomegranate molasses, to drizzle
- handful of crispy fried onions

Serves 4

★V★GF

Begin with the mint and garlic for the garnish. Heat the oil for the Madinian dukkah in a small frying pan and, once hot, add the mint leaves. Fry them for a minute or so until crisp, then transfer them to a plate and set aside. In the same oil, fry the garlic until lightly brown. Remove from the oil with a strainer and put on a plate. Set aside until you are ready to serve.

Return the remaining oil to the heat, add the Madinian dukkah and pul biber, and cook for further 30 seconds before adding harissa paste, brown sugar, and lemon and clementine juices. Sauté on a low for another 4–5 minutes until the juice has reduced a little.

Remove from heat and let it cool down completely. Add the remaining dukkah oil ingredients and mix well, then set aside.

Preheat the oven to 180ºC (350ºF), gas 4.

Halve the halloumi blocks lengthways, then pat them dry as much as possible. Using a small sharp paring knife, score a square (check) pattern, about 1cm (½ inch) deep, on one side of each halloumi slice.

Heat the oil in a non-stick oven-proof frying pan. Add two of the halloumi pieces, so you are not overcrowding the pan, placing them scored side down. Fry for about 2 minutes until golden, then flip over and fry until golden brown on the other sides. Remove from the pan while you cook the remaining two halloumi slices, then return all the halloumi to the pan, scored sides up. Drizzle the runny honey over the halloumi, then transfer the pan to the preheated oven and bake for 8 minutes until very soft in the centre (if you don't have an oven-proof pan, transfer the halloumi slices to a small baking tray along with the oil)

Transfer the baked halloumi slices to a serving plate and pour over any liquid from the tray. Drizzle over the prepared dukkah oil, scatter with the pomegranate seeds and drizzle with pomegranate molasses. Finally, sprinkle the fried garlic, crispy fried onions and mint leaves over. Serve straight away.

FUL 2 WAYS

Ful was once classed as a poor man's breakfast in Egypt (from where it originated) but times have changed and this delicious dish has been popularized by fellow Arabs and ful enthusiasts like me in the West with endless combinations, all vegan and loaded with various sorts of protein. Ful has become the definition of all-day breakfast. It can be eaten at any time of the day; there are no rules. Particularly in Saudi Arabia, it is served during Ramadan at the Iftar spread (to break the fast) along with an array of condiments such as Madinian Dukkah, Kammouneh, finely diced tomatoes, onions and shatta, and eaten with warm khobz.

Here are my two favourite takes on a ful medames from both sides of the Red Sea. Ful Iskandarany (with whole beans) hails from the port of Alexandria, Egypt, and Ful Hasawi comes from the largest oasis in the world located in the eastern region of Al-Ahsa.

FUL ISKANDARANY (Plain, pulverized and topped with tahini and Madinian Dukkah)

INGREDIENTS:

- 1 × 400g (14oz) can of whole fava beans (ful medames; I use Californian Gardens brand)
- 1 small tomato, chopped
- 1 small red onion or shallot, finely chopped
- 1 mild green chilli or jalapeño pepper, finely chopped
- 2 tbsp lemon juice
- 1 fat clove of garlic, crushed
- Fine sea salt, to taste
- 1 tsp roasted ground cumin
- 1 tsp ground black pepper

To serve:

- 1 tsp pul biber (Aleppo pepper flakes)
- Extra virgin olive oil, to drizzle
- 2 tbsp chopped coriander or parsley
- Tahini, to drizzle
- Madinian dukkah, to sprinkle
- Lemon wedges (optional)
- Pitta (page 166) or Mlawa (page 165)

Serves 4

★V★DF★GF

This one is pretty straight forward and easy. Simply empty the whole can of beans (including the liquid) into a microwaveable bowl, cover and heat it through until hot and bubbling – around 2 minutes in the microwave. This can be done in a frying pan as well – just add a splash of water to loosen the beans up a bit.

Once the beans are nice and warm, transfer them to a serving bowl, add the rest of the ingredients and mix well.

Garnish with the pul biber flakes, a good drizzle of olive oil and the chopped coriander or parsley. Drizzle with tahini and sprinkle with Madinian dukkah. Serve with a wedge of lemon and pitta bread or mlawa. It can be enjoyed on its own as well.

MY FUL HASAWI (chunky fava beans)

INGREDIENTS:

- 2 tbsp olive oil
- 1 small onion, very finely chopped
- 1–2 fat cloves of garlic, crushed
- 1 tsp tomato purée (paste); optional but it gives depth to the flavour
- 1 × 400g (14oz) can of whole or crushed fava beans (ful medames)
- 1 tsp Madinian Dukkah (see page 187)
- Juice of ½ lemon
- ¼ tsp sumac
- Sea salt and freshly ground black pepper

To garnish:

- 1 tbsp tahini sauce
- 1 tbsp pomegranate molasses
- Extra virgin olive oil, to drizzle generously
- 1 tbsp finely chopped parsley
- 2–3 tbsp crispy fried onions (homemade or store-bought)
- 1 tbsp chunky Daqqus (see page 183)
- 2 soft-boiled eggs, cut in half lengthways
- A pinch of sumac
- A pinch of za'atar
- Bread of your choice, such as thin Lebanese pitta bread, pitta chips, Mlawa (see page 165) or paratha, to serve

Serves 4

★V★DF★GF

In a shallow frying pan, heat the olive oil on a medium heat, then add the chopped onion and sauté until translucent. Add the crushed garlic and sauté for a further 30 seconds until fragrant. Add the tomato purée, if using, and sauté for 30 seconds.

Now tip in the beans; if using whole beans, gently press them against the pan with a spatula to make a mush. Season with salt and pepper, mix well, then add the dukkah followed by the lemon juice and sumac.

Once the bean mixture is smooth and hot, transfer it to a wide serving bowl. Drizzle the tahini, pomegranate molasses and a good glug of olive oil over the top and sprinkle with the parsley and fried onions. Spoon the daqqus in the middle, top with the boiled egg halves and sprinkle with sumac and za'atar.

Serve warm or cold with your choice of bread.

A VERY RELAXED AUBERGINE FATTEH
(A recipe for when you don't want to cook)

A showstopper vegetarian main, fatteh means "to stack up" in Arabic. There are countless varieties of fatteh but the most popular one, specially in Saudi Arabia, is an aubergine and mince fatteh, aka *fatteh bātinjān wa lahm mafrooma.*

I love a well-made aubergine fatteh, but sometimes life seems too short for a well-layered fatteh when the craving is unbearable, so here is my very laid-back – in fact lazy – meat-free aubergine fatteh, where you just dollop all of the prepared ingredients (which can be made ahead of time), loaded with noodle croutons and pomegranate seeds, on your plate, curl up on a sofa or a beanie and enjoy this moreish, hearty vegetarian dish, hot or cold: your call.

INGREDIENTS:

- 2 large/globe aubergines (eggplants)
- 8 baby/fairytale aubergines (eggplants)
- Vegetable oil, for deep frying
- 2 large Lebanese pitta breads
- Fine sea salt and black pepper

For the chickpea sauce:

- 2 tbsp olive oil
- 1 tbsp ghee
- 1 large brown onion, finely chopped
- 5 cloves of garlic, crushed
- 500g (1lb 2oz) cooked chickpeas
- 1 tsp ground allspice
- 1 tsp ground cinnamon
- 1 tsp paprika
- 1 tsp freshly ground black pepper
- 2 bay leaves
- 8 medium tomatoes, peeled and blended into a purée
- Fine sea salt

For the tahini yogurt:

- 125g (4½oz) tahini
- 80ml (2½fl oz/⅓ cup) lemon juice
- 2 cloves of garlic, crushed
- 600g (1lb 5oz/2⅔ cups) Greek yogurt

To garnish:

- Seeds from 1 small pomegranate
- 1–2 tbsp chopped flat leaf parsley
- 3 tbsp olive oil
- 100g (3½oz) pine nuts (preferably the long Pakistani ones)

Serves 4

★V

Make a start by preparing the chickpea sauce. In a shallow frying pan, heat the olive oil and ghee. Once the ghee has melted, add the chopped onion and sauté for a few minutes until translucent. Add the crushed garlic and sauté until fragrant – about 30 seconds to 1 minute.

Now tip in the chickpeas, along with all of the spices and the bay leaves, and sauté for 1–2 minutes. Add the puréed tomatoes, mix well and let it cook on a medium heat until the tomato purée is reduced by half and has achieved a richer colour and oil starts to appear at the edges of the sauce, about 5–7 minutes. Season to taste with salt, cover the sauce and set aside. (Note: this sauce can be made ahead of time and kept in the fridge for up to 3 days; when serving, just reheat it.)

Moving on to the tahini yogurt, in a jug or a bowl, mix the tahini and 60ml (2fl oz/¼ cup) water together – don't worry if it looks split at this stage, it will come together in a minute. Add sea salt to taste, and the lemon juice and crushed garlic, and mix in. Pour in the yogurt and give it a good mix until nice and smooth – this may take around 5 minutes, but keep mixing and it will all come together.

Once the sauces are made, move on to the aubergines. Peel the large aubergines, cut the round bottom parts into 1.5cm (⅝-inch) discs and the top parts into roughly 2cm (¾-inch) cubes.

Cut the baby aubergines lengthways, leaving the green stem attached and skin on.

Place all of the aubergines in a tray lined with paper towels and sprinkle with fine sea salt. Let them sit for 20–30 minutes so that the excess moisture is drawn out; this step will help the aubergines absorb less oil during frying.

In a deep saucepan, heat the vegetable oil to 170°C (325°F). Pat dry the aubergines and season with black pepper. Fry them in the hot oil, cooking the discs first, then the cubes followed by small aubergines, until golden brown. Fish them out with a slotted spoon and place on a tray lined with paper towels to drain any excess oil. Each batch will take around 3–4 minutes.

To prepare the noodle croutons, cut the Lebanese pitta in half, then slice them thinly to the width of fettuccine pasta – about 3mm (⅛ inch). Fluff them up with your hands so that they are not sticking together. In the same oil used to fry the aubergines, fry the bread slices in batches. Once golden brown, transfer them to another paper-towel-lined tray.

Time to assemble the fatteh: spoon some of the tahini yogurt onto four dinner plates, followed by 2–3 aubergine discs. Top with a spoonful of the chickpea sauce, then some cubed aubergines, followed by another drizzle of tahini yogurt, a few noodle croutons and another spoonful of chickpea sauce. Place the sliced and fried aubergines on top, drizzle with more tahini yogurt, then sprinkle with the pomegranate seeds and chopped parsley.

Heat the olive oil in a small frying pan, add the long pine nuts and fry them until lightly golden – around 1–2 minutes. Sprinkle these onto the prepared fatteh plates, add small handful of noodle croutons and serve immediately.

TIP: Both the chickpea sauce and the tahini yogurt can be made ahead and kept in the fridge for up to 3 days. The noodle croutons can also be fried ahead of time and stored in an airtight container for up to 8 weeks

TAHINI AUBERGINE AND CAULIFLOWER TRAY BAKE
(Shhhh... it's vegan)

This is a simple yet very flavourful, hearty vegan dish that can be enjoyed as a main on its own or as a side dish to another main course. This tray bake is a reflection of contemporary Arab cuisine deviating gracefully from meat-laden main courses, as well as being time savvy. Perfect for packed lunches and a breeze for people who are just starting to cook more often at home.

Back in my college years, this dish was a regular request on my weekly menu. As I was the head chef of my flat, my flatmates used to come home early whenever this was cooking just to claim the crunchy cauliflower bits on the top. For a moment I would feel like the most powerful person on earth, dishing equal portions out of the tray.

I usually made this in two 23cm (9-inch) rectangular pyrex dishes because that was what I had in those days. One could be consumed on the same day and the second one kept for later – and guess what, it tasted even better the next day! Winner winner, it's cauli for dinner.

INGREDIENTS:

- Oil, for shallow frying
- 750g (26½oz) cauliflower florets
- 2 aubergines (eggplants), cut into chunky cubes
- 2 onions, finely chopped
- 120g (4¼oz) tahini
- 60ml (2fl oz/¼ cup) lemon juice
- 1 tbsp freshly minced garlic (about 3 fat cloves)
- 2 tbsp olive oil
- ½ tsp freshly ground black pepper
- 1 tsp pul biber (Aleppo pepper flakes)
- ¼ tsp paprika
- 1 tsp ground cumin
- Sea salt

To garnish:

- 50–100g (1¾–3½oz) pomegranate seeds, as per your preference
- 1 tbsp chopped flat leaf parsley
- 2 tbsp roasted/fried pine nuts, almonds or cashews
- Crispy fried onions (homemade or store-bought), to sprinkle
- Pinch of pul biber (Aleppo pepper flakes), to sprinkle (optional, but looks nice!)
- Fried pitta bread croutons (triangles or strips), or any other croutons will do
- Pomegranate molasses, to drizzle (optional)

Serves 4 generously

★V★DF★GF

Line a baking tray with paper towels. Preheat the oven to 180°C (350°F), gas 4.

Heat enough oil for shallow frying in a frying pan and set over medium-high heat.

Cut any larger cauliflower florets into bite-sized pieces. Working in batches, fry the florets until nicely golden brown. Scoop out the florets with a slotted spoon and place on the paper towels to soak up any extra oil.

Next, fry the aubergine cubes until they brown nicely. Once done, take them out and place on the paper towels as well. Season everything with a sprinkle of sea salt.

To the same pan, add a little more oil and fry the chopped onions until lightly caramelized at the edges. Transfer to a bowl along with the fried aubergine and cauliflower. Mix and set aside.

Make the tahini sauce by mixing the tahini with the lemon juice, garlic and salt to taste. Mix well; it will turn thick and grainy, but don't worry. Add up to 325ml (11fl oz/1⅓ cups) water, a little at a time, and mix well until smooth. A hand-held blender comes in really handy at this stage, or you can whisk it with a hand whisk until smooth. Now add the olive oil, black pepper, pul biber, paprika, and ground cumin and mix in.

Divide the cauliflower, aubergines and onions equally between 2 rectangular baking dishes 23cm (9 inches) long. Pour over the tahini mixture, ensuring everything is coated well. Bake in the preheated oven for 35–40 minutes or until the top is nicely browned.

Scatter over any garnishes you wish to use, finish with a drizzle of pomegranate molasses, if using, and serve.

Darryl and I posing for cookbook's shoot

FOR THE LOVE OF SEAFOOD

December 1985, on a bright, sunny weekend morning. I woke up at the crack of the dawn, very excited. It was my birthday and Aba Jan had promised me he would buy me a pet fish for my birthday present. I was only interested in my present, not at all in my birthday party in the afternoon. Little did I know what tragedy was about to unfold that day.

Without wasting any time, Aba Jan did his Fajr prayer and we both left in his beloved Mazda 626, as the fish market was right at the edge of the sea, about 45 minutes from suburban Yanbu where we lived. I sat in the front passenger seat with two giant pink embroidered cushions underneath me, secured with a seat belt. Listening to the national radio and singing along to the national anthem, off we went to the fish market by the darling Red Sea.

As we entered the market, the fish auction was in full swing. Aba Jan bought a box of armour-clad click-clack giant lobsters tightly shut in polystyrene boxes. I have never seen such humongous lobsters anywhere else in four decades of my life. He got equally massive Jingari prawns, still wriggling around in crystals of ice cubes. Most beautiful of all were the turquoise blue parrot fish, Najal fish cloaked in burgundy scales and Hamour, a fish of reverence across the Red Sea coastline, with buttery, chunky flesh. I wish I could have them all as pets; they looked like fairytale mermaids to me.

As we were leaving the market, I nudged Aba Jan to get me my birthday present. So we went to the nearby stall run by a young man with a kaffiayah wrapped around his head. Sort of like Antonio Banderas (that's one of the reasons I still remember his face). He showed us around the range of pet fish he had in big plastic bags filled with water for me to choose from. I told him it was my birthday. He stood silent for a moment and then took a bag from underneath his table with two stunning little clownfish with blue, white and yellow stripes swimming happily in the water.

I became fixated on those fish, and we bargained. The handsome man gave me a BOGOF (Buy One Get One Free) deal as it was my birthday.

We had Mutabbaq (page 46) from a local shack and went back to our car. At this point it was about 10 in the morning and things were starting to get hot. Dad's seafood haul for the party was in the car boot. My two new friends (clownfish) on my lap, off we went towards home.

Here is the tragic turn in the story. About halfway through our singalong journey, the car stopped in the middle of literally nowhere. Just sand and a long stretch of road with sharp sun above our heads. Aba Jan tried his best to rescue his darling Mazda 626, but it gave up. We had no other option but to walk towards the town, hoping we may get a lift on the way.

Aba Jan was carrying his load of fish and I was carrying mine. I was getting very thirsty and sweaty. My ankles were now very sore and bleeding from the friction of my shoe straps, and then I stumbled on a pebble and fell over into some small green shards of broken glass that were covered in sand. My fish bag popped and the two clownfish spilled out onto dry sand, frantically moving their gills for their last breath and finally collapsing. They left me like Aba Jan's 626. I was tethered to the ground, staring at their lifeless bodies.

I cried bitterly without even noticing that I had a deep cut to my leg and I was bathing in a pool of my own blood. I don't know which pain was greater, the wound or losing my fishy friends.

Aba Jan was anxiously trying to stop my bleeding. Then I heard a loud, desperate roar as he screamed for help. His cry echoed through the wilderness of the desert. I never saw him in such agony again in my life, not even when he lost his mother. And I felt that haunting pain when my son fell to sepsis. It's the fear of losing your child, that's how it feels.

Out of nowhere, my Saudi Antonio Banderas appeared with his pickup. He saw us from a distance, pulled his car up and ran towards us to the rescue. By that time I had lost consciousness.

The next thing I remember was me lying down on the painfully white hospital bed with my stitched-up leg and bandaged ankles. Outside, the sky turned amber as the sun began to set. On the side table was a big fish bowl with half a dozen multi-coloured clownfish staring at me. My Saudi Antonio left me another birthday present. He delivered all of Aba Jan's plethora of fish and his Mazda 626 to our home with the help of Aba Jan's friends while he was at my bedside. If humanity had a face, it would be like him.

My birthday was postponed by a couple of days. To make up for the missed occasion, Aba Jan cooked his speciality lobsters and coconut-crusted prawns. Mama made the rest of the fish feast, along with other friends, and my uncle Razaq bought me my favourite Pineapple Fresh Cream Cake (page 232).

I was still a bit knocked out on my big day but as soon as I took a bite of sassy fried prawn and lobster cooked in citrusy butter, something struck inside me. For a moment, the ruby-red juicy prawns and rich, sweet lobsters glistening in butter overtook the pain of my aching ankles and still fresh wound. That taste still lingers in my memories and that wound scar still tingles when I recall that eventful day.

I have penned all these recipes in this chapter for you to recreate the magic at your own home and bring in the party spirit.

I guarded my pet fish with my life. Then we moved to Jeddah a few months later.

This is a story of love, despair and humanity. This for my Saudi Antonio Banderas.

GRILLED/BROILED LOBSTER AND PRAWNS
(With a citrusy, garlicky brown butter)

This is a trendy, zingy and zesty seafood boil. Proper party stuff. Serve it on its own or along with heritage tomato salad and giant autumnal couscous (see page 173). This recipe is my ode to the endless bounty of the Red Sea and my undivided loved for Saudi seafood. The lobsters, prawns and crabs found there are just unparalleled both in size and taste. I have tried my best to re-create the taste of these delicacies sold at little shacks along the Red Sea shores. I know you will love it. Just give it a try for my Saudi Antonio Banderas.

INGREDIENTS:

- 4 large lobster tails in their shells
- 8 jumbo prawns (shrimps)

For the marinade:

- 60ml (2fl oz/¼ cup) olive oil
- Juice and zest of ½ lemon
- Juice and zest of 1 lime
- A small handful of fresh coriander (cilantro), chopped
- ½ tsp chilli powder
- A pinch of paprika
- 1 tsp garlic granules
- 1 tsp onion granules
- Sea salt and black pepper
- 1 tsp palm sugar

For the citrusy garlic butter:

- 250g (9oz/1 cup) unsalted butter, well softened
- 1 small onion, very finely chopped
- 4 cloves of garlic, minced
- Zest and juice of ½ lemon
- Zest and juice of 1 small orange
- Handful of flat leaf parsley, chopped
- 5cm (2-inch) piece of ginger, peeled and grated
- 1 tsp fish sauce or soy sauce

To serve:

- Handful of chives and parsley, chopped
- Lemon wedges
- Zest of lime and orange (optional)

Serves 4

★GF

Preheat the oven to 190°C (375°F), gas 5.

Prepare the marinade by mixing all of the marinade ingredients in a bowl. Set aside.

To prepare the citrusy garlic butter, whip the butter until light and fluffy. Add all the remaining ingredients except the lemon and orange juices. Now drizzle in the juices slowly, mixing continuously so that the butter doesn't curdle. Cover and set this aside too but not in the fridge.

For the lobster tails, first remove the little legs, if any, then with the help of kitchen scissors, cut straight down in the middle of the back, all the way to the very end of the tail. Make a small cut on both sides of the tail. Stick your thumb between the lobster meat and the shell, move it around and pull the meat out of the shell but keep the end of the tail intact with the shell. Lay the lobster meat back onto the now closed shell, then lay it down on a baking tray and fan the tail out (this process is commonly known as butterflying). Your lobster is now ready for marinating.

Now prepare the prawns (shrimps). Wash and pat dry, then, keeping the heads intact, slit the prawns down the back and devein. Remove the shells, leaving the heads and tails intact. Place them, cut sides up and opened wide, on the baking tray along with the prepared lobster tails.

Preheat the grill (broiler) to high heat. Brush the marinade generously over the prawns and lobster tails, then grill (broil) for 12–14 minutes until the meat is opaque in colour. Keep an eye so that it doesn't burn.

Once cooked, take the lobster and prawns out of the oven and generously smother them with the citrusy garlic butter, putting any extra in a small bowl to serve on the side. Sprinkle with the chives and parsley, the grated lime and orange zest, and dive into a pool of exotic flavours.

SALOONAT RUBYAN
(Prawn curry)

A hearty prawn curry from the eastern coast of Saudi Arabia but popular across the country, this is an everyday, any day kind of recipe. A very simple prawn curry that is zingy and tangy, a medley of subtle flavours with sweetness of the buttery prawns coming through. It can be pulled together in under 30 minutes from start to finish.

INGREDIENTS:

- 2 tbsp olive oil
- 1 small onion, finely chopped
- 500g (1lb 2oz) king prawns (shrimps), head removed, peeled and deveined (the weight is after the prawns have been cleaned and prepared)
- 1 tbsp garlic paste
- ½ tsp green chilli paste (optional)
- ½ tsp roasted ground cumin
- ½ tsp ground green cardamom
- 1 tsp red chilli powder (or to taste)
- ½ tsp ground turmeric
- ¼ tsp freshly ground black pepper
- 2 medium tomatoes, finely chopped
- 30ml (1fl oz/2 tablespoons) tamarind pulp
- 2 tbsp lemon juice
- Salt

To serve:

- A handful of fresh coriander (cilantro), chopped
- Lemon wedges
- Hot Pitta Bread (see page 166) or carrot rice (Aish al Jazar, page 169)

Serves 4

★DF★GF

Pour the oil into a large frying pan and sauté the onion over a medium heat until it starts to caramelize a little – about 3–5 minutes.

Add the prawns (shrimps) and turn the heat up to high to flash fry them without letting them get watery – about 2 minutes on each side, until they turn pink.

Add the garlic paste, green chilli paste (if using), ground cumin, cardamom, red chilli powder, ground turmeric and black pepper, reduce the heat to medium and stir well to mix.

Now tip in the chopped tomatoes followed by the tamarind and lemon juice, and season to taste with salt. Stir until all well combined, then cover the pan and cook for a couple of minutes until saucy and everything starts to come together.

Turn off the heat, transfer the prawn curry to a serving dish and garnish with the chopped coriander and lemon wedges. Serve with fresh hot pitta or, my favourite, carrot rice.

PAN-FRIED RED MULLET WITH CRUSHED SPICY POTATOES & TAHINIYA SAUCE

There are many small rustic restaurants and fish outlets who also tend to serve cooked food and catch of the day throughout the coastal line of the Red Sea. This recipe is a dedication to one such tiny restaurant/fish outlet in Yanbu, which serves catch of the day to an outdoor seating area for four. It's been nearly four decades since my last visit. I'm not sure whether it's still there or not, but the taste of the fish served there is still fresh in my memories.

I visited Jeddah while penning down my memories for this book. There, on a balmy afternoon, I was sitting with my eldest son in a fancy restaurant, overlooking the beautiful shores of the Red Sea, eating this inexplicably delicious and fresh pan-fried red mullet. The crisp fish with a perfectly balanced, citrusy, light tahini sauce and fluffy, lightly spiced potatoes, the smell of the sea, the beautiful bright blue skies and a gentle breeze every now and then... It took me back 40 years to Yanbu, to the same shop where we (Mama, Aba Jan and I) always stopped on our regular weekend meal when I was a child. The sheer joy of it! I wanted to cry my heart out.

Serve this dish with Heritage Tomato and Olive Salad (see page 72)

INGREDIENTS:

- 4 large or 8 small red mullet fillets, skin on
- 2–3 tbsp olive oil, for frying the fish
- Fine sea salt and freshly ground black pepper

For the spicy potatoes:

- 500g (1lb 2oz) roasting potatoes (such as Maris Piper)
- 4 tbsp olive oil or groundnut oil
- 2 tsp black mustard seeds
- 1 small onion, finely chopped
- ½ tsp Kammouneh (see page 196)
- 1 green chilli, finely chopped
- 10g (⅓oz) fresh flat leaf parsley, finely chopped
- 10g (⅓oz) fresh chives, finely chopped
- 10g (⅓oz) fresh dill, finely chopped
- 1 tbsp unsalted butter

To serve:

- Heritage Tomato and Olive Salad (see page 72)
- Tahiniya sauce (see page 184)
- Lemon wedges

Serves 4

★GF

Start by boiling the potatoes, skins on, in a large pan of salted water until they are tender enough that there is no resistance when a knife is inserted into them. This can take up to 20 minutes, depending on the size of the potatoes.

Let them cool down slightly, then peel and place them in a bowl. Crush them to a chickpea-sized crumb with a fork. Dress them with 2 tablespoons of the oil.

In a shallow frying pan, heat the remaining 2 tablespoons of oil, add the mustard seeds and let them crackle for 30 seconds, then add the chopped onion and sauté for 1–2 minutes on a medium heat until translucent.

Tip in the kammouneh and green chilli and sauté for another 30 seconds, then add the potatoes, mix thoroughly and season with sea salt and black pepper. Take the pan off the heat and add the parsley, chives and dill, along with the butter. Mix and fluff up the potatoes so they are well seasoned and coated with all the herby goodness. Cover with a lid and set aside.

If you have large red mullet fillets, score four equal slits in the top of each – this helps them cook better. Heat the oil on a medium heat in a non-stick frying pan that is large enough to accommodate two large or four small fillets at a time. Place the fish fillets in the pan, skin side down, and cook for 3 minutes, pressing ever so gently on the top of the fillets with your fingers for the first 30 seconds, so the fish doesn't curl up too much.

Turn the fillets over and cook for another minute or until cooked through. Season with sea salt and freshly ground black pepper to taste. Repeat to cook the remaining fish fillets.

To serve, plate up the fish fillets with the crushed potatoes and tomato and olive salad. Serve with the tahiniya sauce, either on the side or drizzled on top, and with wedges of lemon for squeezing over.

SHAOOR/NAJAL MAGHLI
(Fried Emperor/Coral Trout Fish)

This was my weekend dining-out experience as a child. Aba Jan and I, along with his friends, would sit on those old wooden ottoman-style benches called *majlis* and enjoy the most flavoursome fish. It was perfectly cooked: crispy on the outside, fluffy and moist on the inside, served with fresh pitta bread, pitta squares (fried in the same salty, fishy oil), fresh tomato salad, daqqus, humr (tamarind sauce) and plain or fisherman's/ Siyadiah rice. It was often served on a large silver or steel platter that you wouldn't want to share with anyone because the whole experience is priceless.

Take one bite and your tongue becomes a dance floor of these mingling flavours. The fish is usually enjoyed on its own, and the sides are more of a consort rather than fully fledged side dishes.

It is a must-have if you are visiting Saudi Arabia. I still won't board the plane back home without having it!

Finding emperor fish or coral trout can be challenging outside KSA, so I usually substitute it with freshly caught sea bass or red snapper.

INGREDIENTS:

- 1–1.25kg (2lb 4oz–2lb 12oz) whole emperor fish or sea bass, descaled, gutted and cleaned
- Generous amount of salt to season
- Oil, for frying

My seasoning mix:

- 1 tbsp sumac
- 2 tbsp ground coriander
- 1 tbsp ground cumin
- 1 tsp ground fennel seeds
- 1 tbsp ground black pepper
- 1 tsp lemon salt (citric acid)
- 1 ground dried white or black lime (loomi)
- 1 tsp chopped coriander (cilantro)
- 2 tsp sea salt (or to taste)

To serve (suggested):

- Jewelled Rice (see page 168) or white rice
- Fresh pitta or pitta chips
- Tahiniya sauce (see page 184)
- Daqqus (see page 183)
- Humr sauce (see page 188)
- Fresh chunky salad (tomatoes, spring onions/scallions, cucumbers, olives, whole green chillies and lemon wedges)

Serves 4

★DF★GF

For the seasoning mix, grind all the ingredients to a fine powder. This can be stored in an airtight jar for up to a week in the fridge or up to a couple of months in the freezer, but it is best used on the day of preparation (see tip below).

For the fish, score it bone-deep in crosshatched lines. Sprinkle with a generous amount of salt, then let it sit for 10–15 minutes. Wash and pat dry.

In a wide wok or pan, heat enough oil to cover the fish two-thirds of the way up. Use a kitchen thermometer to check that the oil is at least 200°C (390°F).

Give another sprinkle of salt to the fish and gently place it in the hot oil. Fry for 5–7 minutes on each side (or until golden brown on each side).

Carefully take the fish out of the oil and place on a wire rack to drain. Give it a good dusting of the prepared seasoning. Serve with your choice of suggested accompaniments and enjoy.

TIP: Leftover seasoning can be used as a rub for meats or as a sprinkling for potato chips (fries).

SAMAK HAMOUR

This very simple fisherman's curry from the southern parts of the Red Sea is literally made up of whatever the fishermen catch on the day. Often cooked in a specific stoneware pot, in a punchy and tart base of simple spices, onions and tamarind, it can be served with rice or bread. A simple everyday kind of curry.

INGREDIENTS:

- 125ml (4½fl oz/½ cup) cooking oil, plus 4 tbsp for frying the fish
- 2 medium onions, sliced
- 2 cloves of garlic, minced
- ½ tsp ground turmeric
- ½ tsp chilli powder
- ½ tsp ground coriander
- 1 stick cinnamon
- 4 green cardamom pods
- 4 cloves
- 2 black cardamom pods
- ½ tsp Baharat spice mix
- 1 tsp crushed dried fenugreek leaves
- 125g (4½oz/½ cup) natural yogurt, at room temperature
- 2 tbsp fresh tamarind pulp or 1 tsp tamarind paste
- 1kg (2lb 4oz) white fish (such as king, swordfish, halibut etc), cut into roughly 10cm (4-inch) slices
- Sea salt

To serve (choice of the below):

- Plain Naan (see page 160)
- Pitta Bread (see page 166)
- Carrot Rice (see page 169)
- Plain Rice (see page 18)

Serves 4–6

★GF

In a heavy-based deep saucepan, heat the oil on a medium heat, then add the onions and fry until they are light brown in colour – around 5–7 minutes. Once the onions are nicely browned, take them out and blend them with a splash of water into a smooth paste. Return the onion paste to the pan.

Add the minced garlic and all the dried spices and season with salt, then sauté for about 5 minutes until oil starts to appear at the edges of the pan.

Add the yogurt and sauté for further 5 minutes. Add the tamarind and sauté for 30 seconds, then set aside off the heat.

In a non-stick frying pan, heat the 4 tablespoons of oil and, working in batches so you don't overcrowd the pan, fry the fish, skin side down first, for 5–7 minutes until crispy and golden. Flip over and fry for a further 2–3 minutes until the fish is nearly done.

Transfer the fish to the pan with the prepared curry base. Add 250ml water and gently mix, then cover and let it simmer for 3–5 minutes until the fish is cooked through and the flavours have all mingled.

Serve the curry with your choice of bread and/or rice.

DATES: THE DIVINE FRUIT

"A date palm is the only creation of God that resembles man. Unlike other trees, a date palm gives more as it grows older" (Egyptian proverb)

It is likely that the date palm is native to the Arabian Peninsula, with rock carvings of them found dating to over 8000 years BC at Jabal Umm Salim. That alone illustrates the importance of dates in prehistoric Arabia. Some archaeologists think it may have all started in the ancient oasis of Al-Ahsa region (a UNESCO heritage site). A date palm tree is not just ancient, it's biblical. The tree is mentioned in the Torah, Bible and even 22 times in the holy book of Qur'an. Allah instructed Maryum (Virgin Mary), the mother of Jesus, to consume dates when giving birth: "Shake the trunk of the Palm tree towards yourself and fresh and ripe dates shall fall upon you. So eat and drink and cool your eyes."

Dates, revered as the dessert fruit by the Bedouins, now cover an estimated 108,000 hectares of Saudi Arabia. There are about 300–400 varieties. The main cultivating areas are Al-ahsa, Al-Qaseem and Al-Medinah regions. How could I write about Saudi Arabia and not mention dates, when it is the largest exporter of dates? I also have very reverential feelings towards the fruit and the wilderness of date palm gardens in Madinah al-Munawwarah since my earliest memories. The English vocabulary fails me in explaining my love for this oasis. It is divine love. A significant part of my beloved memories with Aba Jan belongs to these gardens.

One of them is the Gardens of Salman Al Farsi (Companion of Prophet Muhammad). The date palms stand tall and majestic, with their slender trunks etched with the memory of countless fruit bearings, their crowns fanning out into feathery green fronds and clusters of golden-brown fruit hanging heavy, like drops of gold. Beneath them, a young girl roamed, hugging every single tree in a row. Trying to climb them and falling down breaking her back: yes, that was me.

For me, Date palms are living poems – the whirling dervishes that have been whirling selflessly since their existence, and with them my soul begins to whirl filled with divine love as soon as I set my foot there. And when the night approached, I often laid down on Aba jan's Nissan Datsun bonnet stargazing with him, in the quiet of this sanctuary, sipping Qahwa and munching on fresh juicy dates. Sometimes Aba Jan put on his favourite track of all time, 'Stand By me' by Ben E King, on our way back, passing through these BFGs (my Big Friendly Giants). I knew this song by heart. I can write volumes on date palms but for now, this is it. You will find a couple of date recipes in this book and, yes, do try to drizzle or glaze lamb with date molasses (see page 104); it's a game changer.

Breaking bread together

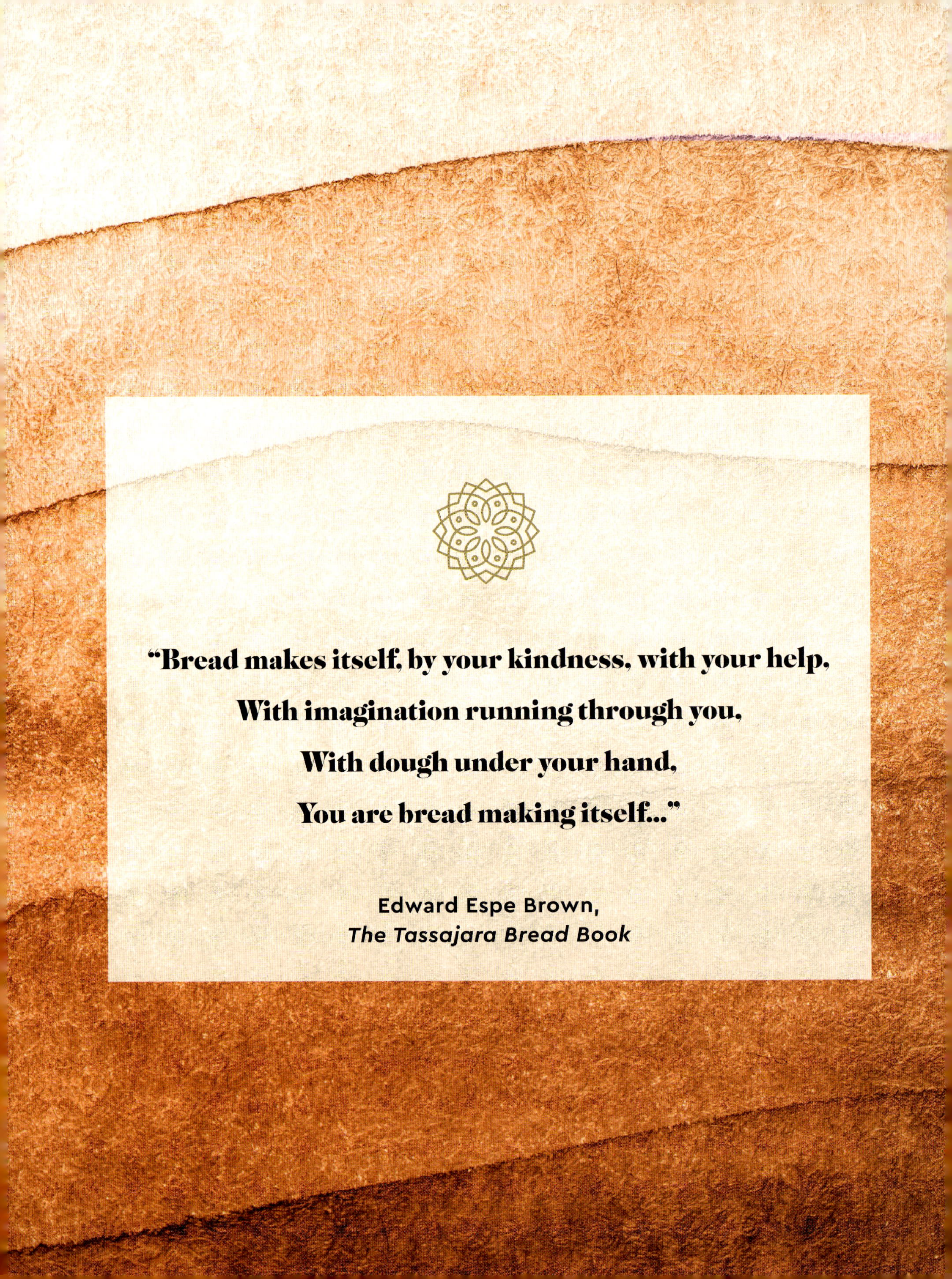

"Bread makes itself, by your kindness, with your help,
With imagination running through you,
With dough under your hand,
You are bread making itself..."

Edward Espe Brown,
The Tassajara Bread Book

The thought of breaking bread takes me back to the sweaty summer evenings in Jeddah and Medina, cramped in the backseat of Aba Jan's car with my cousins and groceries, heart racing at the thought of the first bite. Every Friday, the same ritual, the smell of wood fire in the air, the hum of the neighbourhood, and that impossible choice: which type of bread and pastries would I pick this time. But what truly matters was the bread sharing.

It's home, comfort and a little piece of Saudi Arabia that I still carry with me. These were, hands down, the best breads I have ever had, or maybe it's the best memories that make the bread so special.

In this book, I have tried to bring that spirit back with almost no recipes that require rigorous kneading, which anyone can pull off. No mixers, no fancy machines, no sweat, no tears – just a bowl, flour, water and a little time. The result is an airy, fluffy bread encased in a thin, crispy, crusty canvas, unapologetically simple. The kind of bread that can give any bulk-producing brand a run for its money.

There are a handful of bread recipes ranging from the simplest of pitta breads that puff up like balloons to fluffy naans, perfect for mopping up curries and dips, to a very revered Fatoot designed for communal feasts.

Both bread and rice are quintessential to any Saudi table. While bread symbolizes the strengthening of relations, the word *aish* (Saudi dialect of Arabic) literally translates to "life". The word is used for both bread and rice, emphasizing their importance to the Arab world.

I am a bit of a rice fanatic. Fluffy, steamy, fragrant, with each grain telling its own story, inviting you to "come and eat me". So along with bread recipes, I have included two of my personal favourite rice recipes (there are two in the Mains chapter as well) and a giant couscous (maftoul) recipe too, which can be showstoppers on their own or best mates with any main.

Follow my recipes to the tee and you will fall in love with rice all over again.

2 TYPES OF NAAN:
Butter Naan & Garlic Naan

Serve these naan with your favourite curries, or with honey and *qashta* (clotted cream), preserves of your choice and/or tea.

How to make the Butter Naan

INGREDIENTS:

- 500g (1lb 2oz/3⅔ cups) strong white bread flour or maida
- 1 tsp dried instant yeast
- 1½ tsp sugar
- ½ tbsp salt
- 1 tsp bicarbonate of soda (baking soda)
- 100g (3½oz/½ cup) natural yogurt at room temperature
- 125ml (4fl oz/½ cup) melted ghee, plus extra for brushing
- 250ml (9fl oz/1 cup) tepid water
- 1 egg yolk
- 2 tbsp milk
- Sesame seeds, to sprinkle

Makes 5 medium naans

★V

In a large mixing bowl, combine the flour, yeast, sugar, salt and bicarbonate of soda. Add the yogurt and 2 tablespoons of the melted ghee and mix with your hands until roughly combined.

Add the tepid water, a little at a time, and bring the dough together. It will be very sticky (and it should be). Drizzle with all the remaining ghee so that it's well covered, cover the bowl and let it rest for 20 minutes.

After resting, give the dough a good knead until all of the ghee is absorbed into the dough – this will take about 2 minutes. Cover the bowl and let it prove for 1–1½ hours until roughly doubled in size.

Towards the end of the proving time, preheat the grill (broiler) function of the oven to 250°C (500°F), gas 9 (or the closest you can get) and mix together the egg yolk and milk to make an egg wash.

Place an oven-proof frying pan over a low heat and get it hot. Divide the dough into five equal balls. Stretch a portion out with your hands (or use a rolling pin) to the size of your hand. Place it into the hot pan, brush it with the egg wash and sprinkle with sesame seeds. Cook for 3 minutes, then transfer it to the preheated oven and grill for a further 3–5 minutes, until lovely golden in colour. Repeat to cook the remaining dough balls.

Brush the bread with more ghee and serve.

How to make the Garlic Naan

The base recipe is the same as the butter naan, but with additional ingredients.

INGREDIENTS:

For the dough:

- 1 bulb of garlic for roasting
- Olive oil, for drizzling
- 500g (1lb 2oz/3⅔ cups) strong white bread flour or maida
- 1 tsp dried instant yeast
- 1½ tsp sugar
- ½ tbsp salt, plus extra for the garlic
- 1 tsp bicarbonate of soda (baking soda)
- 100g (3½oz/½ cup) natural yogurt at room temperature
- 125ml (4fl oz/½ cup) melted ghee, plus extra for brushing
- 250ml (9fl oz/1 cup) tepid water
- 1 egg yolk
- 2 tbsp milk

For the garlic butter:

- 125g (4½oz/½ cup) salted butter, softened
- 2–3 cloves of garlic, minced
- 2–3 tbsp finely chopped coriander (cilantro)

Makes 5 medium naans

★V

Preheat the oven to 180°C (350°F), gas 4.

Cut the top off the garlic bulb to expose the tops of the cloves a little. Place the bulb on a sheet of foil, drizzle with some olive oil and sprinkle with sea salt. Wrap it up in the foil and bake it in the oven for 30–40 minutes, depending on the size of the bulb. Let it cool down for a few minutes before unwrapping.

While the garlic is cooking, prepare the naan dough following the steps opposite.

Once slightly cooled down, squeeze the soft roasted garlic cloves out of their skins and into the naan dough after its first 20 minutes of resting. Fold the garlic through the dough, then leave to prove for 1–1½ hours.

Meanwhile, to make the garlic butter, simply mix the butter, minced garlic and chopped coriander together.

Follow the rest of butter naan steps opposite to roll out and cook the naan breads.

Once out of the oven, brush the naans generously with the garlic butter and enjoy.

FATOOT
(An Arab version of the seeded spiced round bread baked in communal ovens)

A staple of Madinah region, no *ta'teema* or *asariya* (afternoon tea gathering) is complete without fatoot. It is a spiced enriched bread named for its crumbly texture.

Traditionally, it was kneaded with the melted tail fat of a sheep, leavened up with Hajj yeast and baked in the neighbourhood's communal ovens, as there were no ovens for domestic use. Nowadays, fatoot is readily available from bakeries.

It is a serene moment to witness when Iftar spreads are laid out in endless row upon row in the courtyards of Madinah, just before the call of Maghrib prayer (sunset, when Muslims break their fast). Fatoot sits majestically before each person, along with its typical accompaniments of dates, a pot of yogurt, some fresh fruits, cheeses, olives, milk and Madinian Dukkah (see page 187), all free for the people visiting the Holy Prophet's mosque during that time – a gesture of true generosity embedded in the Saudi culture for centuries.

I remember vividly a four-year-old version of me standing on my toes, jumping as high as I could to see inside an old bakery in Madinah – a hole-in-a-wall kind of place – while Aba Jan placed an order for fatoot and its accompaniments. Me being me, a very greedy, crowd-puller of a child, I would wriggle my little hands into the bags of warm wholesome and hearty fatoot bread and grab my share to enjoy on the way back to our holiday home. That spiced aroma of freshly baked bread still resonates in my senses.

I serve these fatoot warm with *shai* (Arab/Turkish minty black tea) or at room temperature with assorted accompaniments of dates, olives, cheeses, olive oil, date molasses, pickles and fruit preserves, ideal for British summer picnics and packed treats.

Left: Masjid Al Nabawi, Madinah

INGREDIENTS:

- 14g (½oz) dry active yeast
- 30g (1oz/2½ tbsp) sugar
- 60ml (2fl oz/¼ cup) warm water
- 500g (1lb 2oz/3¾ cups) wholemeal flour
- 250g (9oz/1¾ cups plus 2 tbsp) plain (all-purpose) flour (I use Turkish branded flour)
- 1 tbsp sea salt
- 1½ tsp Baharat spice mix
- ½ tsp ground star anise
- 1 tsp roasted cumin seeds
- 2 tsp ground mahlep (or a couple of drops of almond extract)
- 250ml (9fl oz/1 cup) whole milk
- 250ml (9fl oz/1 cup) full-fat yogurt
- 1 large egg, beaten
- 100g (3½oz/scant ½ cup) ghee or butter, melted
- 200ml (7fl oz/¾ cup plus 2 tbsp) vegetable oil, plus extra for greasing
- 1 tbsp nigella seeds, lightly ground
- 1 tbsp fennel seeds, lightly ground

For glazing the breads:

- 1–2 egg yolks, lightly beaten
- 1 tsp milk
- Sesame, fennel and nigella seeds, to sprinkle on top

Makes 5

★V

Activate the yeast by combining it with the sugar and warm water in a small bowl. Let it sit until it's frothy – about 5–10 minutes.

In a large mixing bowl, combine both flours, salt, Baharat, star anise, cumin and mahlep and mix well so that the dry ingredients get to know each other.

Make a well in the middle and pour in all of the wet ingredients and seeds, along with the bloomed yeast mixture. Mix well and knead for 5 minutes or so until smooth and elastic.

Grease a clean bowl with a little bit of oil and transfer the dough into the bowl. Cover and leave it to prove for about an hour, or until it has doubled in size.

Gently knock the air out of the risen dough, then divide it into five equal balls. Roll each ball into a circle about 15cm (6 inches) in diameter and 1cm (½ inch) thick and let rest for 10–15 minutes.

Preheat the oven to 180°C (350°F), gas 4, and line a baking tray with baking paper. Mix together the beaten egg yolk and milk for the egg wash.

Transfer the breads onto the lined tray, brush with egg wash and sprinkle with the seed mix.

Bake for 12–15 minutes until a lovely golden colour.

Serve warm (that's how I like it) with your choice of condiments.

MLAWA
(Yemeni paratha flat bread)

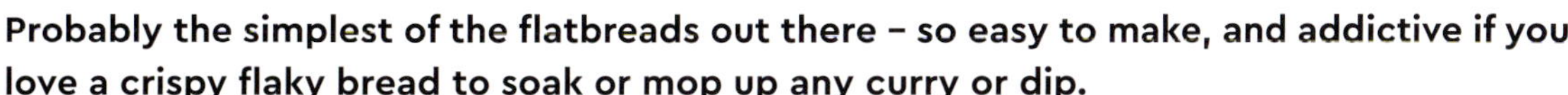

Probably the simplest of the flatbreads out there – so easy to make, and addictive if you love a crispy flaky bread to soak or mop up any curry or dip.

INGREDIENTS:

- 250g (9oz/1¾ cups plus 2 tbsp) plain (all-purpose) flour (I use Turkish brand flour because of its superior quality for these kind of breads)
- 1 tsp salt
- 250ml (9fl oz/1 cup) warm water
- Any flavourless oil, to drizzle
- 125g (4½oz/½ cup) butter, softened
- Nigella seeds, to sprinkle

Makes 3

★V

Mix the flour and salt in a bowl, bring it together with the water, a little at a time, and knead it for 5 minutes, then cover with a tea towel and leave it to rest for 10 minutes.

Knead the dough again for 5–7 minutes so the gluten develops and the dough is stretchy. Drizzle some oil over the dough, cover the bowl and let it rest for 30 minutes to 1 hour – the longer the better.

Divide the dough into three portions, then roll them into balls. Lightly grease the work surface with oil or butter. Working with one portion of dough at a time, start stretching the dough out with your hands as thinly as possible. You should be able to read through it.

To laminate the dough, spread one-third of the butter across the stretched dough. Crinkle-fold this thin sheet of dough (as you would to make a paper fan), so that you have a strip of pleated dough. Hold one end of the pleated dough and wrap the strip around your index and middle fingers into a swirl shape resembling a cinnamon bun, tucking the other end under the spiral as you release your fingers from it. Repeat to shape the remaining two dough portions, then let them rest for at least 10 minutes.

Use your hands to spread each of the laminated dough portions into thin round discs about 25cm (10 inches) in diameter. Sprinkle some nigella seeds over each disc.

Heat a large, round, flat pan (also known as a tawa), and place a mlawa onto it. Cook until bubbles start to appear, then flip it over and cook until the bubbles start to brown – about 3 minutes in all. Remove to cook the other two discs, then enjoy with your favourite curries.

PITTA BREAD
(That anyone can make; AKA Khobz Al-Arabi)

These are a far cry from those abominable, thick, sorry-looking slabs of dough that are sold to us in supermarkets. I have specifically developed this recipe with my eldest, 11-year-old son, Sinan. If he can make it successfully, I think anyone can.

Enjoy homemade pittas with any dip or curry of your choice or stuffed with falafel, pickles and salads – there are plenty in this book.

INGREDIENTS:

- 350g (12oz/2⅔ cups) plain (all-purpose) white or wholemeal flour, plus extra for dusting (I use Turkish brand for a superior bread)
- 1 × 7g (¼oz) sachet of dry active/instant yeast
- 1 tbsp granulated sugar
- 200ml (7fl oz/¾ cup plus 2 tbsp) warm water
- 70g (2½oz/5 tbsp) thick Greek or natural yogurt, at room temperature
- 20ml (⅔fl oz/1½ tbsp) olive oil (or any neutral oil)
- 1 tbsp milk powder
- 1 tsp salt

Makes 9
⭑V

Start by putting the flour in a mixing bowl. Make a well in the middle and add the yeast, sugar and warm water. Let it rest for 10 minutes to activate the yeast, then add the rest of the ingredients and knead gently until everything comes together into a soft dough.

Tip the dough onto a work surface and knead for about 10–12 minutes. If the dough becomes too sticky, sprinkle some flour on the work surface. Let the dough rest for 45 minutes to 1 hour until roughly doubled in size.

Roll the dough into a log, then cut it into 9 equal balls. Cover the balls with a damp cloth or cling film (plastic wrap) and let them rise for about 20 minutes.

Dust a little flour on the work surface and roll each dough ball out to a circle with a diameter of around 15cm (6 inches).

Let the rolled-out pittas sit for 15 minutes, covered with a cloth or cling film.

Meanwhile preheat the oven to 250°C (500°F), gas 9, placing a hot stone or marble slab, pizza stone or heavy baking tray on the middle shelf of the oven to heat up with it (the stone will give superior results in proper ballooned-up pittas). Once hot, bake the pittas on the stone or tray for 4–5 minutes.

As soon as the tops of the pittas turn light brown, take them out. Don't wait for the bread to turn a rich brown or they will go dry and hard. Enjoy warm.

LOADED JEWELLED RICE

INGREDIENTS:

- 1 tbsp white vinegar
- 5–6 green cardamom pods, lightly pounded to open up the pods
- 750g (1lb 10oz) easy-cook basmati rice (I use sella), soaked in warm water for 1 hour
- 3 tbsp oil (any sort)
- 2 tbsp ghee
- 70g (2½oz/½ cup) blanched almonds
- 70g (2½oz/½ cup) cashews
- A handful of pine nuts (preferably the long Pakistani ones)
- Zest and juice of 1 small orange
- 70g (2½oz/½ cup) mix of raisins and dried cranberries
- 1 small onion, finely chopped
- 2–3 whole jalapeño chillies (optional)
- 250ml (9fl oz/1 cup) chicken or vegetable stock (or use the reserved liquid from Lamb Mandi, page 104)
- 1 tsp Baharat spice mix
- A few strands of saffron soaked in 2 tbsp kewra (screwpine) water
- Sea salt
- Slivered pistachios, to garnish
- A few pomegranate seeds, to garnish

Serves 4–6
★V★GF

Get a large, wide pot of water boiling and season it well with salt, the vinegar and the cardamom pods. Tip in the soaked rice and simmer until 80 per cent cooked – tender, but still al dente. Drain the rice and set aside.

In the same wide pot, heat the oil and ghee, then fry the almonds, cashews, pine nuts, orange zest and raisin and cranberry mix for 3–4 minutes, or until they start to puff up a little and your whole kitchen starts to smell like an orchard. Remove them with a slotted spoon and drain on paper towels.

In the same oil, on a medium heat, sauté the chopped onion until soft, then add your jalapeño chillies, if using.

Pour in the stock and orange juice and add the Baharat spice mix. Taste and adjust the salt if required. Give it a stir, then tip in the boiled rice and fried nuts and fruit, reserving a few for garnish. Gently mix together in a folding motion, then add the saffron mix in a swirling motion too.

Let the rice cook on a very low heat until all of the liquid has been absorbed and the rice has fluffed up – about 7–10 minutes.

Dish the rice out onto a serving plate and garnish with pistachios, pomegranate seeds and the reserved fried nuts and fruit.

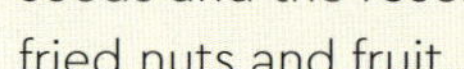

AISH AL JAZAR
(Carrot rice)

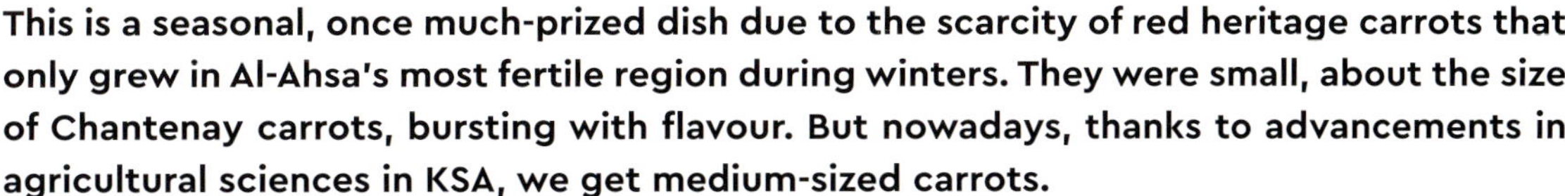

This is a seasonal, once much-prized dish due to the scarcity of red heritage carrots that only grew in Al-Ahsa's most fertile region during winters. They were small, about the size of Chantenay carrots, bursting with flavour. But nowadays, thanks to advancements in agricultural sciences in KSA, we get medium-sized carrots.

These carrots reminded my mama of her early days in Saudi Arabia, and of Pakistani carrots filling the donkey carts everywhere. I remember watching her sob in silence one day our lovely Saudi neighbour cooked this memory-laden rice dish and served it with jajeek and daqqus. Since then, it has been an integral part of our lives. Mama makes it for my children while narrating the whole story again and again. That is all that is left of her fading memories.

Aish al jazar is a complete meal on its own, but it can be served as a side to other main meals as well.

INGREDIENTS:

- 60g (2oz/¼ cup) unsalted butter
- 1 tbsp olive oil
- 1 brown onion, finely chopped
- 2 tbsp concentrated tomato purée (paste)
- 300g (10½oz) bright red carrots (not the purple ones) or regular carrots, peeled and diced into cubes
- 15g (½oz/4 tsp) sugar
- 1 tsp saffron strands, bloomed over a cube of ice (see page 246)
- 5cm (2-inch) cinnamon stick
- 1 tsp whole black peppercorns
- 1 tsp cloves
- 1 tsp roasted ground cumin
- ½ tsp ground cinnamon
- 1 tsp Baharat spice mix
- ½ tsp ground cardamom
- 200g (7oz) tomatoes, diced
- 300g (10½oz) green beans, trimmed
- 500g (1lb 2oz) basmati rice, soaked for 30 minutes
- 3–4 large (US extra-large) eggs
- Sea salt

To serve:

- Chopped coriander (cilantro)
- Jajeek (see page 190, optional)
- Daqqus (see page 183, optional)
- Shatta (see page 195, optional)

Serves 4–6

★V★GF

In a large pan (big enough to eventually accommodate the rice), melt the butter and olive oil together over medium-high heat. Add the chopped onion and sauté until it starts to turn golden, then sprinkle with salt. Add the tomato purée and sauté for another 30 seconds.

Add the carrots and sugar to the pan and cook until the carrots start to caramelize a little.

Add the spices and chopped tomatoes and cook until the tomatoes have completely broken down – about 7 minutes.

Meanwhile, blanch the green beans in boiling water for 5 minutes until cooked but still firm, then drain.

Now add the blanched beans to the carrot mixture and stir in gently, then add the soaked, drained rice. Give the rice a mix and add 800ml (28fl oz/3½ cups) water, cover the pan and cook on a medium-high until 75 per cent of the water has been absorbed by the rice.

Turn the heat right down to its lowest setting, add the saffron water, and place the lid tightly on the pan so no steam escapes and let it cook for 15–20 minutes, or until the rice is fully cooked, rotating the pan every now and then so that the rice cooks evenly.

While the rice cooks, boil the eggs for 6 minutes and 45 seconds exactly to achieve a soft runny yolk in the middle.

Serve the rice with the halved boiled eggs and a sprinkle of coriander on top, with jajeek, daqqus and/or shatta on the side.

ROASTED AUTUMNAL VEGETABLE MAFTOUL
(Giant couscous)

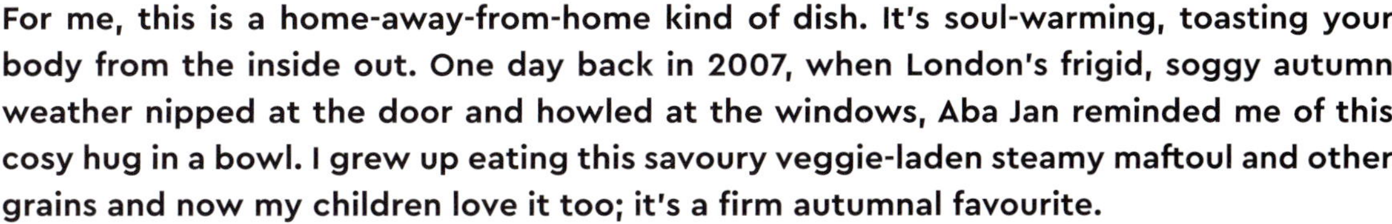

For me, this is a home-away-from-home kind of dish. It's soul-warming, toasting your body from the inside out. One day back in 2007, when London's frigid, soggy autumn weather nipped at the door and howled at the windows, Aba Jan reminded me of this cosy hug in a bowl. I grew up eating this savoury veggie-laden steamy maftoul and other grains and now my children love it too; it's a firm autumnal favourite.

Now, you may be overwhelmed at first glance, but trust me, it is a very straightforward, easy recipe. It's a perfect vegetarian main meal, or serve it as a side. It encapsulates so many textures and flavours, yet they live in perfect harmony, and the best part is, you can prepare it well in advance if you are hosting a large gathering and just heat the dish before serving. Job done, family happy! I serve this dish with the classic culprits, namely shatta and jajeek, when serving on its own, or as a side to a fish course. A chef's kiss it is.

INGREDIENTS:

For the roasted vegetables:

- 2 aubergines (eggplants), cut into 4cm (1½-inch) cubes
- 2 courgettes (zucchini), cut into 4cm (1½-inch) cubes
- 3 (bell) peppers (any colours) cut into 4cm (1½-inch) squares
- 500g (1lb 2oz) – prepared weight – dark green squash/little pumpkin with the most orange flesh possible, cut into 2.5cm (1 inch) thick slices
- 2 parsnips, peeled and cut into 2.5cm (1 inch) thick slices
- 2 carrots, peeled and cut into 2.5cm (1 inch) thick slices
- Olive oil, to drizzle generously
- Salt and freshly ground black pepper

For the maftoul:

- 3 tbsp olive oil or ghee (or any light neutral oil)
- 1 large white onion, very finely chopped
- 2 fat cloves of garlic, minced
- ½ tsp ground allspice
- ¼ tsp ground ginger
- ½ tsp ground turmeric
- 5cm (2-inch) cinnamon stick, broken into smaller pieces
- 1 medium tomato, skin removed and finely chopped
- 500g (1lb 2oz) maftoul
- 1.25 litres (44fl oz/5½ cups) vegetable stock
- 1 × 400g (14oz) can butter (lima) beans, rinsed
- 50g (1¾oz) flat leaf parsley, chopped
- 50g (1¾oz) coriander (cilantro), chopped
- 2 tbsp toasted pumpkin seeds (optional but highly recommended)

To serve:

- 25g (1oz) mint leaves
- 2 tbsp neutral oil
- Handful of pomegranate seeds
- Pomegranate or grape molasses (optional but highly recommended if serving the dish on its own)
- Shatta (see page 195) and/or Jajeek (see page 190) (optional but recommended)

Serves 6–8

★V★DF

Preheat the oven to 180°C (350°F), gas 4.

Arrange the veggies on a foil- or baking-paper-lined roasting tray which is large enough to fit all of them and also fit in the oven. Sprinkle some salt and pepper over the veggies and drizzle generously with olive oil, tossing to ensure all of them are coated well. Roast for 45 minutes to 1 hour, or until the veggies are thoroughly cooked and very soft, turning them halfway through roasting so that they cook evenly.

In the meantime, prepare the maftoul. Heat the olive oil or ghee in a large saucepan over a medium–high heat. Add the chopped onion and sauté for 3–4 minutes until soft and translucent.

Stir in the garlic, allspice, ginger, turmeric and cinnamon and cook, stirring frequently, for a few minutes until fragrant.

Add the chopped tomato and cook the mixture down until oil starts to appear at the edges.

Add the maftoul to the pot and stir to coat the grains in the spiced oil. Toast for about 5 minutes or until lightly golden and fragrant.

Pour in all but 250ml (9fl oz/1 cup) of the vegetable stock and stir well. Bring to a gentle boil, then reduce the heat to low. Cover, and let it simmer for 12–15 minutes, or until the maftoul has absorbed the liquid and is tender.

At this point, add the butter (lima) beans to the pan and allow them to warm through.

In the meantime, prepare the crispy mint leaves. Wash them and pat dry. Heat the oil in a small frying pan, add the leaves and fry for 1 minute or so until they change colour and crisp up. Be careful, as the oil can splatter a bit. Transfer the crisped-up leaves to a piece of paper towel to drain.

Remove the pan from the heat and fluff up the maftoul. Dish it out onto a serving platter and ladle the remaining stock over it. Stir in the pumpkin seeds and most of the chopped parsley and coriander through the maftoul, reserving a little to garnish.

Top the maftoul with the roasted veggies – you can mix them through if preferred, but I like serving them on top, in all of their caramelized glory.

Sprinkle the reserved herbs and the pomegranate seeds on top and add a little drizzle of molasses. Finish with the crispy mint leaves. Serve it with shatta sauce and jajeek, or as a side to a main course.

A drizzle of magic & a sprinkle of spice

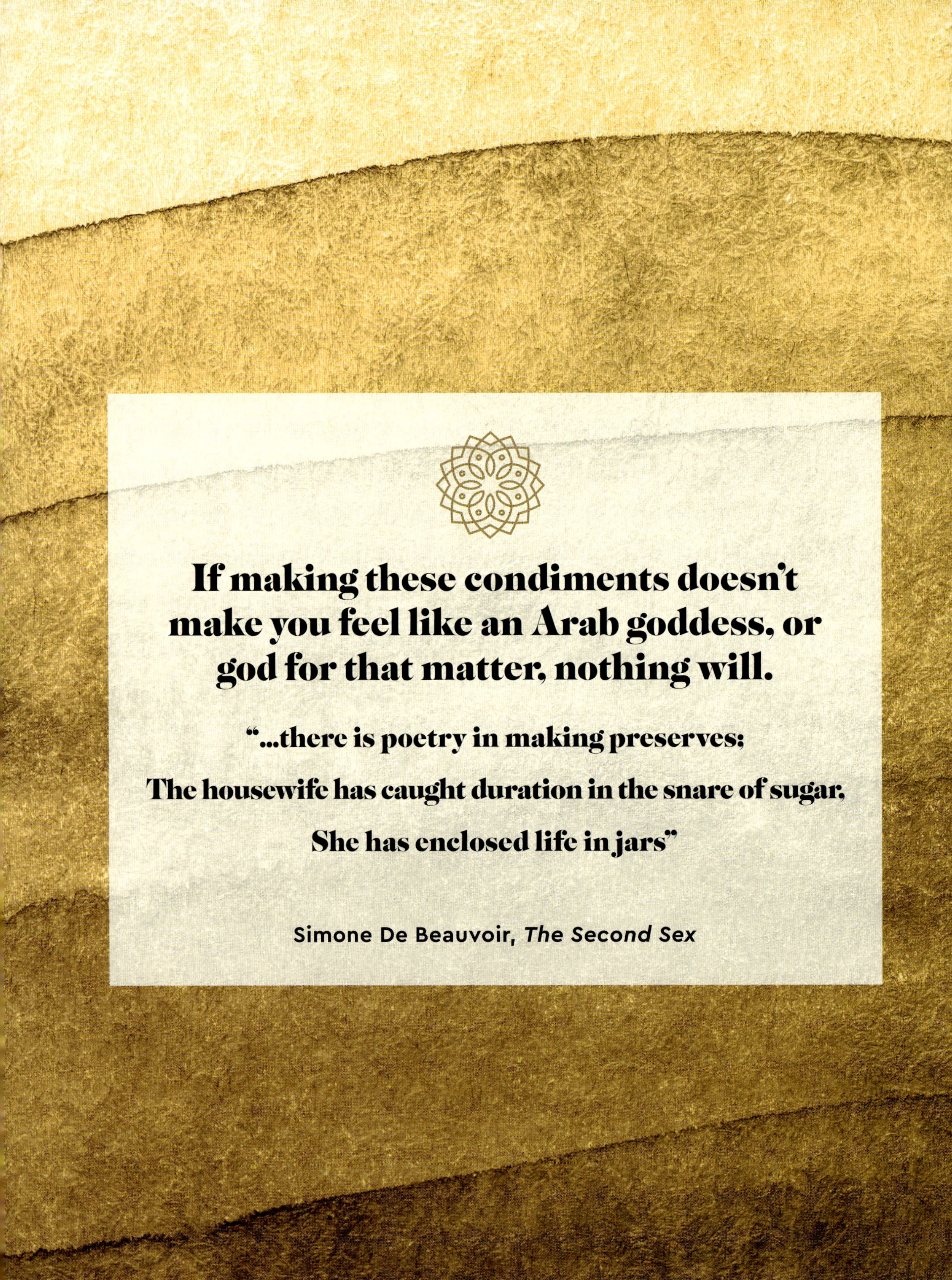

If making these condiments doesn't make you feel like an Arab goddess, or god for that matter, nothing will.

"...there is poetry in making preserves;
The housewife has caught duration in the snare of sugar,
She has enclosed life in jars"

Simone De Beauvoir, *The Second Sex*

Condiments are an integral part of the Saudi culinary scene. There are a few supporting actors and a few that take the lead. I often call these the Three Musketeers of the Saudi table. They are saviours to any dish. For me these are Shatta, Tahiniya and Daqqus or Humr (but you can use any combination of your three favourites). They magically transform the whole feasting experience.

Then there is Hot Harissa Honey, Amba and Zhoug. Oh la la – the flavour profile of these will knock you out of the park! They are feisty, and perfect as dips, drizzles or even marinades. And then you have Tinkerbell's gold dust – Madinian Dukkah (page 187), Hawaij (page 186) and Kammouneh (page 196) – which hold the power to secretly elevate your food to royalty status.

Spices were a sacred part of Silk Route culture – the first engine of globalization. Trading spices was probably the first time in modern history that cultural cross-pollination happened, and hawaij was born out of this generational mingling. From the port of Aden, Yemen, to the shores of Jakarta via the cinnamon quills of Colombo, you have it all in a teaspoon of this powerful spice blend. Before the European invasion and disruption of ancient trade, this spice barter system was harmonious for centuries. Indonesians traded cloves, nutmeg and mace, Vietnam and Cambodia had oud (agarwood), and they exchanged these with Yemenis for their most expensive and proud product – frankincense.

Hawaij is more than just a spice blend, it is a pre-colonial identity in a jar, embodying a blend of customs and cultures from communities across the Indian Ocean. This is the reason I say "the old Silk Route runs through my veins"; in any country across this region that I have lived in or visited, I have felt a strong familiar cultural pull. My identity is intertwined with these spices.

I have shared two of my very favourite preserves. Most people will probably never have heard of Watermelon Pith Jam (page 197), but on a frosty morning, I open up a jar of this jam and inhale the musky fragrance I associate with Aba Jan. It was that time of year when I lost him. I dollop the jam onto toast with clotted cream and take a bite, wiping away bittersweet tears of memories. It is very dear to me, so please do read it. Even if it's just for the story.

1
2
3
4
5
6
7
8

9
10
11
12
13
14
15

1: AMBA
(An Iraqi condiment very popular throughout the Middle East)

This particular condiment is very popular throughout the Middle East and North Africa. No sandwich or fry-up is complete without it. It is the perfect amalgam of spicy Indian influences on the Mesopotamian region over millennia. It is tangy, sweet, zesty, sour, sharp enough to make you wink your eye and pungent like wasabi at the same time.

I love to serve it with ta'miyyah (falafel, see page 58), sabich (a Middle Eastern sandwich) and fried aubergines (eggplants). This is my version and I like it spicy.

INGREDIENTS:

- 2 medium firm green mangoes (ideally from an Arab or Asian grocery store, if possible)
- 80ml (2½fl oz/⅓ cup) white or apple cider vinegar to start (adjust the sourness to taste)

For the amba spices:

- 1 tsp ground turmeric
- ½ tsp yellow mustard powder
- ½ tsp mild curry powder
- 1½ tsp ground fenugreek
- 1 tsp lemon salt (citric acid)
- ½ tsp red chilli powder
- 2 tsp sugar
- ½ tsp chilli flakes (optional)
- 1 tsp salt (or to taste)

Makes 1 medium jar

★V★DF★GF

Start by mixing all the amba spices together in a bowl. Add 200ml (7fl oz/scant 1 cup) of hot water and whisk until combined. Leave it to rest for about 30 minutes, or until it becomes thick and a bit frothy.

Meanwhile, peel and thinly slice the mangoes. In a bowl, soak the sliced mango in the vinegar for 5–10 minutes.

Now whisk the soaked amba spices to a homogenous paste, then add the mango slices, along with their soaking vinegar. At this stage, you can blitz it into a smooth paste or keep it chunky the way it is.

Transfer the mixture to a saucepan and bring it to a boil over a medium-high heat. Let it cook for 5 minutes or so, until it starts to thicken up, then take it off the heat and let it cool down completely.

Store in a clean jar in the fridge for up to a fortnight, giving it a gentle mix every couple of days to let the gas escape.

TIP: You can add other vegetables (such as cauliflower florets or pickled cucumbers or olives) to the amba spice paste instead of mangoes. The spice paste works well on its own as well.

2: DAQQUS
(Saudi salsa)

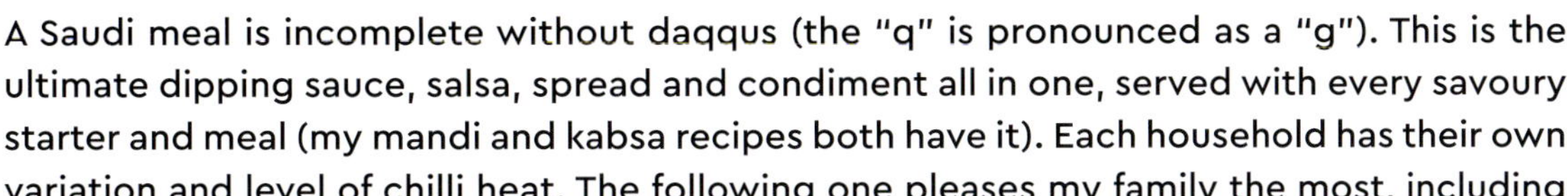

A Saudi meal is incomplete without daqqus (the "q" is pronounced as a "g"). This is the ultimate dipping sauce, salsa, spread and condiment all in one, served with every savoury starter and meal (my mandi and kabsa recipes both have it). Each household has their own variation and level of chilli heat. The following one pleases my family the most, including the children.

INGREDIENTS:

- 2 large beef tomatoes
- 1 hot red chilli
- 1 clove of garlic
- A small handful of fresh coriander (cilantro), with stalks, roughly chopped
- ½ tsp double-concentrate tomato purée (paste); optional, but this gives depth and a beautiful rich colour to salsa
- Juice of ½ lemon
- ½–1 tsp pomegranate molasses
- 1 small banana shallot (or 1 small baby cucumber) finely chopped (optional)
- Salt
- Olive oil, to serve (optional)

Makes about 500ml (17fl oz)
★V★DF★GF

Put everything except the shallot in a food processor and whizz together to your preferred salsa consistency.

Once the desired consistency is achieved, stir in the finely chopped shallot (or cucumber, or both can be added as a variation). Season to taste with salt.

Serve the daqqus drizzled with olive oil. It can live happily in an airtight container in the fridge for up to a week.

3: TAHINIYA
(Tahini sauce)

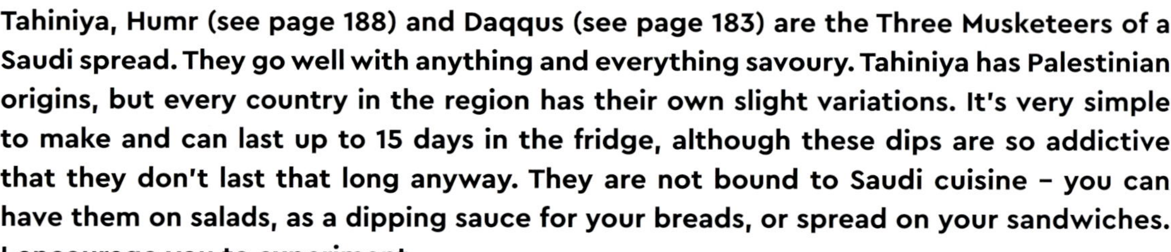

Tahiniya, Humr (see page 188) and Daqqus (see page 183) are the Three Musketeers of a Saudi spread. They go well with anything and everything savoury. Tahiniya has Palestinian origins, but every country in the region has their own slight variations. It's very simple to make and can last up to 15 days in the fridge, although these dips are so addictive that they don't last that long anyway. They are not bound to Saudi cuisine – you can have them on salads, as a dipping sauce for your breads, or spread on your sandwiches. I encourage you to experiment.

INGREDIENTS:

- 4–5 tbsp good-quality tahini paste
- 2 tbsp yogurt
- 1 clove of garlic, crushed
- Juice of 1½ lemons (or to taste)
- ¼ tsp roasted ground cumin
- 2 tbsp chopped parsley (optional)
- Salt

To serve (all optional):

- Olive oil, to drizzle
- Pomegranate seeds
- A pinch of sumac

Makes about 300ml (10½fl oz)

★V★DF★GF

In a bowl, combine the tahini paste, yogurt, garlic and lemon juice. Mix them vigorously – at first the mixture will look curdled, but don't be afraid, you haven't split the sauce.

Now gradually add about 200ml (7fl oz/scant 1 cup) water and keep on mixing until you reach the desired consistency, adding a little more water if needs be.

Add the cumin and parsley, season to taste with salt and give it a good mix – your sauce is ready.

If wished, serve the tahiniya in a bowl, drizzled with olive oil and sprinkled with pomegranate seeds and sumac.

4: HAWAIJ SPICE BLEND

If there is one thing that epitomizes the flavours of the Silk Route, this is it. It is earthy, smoky and aromatic – basically a foundation blend of Yemenite spices that can be used to marinate meat and vegetables or to zhuzh up soups and salads, or even espresso.

So, next time you crave a pumpkin spiced latte and don't have the spice blend to hand, try adding a little bit of hawaij to it and thank me later. It is an invitation to a whole new level of bursting, bright flavours; there's never a dull moment with it.

INGREDIENTS:

- 30g (1oz) black peppercorns
- 25g (1oz) cumin seeds
- 15g (½oz) coriander seeds
- A small cinnamon stick
- ½ tsp whole cloves
- 15g (½oz) green cardamom pods
- 15g (½oz) ground turmeric

Makes 1 small jar

★V★DF★GF

Put all the spices except for the turmeric in a frying pan and set on a medium heat. Roast the spices for 4–5 minutes until fragrant, then tip the roasted spices onto a plate and let them cool down.

Once cool, finely grind the spices in a coffee grinder. Sift the ground spices to separate out any big chunks, returning any larger pieces to the grinder to blitz again. Sift the mixture, then mix in the turmeric.

Put the spice mix in a jar with a tight lid and store in a cool dry place and we are good to go.

5: HAWAIJ SPICED CRUNCHY NUTS

Nuts in all forms are an essential part of the Arab diet – from savoury to sweet, you will rarely find a recipe that is not sprinkled with nuts. Growing up in Balad District of Jeddah (which is now a UNESCO world heritage site), I remember running through the narrow streets of the old souk, shaded with all sorts of stuff, from dried palm leaves to tin sheets. Most of the shops displayed a diverse assortment of spices in large jute sacks, along with a huge variety of nuts at a very affordable price.

The spice-perfumed air and colourful displays of nuts, with faint background voices of spice merchants haggling over prices, still happily live in my memories. To cherish those lost moments in time, I recreated this nut mix in 2017 when I revisited Saudi Arabia and these souks to bring a little piece of those foregone times back to life, at least on my tongue.

Perfect for happy-hour nibbles on a Friday with an icy drink or as a topping to your boring salads and breakfast bowls, this crunchy glory brings the whole dull plate of food to life, as do the people of the Red Sea. I have kept this recipe vegan-friendly, using maple syrup instead of honey. You can use any nuts of your choice but this is my favourite combo. This recipe serves no one and everyone.

INGREDIENTS:

- 50g (1¾oz) walnut halves
- 75g (2½oz) pecan nuts
- 75g (2½oz) almonds
- 100g (3½oz) cashews
- 50g (1¾oz) hazelnuts
- 20g (¾oz) pumpkin seeds
- 60ml (2fl oz/¼ cup) maple syrup
- 2 tsp Hawaij Spice Blend (see page 185)
- 1 tsp cayenne pepper (optional, depending on your heat tolerance)
- 2 tbsp olive oil
- A hefty pinch of sea salt
- Zest of 1 lime
- 10g (⅓oz) sesame seeds

Makes 1 large jar

★V★DF★GF

In a bowl, soak the walnuts and pecans in hot water (from a kettle is fine) for about 15–20 minutes, then drain.

Wash the almonds and pat dry.

Preheat the oven to 180°C (350°F), gas 4 (both top and bottom of the oven if you have a conventional oven) and line a baking tray with baking paper.

Mix together all the ingredients except the sesame seeds in a bowl. Tip the mixture onto the lined tray and spread it out in a single layer.

Bake for 15–20 minutes, or until crispy and dry with a nice golden colour, flipping and mixing the nuts and adding the sesame seeds halfway through cooking.

Once baked, take the tray out of the oven and let the nuts cool down completely – they will crisp up as they cool. Break them into clusters, sized to your liking.

Use straight away or store them in an airtight jar for up to a week – that is, if they last that long.

6: MADINIAN DUKKAH
(Savoury seasoning)

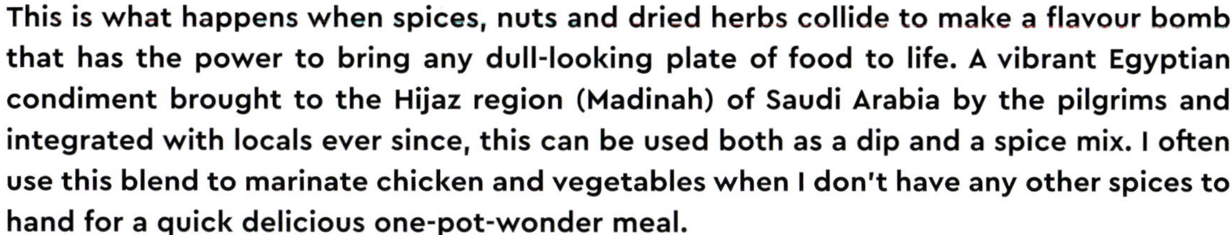

This is what happens when spices, nuts and dried herbs collide to make a flavour bomb that has the power to bring any dull-looking plate of food to life. A vibrant Egyptian condiment brought to the Hijaz region (Madinah) of Saudi Arabia by the pilgrims and integrated with locals ever since, this can be used both as a dip and a spice mix. I often use this blend to marinate chicken and vegetables when I don't have any other spices to hand for a quick delicious one-pot-wonder meal.

It is also a quintessential part of my Arab breakfast spread; I roll various cheeses in this mix and drizzle with honey – heaven!

INGREDIENTS:

- 2 tbsp cumin seeds
- 2 tbsp coriander seeds
- 1 tbsp fennel seeds
- 1 tbsp sesame seeds and/or sunflower seeds
- 75g (2½oz) roasted hazelnuts, peanuts or almonds (or a mix of all three)
- 1 tsp nigella seeds
- 2 tsp dried mint
- 1 tsp salt
- 1 tsp ground black pepper
- 1 tsp lemon salt (citric acid)

Makes 1 small jar
★V★DF★GF

Start by roasting the cumin, coriander and fennel seeds in a pan on a low heat until they start smelling fragrant. This will take about 5 minutes. Take them off the heat and let them cool down.

Meanwhile, in another pan, toast the sesame seeds until lightly brown. Let them cool down.

Now mix the spice seeds and sesame seeds with the roasted nuts and the rest of the ingredients. Coarsely grind the mixture in a pestle and mortar or coffee grinder.

The dukkah can be stored in an airtight jar for up to 2 weeks at room temperature.

7: HUMR
(Hot tamarind dip)

In Saudi Arabia, particularly in Jeddah, you can't have fish in any way or form without this dipping sauce.

INGREDIENTS:

- 200g (7oz) block of tamarind
- 1 small clove of garlic, minced
- 1 tbsp Shatta (see page 195)
- 2 tbsp finely chopped chives or spring onions/scallions (green part)
- ½ tsp freshly ground black pepper
- 1 tsp roasted ground cumin
- 1 tbsp date molasses
- Salt

Makes XXX
★V★DF★GF

Put the tamarind block in a bowl, cover with 400ml (14fl oz/1¾ cups) water and leave to soak for at least 2 hours, preferably overnight.

Rub the softened tamarind block until it breaks down into a muddy situation.

Strain the tamarind through a muslin cloth or a fine sieve into a saucepan, pushing and squeezing every last drop of tamarind pulp out. Discard the seeds and residue.

Bring the tamarind juice to a boil, then let it simmer for 2 minutes. Take it off the heat and let it cool down completely (traditionally, it's not cooked but I do cook it, as it lengthens the shelf life of the sauce).

Add the rest of the ingredients to the pulp and season with salt. Mix well and you have your humr sauce.

The sauce can be stored for up to a week in the fridge, or freeze it in ice cube trays and use a cube as and when needed. Take the frozen cubes out of the freezer and let defrost completely before using.

8: QUINCE PRESERVE

This preserve is an ode to autumnal bounty. In autumn you see crates loaded with these golden lanterns that were once cradled in the crooked arms of age-old trees. I love quince because they are a bit like me: tough on the outside but a big softie on the inside; am I blowing my own trumpet here!

Quince is a fruit requiring patience and care. It cooks on a low and slow heat, but it's well worth the wait when the whole house fills up with scents of honeyed musk and cinnamon, as if it is a temple of peace and calm where your body and soul gets nourished at the same time.

Enjoy this preserve with clotted cream (aka *qashta* or *kaymak*) or serve it on a cheese board with some crackers the next time you host a party.

INGREDIENTS:

- 1kg (2lb 4oz) quince, peeled and cored
- 2.5cm (1 inch) cinnamon stick
- Juice of 1 lemon
- 700g (1lb 9oz) granulated sugar
- A fat pinch of lemon salt (citric acid) (this will extend the shelf life of your preserve)

Makes about a 600ml (21fl oz) jar

★V★DF★GF

Cut the quince into bite-sized cubes and put them in a saucepan with 400ml (14fl oz/1¾ cups) water, the cinnamon stick and lemon juice. Cook on a medium–low heat until tender – this will take around 8–10 minutes.

Strain the quince cubes, reserving the liquid. Set the cooked quince aside and return the liquid to the pan. Add the sugar, bring to the boil and boil for 5 minutes until thick and syrupy.

Now add the cooked quince back to the syrup along with the citric acid and let it cook until it turns a nice rose-gold colour and the syrup has considerably thickened. It will take at least 10–15 minutes on a medium heat, until the syrup is as thick as runny honey.

Once completely cold, transfer it to a jar and keep in the fridge. This preserve can last up to 6 months easily.

9: JAJEEK
(One of the three famous condiments)

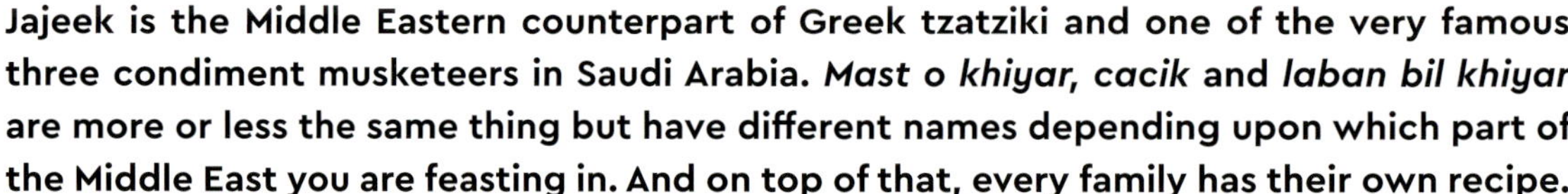

Jajeek is the Middle Eastern counterpart of Greek tzatziki and one of the very famous three condiment musketeers in Saudi Arabia. *Mast o khiyar, cacik* and *laban bil khiyar* are more or less the same thing but have different names depending upon which part of the Middle East you are feasting in. And on top of that, every family has their own recipe.

I have suggested this condiment so many times throughout this book that I thought, let's make it a part of this culinary journey, and as one of the last finishing touches I decided to include it in the book. It would be rude not to.

It is perhaps the simplest of all the condiments and a very forgiving recipe, so do try it and feel free to pair it with any main, or enjoy on its own with a warm pitta bread.

INGREDIENTS:

- 1 large English cucumber or 2 small cucumbers
- 250g (9oz/1 cup) Greek-style yogurt
- A small handful of flat leaf parsley, chopped
- A small handful of mint leaves or dill, chopped
- 1 tsp dried dill (optional but gives a lovely aroma; don't use if using fresh dill)
- 1 fat clove of garlic, crushed
- Juice of ½ lemon
- Sea salt and freshly ground black pepper
- 1 small tomato, deseeded and finely diced, to garnish (optional)
- Extra virgin olive oil, to drizzle

Serves 4

⭑V⭑DF⭑GF

Cut the cucumber in half lengthways, then cut a 5cm (2-inch) piece from one of the cucumber halves, finely dice it and set aside for garnish.

Scoop out the seeds from the rest of the cucumber and discard them. Grate the cucumber on the large holes of a box grater and gently squeeze out any excess liquid. Place the cucumber in a bowl large enough to accommodate all of the other ingredients.

Add rest of the ingredients (except the diced cucumber) and mix well, then season with salt and pepper. Transfer to a serving bowl.

Garnish with the diced cucumber and tomato and drizzle with olive oil. Serve and enjoy!

10: HOT HARISSA HONEY

(For all those sticky and spicy cravings)

If there is one thing I swear by in my pantry, it's got to be my Hot Harissa Honey – or my "3H", as my seven-year-old rainbow baby calls it. Over the years, the world has seen this combination trend like a stock exchange bull. Having consumed and been hooked on this concoction in my teens, I have tried so many of the store-bought versions, but they have all been an utter disappointment. Not punchy enough, not vibrant enough, not pungent enough, not fragrant enough, not sweet enough... enough is enough! Let's make it together and be hooked on it.

My ratio is one part each of harissa, honey and olive oil. It stays good for at least 2 months provided you use a dry spoon to take out the desired amount. Mine never lasts that long as we have a tendency to spoon it over everything, even ice creams and fruit at times. Weird, I know, but life is a one-way trip, so enjoy it and do what makes your soul happy.

INGREDIENTS:

- 170ml (5½fl oz/scant ¾ cup) light olive oil
- 6 cloves of garlic, finely chopped
- 1 × 170g (6oz) jar of rose harissa
- 1 × 170g (6oz) jar of orange blossom honey (I prefer the Greek variety as it is more floral)

Makes about a 450ml (16fl oz) jar

★V★DF★GF

Heat the olive oil in a saucepan over low-medium heat. Add the chopped garlic and sauté for just a minute or so until the raw edge of the garlic has disappeared and turns ever so slightly golden.

Immediately take the pan off the heat, add the harissa paste and give it a good stir. Tip in the honey, stir to incorporate well, then let it cool.

Transfer it to a sterilized jar and keep it in a cold dry place for up to 2 months.

11: ZHOUG
(An ancient Yemenite dip)

This condiment originated from the shores of Yemen and travelled all over the world with Yemenites wherever they went. It left the British audience in awe when I served it with Mutabbaq (see page 38) on MasterChef.

Vibrantly green in colour, zhoug has pungent, heady notes of fresh coriander and parsley, the nuttiness of roasted cumin and coriander seeds, a sharp, spicy kick of chillies and tartness of lemon enough to make your eyes wink. This is all enveloped in a copious amount of olive oil, which means it can last up to three months if kept chilled in airtight jars. It's perfect as it is, served with Mutabbaq, or run through Hummus (see pages 46–53) and Musabaha (see page 37) as I do. Oh, I love batch-cooking and meal prepping!

INGREDIENTS:

- 30g (1oz) fresh coriander (cilantro) with stalks, roughly chopped
- 30g (1oz) fresh parsley with stalks, roughly chopped
- 2 fresh green serrano (or any hot) chillies, roughly chopped
- 1 fresh red chilli, roughly chopped
- 3–4 cloves of garlic, minced
- Juice of 1 lemon
- 1 tsp roasted ground cumin
- 1 tsp roasted ground coriander
- ¼ tsp ground cardamom
- 120ml (4fl oz/½ cup) olive oil
- Salt

Makes 200ml/6¾fl oz

★V★DF★GF

Put all the ingredients except for the olive oil and salt in a food processor or pestle and mortar. Grind it as per your preference – chunky or smooth, it's your call.

Add the olive oil and blend in, then taste and season with salt if required.

Transfer the zhoug to a jar and keep in the fridge for up to 3 months.

12: ROASTED AND SALTED PUMPKIN SEEDS

This is really more of an improvisation then a recipe. A humble snack – similar to Mexican *pepitas* – that is also an answer to zero waste for pumpkins. Each year in the UK, we gut and waste thousands of tonnes of pumpkins in the name of Halloween. I am not saying not to celebrate Halloween, but to be mindful of what we do with the leftover pumpkins. That is the beauty of diverse Saudi cuisine, in which even pumpkin seeds get a VIP treatment.

Roasted pumpkin and watermelon seeds are a readily available nibble in Saudi Arabia, and you can find them in almost every household there. Whether it is friends having a PJ party, binge-watching TV or having a gossip, or people having a serious conversation, there is always a bowl of these glistening salty bits handy, accompanied by dates and Saudi coffee.

INGREDIENTS:

- Pumpkin seeds (from a medium pumpkin), rinsed and stringy bits removed
- Olive oil or any neutral oil, to drizzle
- Salt
- Spice mix of your choice, such as harissa, Hawaij (page 186), or Madinian Dukkah (page 187), to season

Makes 1 small jar

★V★DF★GF

Bring a saucepan of water to the boil and add a good amount of salt (I use about 1½ tablespoons for a medium saucepan). Tip in the pumpkin seeds and bring them to a rolling boil for about 4–5 minutes.

Drain the seeds and pat them dry between two sheets of paper towel. Meanwhile, preheat the oven to 170°C (325°F), gas 3.

Transfer the seeds to a baking tray and drizzle lightly with oil. Season with salt and your choice of seasoning, if you like.

Bake the seeds for around 10–15 minutes until light golden in colour, keeping an eye on them so that they don't burn.

Let them cool down completely before enjoying.

The pumpkin seeds can be stored in an airtight container for up to 15 days.

13: SHATTA
(This is the Middle Eastern hot sauce)

The hero sauce saviour of my home, shatta is spicy, salty and pure. The more you have it, the more you want it. I can't even imagine a rice and meat dish or a sando without it. Every household has their own recipe; this is mine and I love it. Use any type of peppery chillies, depending on the spice level you can tolerate. I use a mix of red chillies available in the supermarket. Just avoid using Scotch bonnet.

INGREDIENTS:

- 500g (1lb 2oz) red jalapeño or serrano chillies
- 1 tbsp (or to taste) sea salt or table salt
- 1 tbsp white or malt vinegar
- 60ml (2fl oz/¼ cup) extra virgin olive oil

Makes 400–500ml/14–17fl oz
★V★DF★GF

Wash and chop the chillies (leaving the seeds in), place them in a food processor and blend to a coarse paste.

Add salt according to your taste (I use 1 tablespoon salt for each 500g/1lb 2oz of chillies) and mix well. Then add the vinegar and half of the olive oil. Give it a good mix.

Spread the paste on a glass dish (you can use ceramic, but it may stain it) or a tray and place it in a cool place or fridge, uncovered, overnight. This will help the paste dry up a little bit and thicken up. The next day, discard any excess liquid.

Drizzle a tablespoon of the olive oil into a sterilized jar and pour in the chilli paste. Drizzle the rest of the olive oil over the top and seal the jar.

Store it in a cold dark place and let it ferment for a week, letting the gas escape by opening the jar lid and giving it a gentle shake every day. The longer it ferments, the deeper the flavour.

Have it on anything and everything and enjoy.

14: KAMMOUNEH
(A savoury Lebanese seasoning)

Lebanese cuisine is so deeply integrated into Saudi cuisine that a spread is just not complete without a Lebanese dish or two. Kammouneh is a Lebanese cumin-based seasoning – a very light and delicate blend of spices – that goes on anything and everything. It's ideal for sprinkling on salads, soups, sandwiches, roasted meat, vegetables and even on baked desserts, or stir it into olive oil and use as a drizzle.

INGREDIENTS:

- 3 heaped tbsp roasted cumin seeds
- 1 tbsp dried mint
- 2 tbsp dried rose buds, stalks removed
- 1 tbsp onion granules
- 1 tbsp dried marjoram
- 1 tbsp dried basil
- 1½ tsp whole black peppercorns
- 2 × 5cm (2-inch) sweet cinnamon quills
- ½ tsp salt (or to taste)

Makes 400–500ml/14–17fl oz

★V★DF★GF

Mix all the ingredients and grind in a spice or coffee grinder to a fine powder. Sift and discard any larger bits. Taste and add more salt, if wished.

Store the seasoning in an airtight container in a cool, dry place for up to 3 months.

15: WATERMELON PITH JAM

I literally spent my childhood emptying the tiny tins of this jam in bulk. I used to eat it by the spoonful. In the 1980s, when things were fairly ok in the Middle East, watermelon pith jam in tins was widely imported into Saudi Arabia from Iraq, where it originated. It was extremely popular – so much so that it was part of everyday breakfasts and brunches, often served with soft creamy cheese or labneh, sandwiched in *samooli* bread.

But trading ties took a turn after the Gulf War and suddenly the supply chain vanished. Watching me sob over the scarcity of this jam, Aba Jan telephoned a few friends here and there to find an alternative. As a result, someone forwarded their family recipe to help us out. We were back on track, churning out tubs of this yummy stuff. I was a happy child again and Aba Jan a very satisfied father. Fast forward to 2014, when the *Paddington* movie was released (yes, I still watch animated movies very fondly). Paddington's addiction to orange marmalade awoke my forgotten desire to make watermelon pith jam again. I called Aba Jan that very night and before even I uttered a single word, he knew why I had called him: "*Don't tell me you are craving watermelon jam at this hour of night? Here is the recipe, Bhungi*!"*

Enjoy this on a slice of sourdough bread or pitta, on scones with clotted cream, or on crackers with a thick slab of goat's cheese, mature Cheddar or Gorgonzola – or be a *bhungi* and simply eat it with a spoon. The combinations are endless.

INGREDIENTS:

- 500g (1lb 2oz) fleshy watermelon pith (from 1 large or 2 small melons)
- 300–350g (10½–12oz/1½–1¾ cups) granulated sugar (depending on how sweet you'd like it)
- 4–5 green cardamom pods
- ¼ tsp salt
- ½ tsp lemon salt (citric acid)

Makes 2–3 medium jars

★V★DF★GF

Peel away the fibrous green skin of the watermelon and also as much red flesh as possible. (A little bit of red is okay.) Slice the white pith into matchstick strips.

Bring a large saucepan of water to the boil and add the sliced watermelon pith. Let it boil for 5 minutes, then drain out the water, leaving about 100ml (3½fl oz/ scant ½ cup) of water in the pan.

Add the sugar and cardamom pods, cover and let it cook for 1 hour on a very low heat. Add the salt and lemon salt, give the mixture a good stir, and cook for another 1 hour, still on the same low heat.

Once the consistency is like thick runny honey, take it off the heat and let it cool down before transferring to jars. Store in the fridge for up to a month.

*(*Bhungi means "druggy", in the nicest way possible! It is usually used affectionately for someone who dresses like a hippy and is a bit of a couch potato, which I am [but I never did drugs]. Only my dad called me that nickname. I never allowed anyone else to call me by that name after him.)*

Cakes, bakes & all things great

I have always loved a cake. In fact my cooking journey began with a cake, so it was a baking journey rather than a cooking one.

I started baking when I was eleven. I made my very first orange cake in a round biscuit tin as old as time, rather than a fancy loaf tin, because that's all we had at that time. Nevertheless, that thick, fragrant waft of orange still remains with me.

There is a Pineapple Fresh Cream Cake (page 232) in this chapter. The OG version is a centrepiece at every single birthday at mine. I made this cake for the MasterChef UK 2021 semi-finals and the whole studio was infatuated by the enchanting tropical aroma – so much so that the cake disappeared in minutes, landing me a position in the finals. Obviously, it was a hit with the judges. What else can a cake girl ask for?

Some trends are short-lived; they spiral out on social media and then they fade away as though nothing happened, but that Dubai pistachio kunafa chocolate, OMG it has become a legend now. That trend is here to stay. The irony is that it has always existed in the Arab world in one form or another. (I think the Middle East should be a continent on its own as it has so much diversity.) I finally gave in and created my own piece of edible art. There are so many reasons why you should make this Iconic Kunafa Chocolate Bar Basque Cheesecake (page 228) for your next celebration – or just make it for no reason at all to enjoy by yourself, because it is so good. The vibrant green hue of pistachio cream against the rich dark brownie and burnt top with golden shards of filo is visually spectacular and pulls a crowd (the shards aren't included in the photo; please add them if you fancy). It's a dessert that looks as impressive as it tastes: a showstopper.

I make cake for anyone who politely requests me to do so because I love making and sharing a cake. Sharing a cake appeals to me.

You probably know Om Ali (page 226), but do try my version; it's simple and finger-licking good. There are other bakes and cookies, like Keleeja (page 223), Saudi Arabia's national cookie and worth living for. And a Ma'amoul Tray Bake, a cookie big enough for the cookie monster.

If you are looking for something savoury, you will find Farmouza (page 209) and Muhammara Parcels (page 217) just perfect for any time of day, with a little salad on the side. In this chapter, you will find some of my favourite hot cakes and bakes that are perfect anytime and anywhere; from picnics to packed lunches to munching on the sofa, I've got you covered.

CUCKOO'S CRESCENT
(No cuckoo was harmed in this recipe)

Why is this recipe called a cuckoo's crescent? In Saudi Arabia, dainty little meringues are known as "cuckoo's eggs" due to their small size and colour. Each is suffused with a fragrant cardamom note that bursts into a perfumed cloud as the meringue melts in your mouth as soon as it hits your tongue. They are usually distributed to celebrate a child's birth and during religious festivities. When I was a child, as soon as the narrow streets, decorated with wooden terraces, echoed with the chants "*Cuckoo, beid al-cuckoo*", I would rush out of my house, often barefoot, along with many other children to find the vendor named Khalid (if memory serves me right). Feeble and old, with every wrinkle on his face and hands hinting at an untold story, he walked through the streets carrying a wooden chest with little glass panels on his shoulder, full of these colourful treats. I would get into a brawl with the other children about who should be the first in line to get their hands on cuckoo's eggs. Life was simple and beautiful back then. Vendors like Khalid have since disappeared. Commercial bakeries and patisseries have taken over and selling them as "meringue kisses" but for me these are, and always will be, cuckoo's eggs.

This recipe is my ode to these tiny meringue kisses with the faintest blue or yellow colour. In order to pull out all the stops and wow my guests with a showstopper dessert, I pipe these into a large crescent-shaped pavlova and top it with fruit. A must-have on Eid al-Fitr, to mark the end of Ramadan.

This recipe is best made in a stand mixer, but you can make it using a hand-held electric mixer, although it may take a bit longer. A St Honoré nozzle is ideal for piping the crescent, but again don't hold yourself back. If you don't have one, just use your preferred nozzle.

You will probably never look at meringue the same way again, I promise.

INGREDIENTS:

For the meringue:

- 1 tsp lemon juice
- 120g (4¼oz) fresh egg whites (from about 3 large eggs)
- ¼ tsp ground green cardamom
- 60g (2oz/heaped ¼ cup) granulated white sugar
- 120g (4¼oz/scant 1 cup) icing (confectioners') sugar
- 1 tsp cornflour (cornstarch)
- A drop of blue or yellow gel food colouring (optional)

For the saffron mascarpone cream:

- 25g (1oz/2 tbsp) granulated sugar
- 7 saffron strands
- a few drops of rose water
- 300ml (10½fl oz/1¼ cups) double (heavy) cream
- 120g (4¼oz) cold mascarpone cheese

To assemble:

- Mango, raspberries, blackberries, kiwis or fruit of your choice, sliced if needed
- 1 tbsp apricot glaze or jam, warmed and melted, to brush the fruit

Serves 8–10

★V★GF

Start by making your cuckoo's crescent. Preheat the oven to 90°C (195°F), gas ½. On a piece of baking paper, draw a crescent 30cm (12 inches) long, with a width of 12.5cm (5 inches) at its widest part in the middle. Place the template onto a baking sheet.

Wipe the bowl of your stand mixer clean using the lemon juice and a piece of paper towel to remove any traces of grease. Start whisking the egg whites along with the ground cardamom at low-medium speed until lightly frothy and big bubbles are appearing.

In another bowl, combine both sugars and the cornflour. Turn up the speed slightly and gradually incorporate the mixed sugars while continuously whisking.

Once all of the sugar is dissolved, turn the speed level up slightly again and whisk for another 5 minutes. Then jump to an even higher speed for 5 minutes. Lastly, turn up to the maximum speed level for the final 2 minutes. Add the food colouring gel at this stage, if using. Pinch a little portion of meringue between your fingers and have a feel to ensure that there is no sugar grain left.

Transfer the meringue to a piping bag fitted with a St Honoré nozzle. Pipe the meringue onto the crescent template, filling the whole area, using the feathering motion (classic St Honoré pattern).

Place the tray in the middle of the oven and bake for 2 hours. When the baking time is up, turn off the oven and leave the meringue until it cools down; this will help it dry out and crisp up, and avoid it cracking.

Meanwhile, start your saffron mascarpone cream by grinding together the sugar, saffron and rose water in a pestle and mortar. Combine the saffron sugar and cream, then chill for at least 2 hours in the fridge.

To finish the cream, add the chilled mascarpone to the infused cream and whip until it forms soft, stable peaks. Be careful not to overwhip it – the cream will go grainy very quickly. To assemble, pipe mascarpone cream on top of the meringue. Decorate with your chosen fruits, then brush the fruits with the warm apricot glaze.

RAINBOW TART
(My first taste of a French patisserie in KSA)

This recipe is an homage to one of the very first French patisseries in Saudi Arabia that opened their doors to the general public, La Fraise.

The dough for this recipe freezes very well and lasts in the freezer for up to 3 months, and so I have given a quantity of pastry crust enough to make 3 tarts about 36cm (14 inches) long. This is how I prepare it at home, so that I can quickly make tarts whenever I like, but feel free to adjust the recipe if you only want to make enough pastry for one tart.

I usually freeze the prepared tin and the flour for the crust for at least 30 minutes before baking for better results.

Try using an array of coloured fruits to get that rainbow effect, for example strawberries, raspberries, cherries, plums, apricots, peaches, mangoes, kiwis, grapes, oranges etc.

INGREDIENTS:

For the crème pâtissière filling:

- 500ml (17fl oz/2 cups) whole milk
- 1 vanilla bean or 1 tsp vanilla bean paste or vanilla extract
- 2 tbsp custard powder
- A few saffron strands
- 2 tbsp caster (granulated) sugar
- 200ml (6¾fl oz/scant 1 cup) double (heavy) cream
- 25g (1oz/2 tbsp) butter, softened

For the pastry crust:

- 350g (12¼oz/2⅔ cups) plain (all-purpose) or pastry flour, ice cold
- 50g (1¾oz/½ cup) ground almonds
- A pinch of salt
- 150g (5¼oz/1 cup) icing (confectioners') sugar
- 180g (6¼oz/¾ cup plus 2 tsp) cold unsalted butter, cut into small cubes
- 1 tsp vanilla extract, plus a little extra for the egg wash
- 65g (2¼oz) beaten egg (1–2 large eggs), plus an extra egg yolk for the egg wash
- Fruit of your choice, to decorate.
- 2 tbsp apricot glaze (or smooth apricot jam)

Makes 3 tarts

★V

First prepare the crème pâtissière. Mix all of the ingredients, except the cream and butter, in a saucepan and cook on a medium heat while stirring continuously. Once it starts to thicken and large craters (like the ones on the moon) start to appear, turn off the heat. Transfer the mix to a bowl and cover with cling film (plastic wrap). Set aside to cool.

Once the custard is fully cool, in a separate bowl, whisk the double cream until it forms soft, fluffy peaks. Add the cooled custard (removing the vanilla bean if you have used one) and softened butter, incorporating well so no lumps and bumps remain. Let it chill in the fridge until needed.

Next, make your pastry dough. You can use a stand mixer to make the dough, but I prefer to do this by hand. Into a large clean bowl, tip the chilled flour, ground almonds, salt, sugar and butter. Gently massage the butter into the flour. Once it resembles fine breadcrumbs, add the vanilla extract and the beaten egg.

Gently bring the flour mixture together and lightly knead to form a dough ball. Divide into three balls and wrap two for future use. (Any extra dough lives happily in the fridge for 3 days or in the freezer for up to 2 months.) Cover the remaining ball with cling film and flatten into a rough rectangular shape – this will help you to roll the dough out without any cracks. Let the dough chill in the fridge for a minimum of 2 hours.

Preheat the oven to 180°C (350°F), gas 4. Roll out the dough to a rectangle about 3mm (⅛ inch) thick, then transfer the pastry to a rectangular tart tin 36cm (14 inches) long. Make sure there are no cracks and that every corner is covered. Prick the pastry a few times with a fork. Bake in the preheated oven for 20 minutes until it is golden brown. Remove from the oven and let the pastry case cool down completely.

Beat your egg yolk for glazing with a little vanilla extract. Remove the pastry from the tin and give it a good egg wash on the inside and sides of the pastry, then bake for another 5 minutes. This is an additional step that you could skip, but it gives a very professional look and also prevents the pastry from going soggy.

Once the pastry case is ready and cooled down, fill it in with the crème pâtissière and top it with fruit. Warm the apricot glaze for a few seconds until it is loose enough to brush, then brush the fruit with the glaze and chill before serving.

FARMOUZA
(One-bite mini mince parcels, a well-known street food in KSA)

Farmouza are actually the Saudi (or more specifically, Hijazi) cousin of a Kosovo manti and are very popular, especially during Ramadan. This recipe encapsulates beautifully the merging of diverse cultures – from central Asian and Balkan states – into the very fabric of Saudi cuisine. It is a well-known trait of Saudi hospitality that we welcome any culture with open arms and make them feel at home.

The few ingredients in this bake let the lamb mince sing its song. It is nestled in a traditional, elaborate pastry, the preparation of which resembles the lamination process of making puff pastry. I use puff pastry to cut out the laborious work of making my own pastry and the results are equally good. Trust me, I have got this!

On his way back from Friday prayers, it was a must for Aba Jan to get Friday's lunch treat for us (it was Mama's day off from cooking). It would be either Shaoor Maghli (see page 152) or d'jaj meshwi with bukhari rice (Jewelled Rice – see page 168), accompanied by a portion of piping hot farmouza and the three sauce musketeers: daqqus, humr and tahiniya or shatta. I have burned my mouth many a time while gobbling one or two of them. This was our equivalent of a classic English roast.

These juicy little orbs of love can be enjoyed as part of *asariya* (a tea-time snack), as a starter, an Iftar dish, or as and when you feel peckish. I batch-make them, a very meditative process, I must say! Once baked, they look like little soldiers, and a race to finish those little bundles of steamy farmouza starts among my three young and very hungry fighters. I think they have inherited this greedy gene from me!

INGREDIENTS:

- 1kg (2lb 4oz) puff pastry
- Flour, for dusting
- 1 egg, beaten
- 1 tsp vinegar
- Nigella seeds and sesame seeds, to sprinkle
- Shatta (page 195), Zhoug (page 192), Tahiniya (page 184) or other condiment of choice, to serve

For the filling:

- 400g (14oz) minced (ground) lamb or beef (about 10–15% fat; I use lamb)
- 1 onion, finely chopped
- 3 spring onions (scallions), finely chopped
- 1 tomato, deseeded and very finely chopped (optional)
- 1 tsp freshly ground black pepper
- 1 tsp roasted coarsely ground cumin
- ½ tsp Baharat spice mix (this is my addition, as it gives a nice warmth to mince)
- Sea salt

Makes 80 (enough to satisfy an army of 10–12 hungry little troublemakers)

In a mixing bowl, mix all of the filling ingredients together and season to taste with salt. Set aside.

Roll out the puff pastry on a flour-dusted surface until you have a large rough rectangle. Using a sharp knife, cut it into 5 × 5cm (2 × 2-inch) squares. You should get about 80 squares.

Using a measuring teaspoon as a guide, place 1 teaspoon of the filling in the centre of a square. Bring together two opposite corners of the square and squeeze them together. Repeat with the other two corners and pinch to form a money bag or parcel shape.

Arrange the parcels, seam sides down, in rows on a large baking tray. Tuck them closely together so that there are no spaces between each parcel.

Mix together the beaten egg and vinegar and brush the parcels with the egg wash, then sprinkle with nigella and sesame seeds.

Put the prepared tray in the freezer for about 30 minutes – this step is optional, but it gives the best rise to the pastry.

While they are chilling, preheat the oven to 200°C (400°F), gas 6.

Place the tray in the bottom third of the oven and immediately drop the temperature to 180°C (350°F), gas 4. Cook for 25–30 minutes, until the base of the farmouza is crispy and brown.

Move the tray to the top third of the oven and cook for a further 15–20 minutes, or until the parcels are a gorgeous brown colour all over.

Take them out of the oven and resist the temptation to put them straight into your mouth (I know it's hard but patience is a virtue, remember!).

Serve with shatta, zhoug or tahiniya or whatever you like; even sweet chilli sauce works.

KHALIYAT AL NAHAL
(Beehive bread with assorted fillings: Nutella, pistachio, Biscoff and cream cheese)

I first had this dish at Bilqees's place (our landlords Abui and Umi Qamar's eldest and married daughter), at an afternoon tea party called an *asariya*. Khaliyat al nahal (aka honeycomb bread) is a cotton-candy-soft, sweet tear-and-share bread, very similar to a monkey bread. It's often filled with cream cheese and drizzled with honey and nigella seeds – that's the traditional version Bilqees taught me, which I absolutely love and adore. But, me being me and never settling on one version, I came up with multiple fillings like chocolate, pistachio and even Biscoff spread. On top of that, I just love to drizzle the whole thing with the spreads that I have used as a filling, though traditionally it is drizzled with honey or condensed milk. In the last two decades, this bread has evolved as much as Jeddah itself.

Bilqees was a fond baker and her passion for cooking shined through her love of food. She was like an elder sister to me. During the compilation of this book, I went back to Saudi Arabia to meet her, but Jeddah has changed so much in the last 25 years and the building they lived in was demolished and rebuilt a long time ago. New faces have moved in and no one knows where Bilqees or Umi Qamar went. I tried my best to find them, for days going door to door in scorching humid Jeddawi heat, along with my whole little family. But every time my renewed hope with another vague lead ended up in despair and we were back to square one.

Now back in England and penning down this journey of longing with a very heavy heart; my soul is still hungry for that best friend hugging me tightly with a flicker of hope in my heart that maybe one day we will meet again. Maybe one day my children will get to know and meet their Khaala (aunt). Maybe this book will become my voice to reach her, and find her in peace and happiness. Maybe one day...

I miss you Bilqees; you will always be a loving and caring elder sister to me and I will keep on looking for you until I find you.

This recipe serves a party of 10 – or two introverts curled up on the sofa binge-watching Netflix.

INGREDIENTS:

- 240ml (8fl oz/1 cup) warm water
- 10g (⅓oz) dried active yeast
- 25g (1oz/2 tbsp) granulated sugar
- 1 large egg or 60g (2oz) natural yogurt
- ½ tsp vanilla extract
- 60ml (2fl oz/¼ cup) sunflower oil, or any neutral oil, plus extra for greasing
- 30g (1oz) full-fat milk powder
- 400g (14oz/3 cups) plain (all-purpose) white flour
- 7g (¼oz) table salt
- 100g (3½oz) cheese triangles (I use Laughing Cow or Kiri brands)
- 50g (1¾oz) chocolate spread of your choice (I use Nutella), chilled (so it's easy to scoop out)
- 50g (1¾oz) Biscoff spread or pistachio paste, chilled
- Butter, for greasing
- Toasted sesame seeds, to sprinkle

For the egg wash:

- 1 egg yolk, beaten
- 1 tbsp milk
- ½ tsp vanilla extract

To drizzle/top (your choice of):

- Condensed milk, honey or melted biscoff spread
- Melted chocolate or store-bought chocolate sauce
- Melted pistachio spread
- Toasted pecan or pistachio slivers (or any nut of your choice), to sprinkle

Serves 8–10

★V

Begin by blooming the yeast. In a mixing bowl, combine the warm water, yeast and sugar. Let it froth up for about 5 minutes, then add the egg (or yogurt), vanilla and oil and give it a good mix.

Add the dried milk powder and mix well, then tip in the flour and salt.

Knead for a good 8–10 minutes until a smooth dough is formed. Drizzle a little oil over the surface of the dough, cover and let it prove for about 20 minutes in a warm place.

In the meantime, prepare the fillings. Cut the cheese into roughly 4g (⅛oz) cubes. For the spreads and pastes, use a ¼ teaspoon-sized measuring spoon to make small spheres, then place them on a tray lined with a sheet of greaseproof paper and freeze for 30 minutes or so. This step makes life easier, as the frozen spheres will be a breeze to stuff into the dough.

Grease a 30cm (12-inch) round mould or baking dish with butter.

Now, gently knock the air out of the dough and, using a measuring tablespoon as your scooping guide, scoop out a little piece of dough. Flatten it a bit and place a sphere (or cube) of the desired filling in the middle, then bring in the edges and press them together to seal. Shape the filled dough into a ball and place in the prepared dish. Repeat to fill the remaining dough. Cover and let prove for another 20 minutes, or until doubled in size.

While the bread is proving, preheat the oven to 170°C (325°F), gas 3. Combine all the ingredients for the egg wash in a small bowl.

Brush the dough with the egg wash and sprinkle with sesame seeds, if you like. Bake for 20–25 minutes, or until a bright golden colour. Take out of the oven and let the bread cool down slightly. Drizzle it – or as I do, drench it – with condensed milk, melted chocolate or Nutella, and pistachio spread. Sprinkle over the nuts and enjoy with a cuppa, espresso or Saudi coffee.

MA'AMOUL TRAY BAKE
(A giant cookie with dates sandwiched inside)

Traditionally, ma'amoul is a very short, stout and delicately carved cookie made by using traditional wooden moulds bearing a specific geometric design. It sits like a relic on silver trays, marking the end of Ramadan and welcoming Eid, a symbol of celebration, a taste of belonging – it is a small, golden memory, crumbling sweetly on the tongue, echoing across generations.

Inside, is the heart: a filling of velvety mashed dates or ground pistachios or walnuts, often dusted with cinnamon and sugar. The bite is gentle with a soft snap, a buttery melt, and then the flood of spicy warmth from within. It is humble and ornate at the same time; born of everyday ingredients but shaped with reverence.

As a 5-year-old girl with goldilocks hair, I – along with Aba Jan and my little cousins – religiously visited the local bakery, named Hannah Bakery, the night before Eid. With wide eyes I would reach for the warm little ma'amoul displayed on a baking tray at the counter; sneaking one or two in my mouth while Aba Jan was busy getting other goodies for Eid morning celebration. With a sudden inquisitive gaze from Aba Jan, my cousins and I would put on our most innocent faces as though nothing had happened, but our lips, already dusted with powdered sugar, gave it all away. A very gentle reprimand would follow.

Years later, I found out that the bakers specifically placed that one tray of ma'amoul for children to come and enjoy the Eid celebration, regardless of purchasing them or not – a simple symbol of generosity, affection and love towards children.

INGREDIENTS:

For the semolina cookie dough:

- 170g (6oz) fine semolina
- 1kg (2¼lb) medium semolina
- 650g (23oz/3 ½ cups) caster (granulated) sugar
- 50g (1¾oz) full-fat milk powder
- 7g (¼oz) instant dried yeast
- 625g (1lb 6oz/2¾ cups) unsalted butter, melted, plus extra for greasing
- 125ml (4fl oz/½ cup) orange blossom water
- 125ml (4fl oz/½ cup) rose water

For the spiced date filling:

- 1kg (2¼lb) date paste block
- 60g (2oz/¼ cup) unsalted butter, melted
- ½ tsp mahlep powder, 3–4 mastic resin drops, ground, or ½ tsp ground green cardamom
- Pinch of ground sweet cinnamon
- Pinch of ground cloves (optional)

Makes 10–12 bars

★V

In a large bowl, mix together all of the dry ingredients for the dough and make a small well in the middle.

Add the melted butter, orange blossom and rose water to the well and mix the ingredients by rubbing them between the palms of your hands until they form into a very soft, crumbly, sandy dough. Don't knead the dough at this stage – just let the flavours marry each other. Cover the bowl tightly with cling film (plastic wrap) and set aside at room temperature for at least 2 hours.

Once the cookie dough has visibly risen, lightly wet your hands with water and knead the dough until smooth – this is very therapeutic. Cover and let it rest again for 20 minutes.

In the meantime, mash the date paste block in a wide mixing bowl until it becomes loose. Once it is loose enough to break into chunks, pop it in the microwave and heat in 20–30-second bursts, 2–3 times, which will soften it enough to combine with the other ingredients.

Now, add the melted butter, mahlep powder (or cardamom powder or ground mastic, whatever you are using) and the other spices. Knead until everything is fully incorporated into the date paste.

Preheat the oven to 180°C (350°F), gas 4. Grease a 38 × 28cm (15 × 11-inch) baking tray with a generous dollop of melted butter so that the cookie doesn't stick.

Divide the cookie dough into two portions, one slightly bigger than the other.

Spread the larger dough portion across the prepared baking tray to about 1cm (½ inch) thick, making sure that the base and sides of the tray are fully and evenly covered. Wet your fingers every now and then, if needed, to spread the dough and stop it sticking to your hands.

On a piece of cling film roughly the size of the baking tray, flatten out the date mixture to make a layer the size of the cookie. Now, transfer the date paste to the prepared cookie dough, remove the cling film and make sure that the date paste is covering all of the dough base.

Now spread the remaining cookie dough over the dates to form the top layer, leaving no gaps. Wetting your fingers now and then will help you to spread it out.

Now, decorate the top cookie. You can go fancy with a design of your choice; I just draw parallel lines with a fork, but you can score squares, rectangles or triangles if you want to make nice and neat portions out of it.

Put the cookie tray into the preheated oven and bake for 30–40 minutes, until the top is a rich golden colour. Don't be greedy; I know, at this point the whole house will be smelling of warm sweet toasty spices and semolina, but resist the temptation and let it cool down completely before digging in.

The cookie slices can be stored in an airtight container in the fridge for up to 4 weeks.

MUHAMMARA PARCELS
(Puff parcels with a creamy red-pepper filling)

There is no doubt that I am a hummus girl through and through, but I think we need to have more muhammara in our lives too. It is a very versatile Middle Eastern roasted red pepper and walnut dip, packed full of fruity, tangy fresh flavours. There are endless possibilities to use it: as a dip, as a main, with bread as a spread and sandwich filler, or as I have done in this recipe, as a tantalizing stuffing, along with some feta cheese, encased in a puff pastry parcel. These are perfect for packed lunches or summer picnics. Thank me later.

From the mountains of Latakia to the bustling streets of Damascus, you will find this simple but flavourful delicacy everywhere. It has been filling people up for centuries. I was taught this recipe by a Syrian friend residing in KSA – using locally grown gigantic fruity, almost sweet, red peppers – a long time ago, and today I share this with you in my own nerdy creative way by putting a gorgeous dip like muhammara into a fancy pastry case. It is probably the first of its kind.

Muhammara is quintessentially an ancient Syrian dip, traditionally made in a stone pestle and mortar, but a food processor will help you to create this vibrant dip in a jiffy. There is a tangy Lebanese twist of added citrusy sumac that is found in almost every café of the Hijaz region. Pure nostalgia at first bite.

This vegetarian treat is a joy to eat and can easily be veganized. Next time, give hummus a miss and try something different like this dip – you will fall in love with it. I promise. Enjoy!

INGREDIENTS:

- 2 × 320g (11¼oz) ready-rolled puff pastry sheets
- 200g (7oz) feta cheese, crumbled
- 1 egg yolk
- 1 tbsp whole milk
- Roasted cumin seeds, to sprinkle
- Za'atar, to sprinkle
- Pomegranate molasses, to drizzle
- Leafy salad, to serve

For the muhammara:

- 1 × 450g (1lb) jar of chargrilled red peppers (350g/12oz drained weight)
- 75g (2½oz) walnuts
- 1–2 cloves of garlic
- Juice ½ lemon or 1 lime
- 100g (3½oz) bread sticks or ka'ak (traditional Syrian bread sticks)
- ½ tsp sea salt or table salt (or to taste)
- ½ tsp sumac
- ½ tsp ground cumin
- ¼ tsp paprika
- ½ tsp pul biber (Aleppo pepper flakes, optional)
- 1 tsp Turkish red pepper paste (biber salcasi)
- 2 tbsp pomegranate molasses
- 2½ tbsp extra virgin olive oil
- 2 tbsp good-quality tahini

Makes 6

★V

To make the muhammara, put all of the muhammara ingredients in a food processor and pulse until grainy, or blitz a bit more if you like a smoother consistency.

Preheat the oven to 190°C (375°F), gas 5, and line a large baking tray with baking paper.

Cut one of the puff pastry sheets into six equal rectangles, but don't move them so they stay together in one large rectangle. Dollop a heaped spoonful of muhammara in the middle of each rectangle and crumble on some feta.

Using a lattice pastry cutter, draw the lattice on the second puff pastry sheet. Stretch the pastry so that the lattice pattern is visible.

Place the stretched pastry sheet on top of the filled rectangles, so that it covers them all. Then press it down firmly around the edges of the filling, following the original pastry rectangles beneath. Cut the top sheet to separate the rectangles as neatly as possible. Press the sides of each rectangle to ensure that they are sealed well.

Mix together the egg yolk and milk to make an egg wash, then brush the parcels with the wash and sprinkle with some cumin seeds and za'atar. (The parcels can be frozen at this stage for up to 2 months and can be baked straight from freezer or even air fried.)

Bake in the preheated oven for 20–25 minutes, or until puffed and a nice golden colour is achieved. Serve with a drizzle of pomegranate molasses and leafy salad of your choice (there are plenty in this book).

TIP: Any leftover lattice pastry can be egg washed and sprinkled with za'atar, then baked along with the parcels. It is delicious to dip in the leftover muhammara and enjoyed with a nice cup of Turkish tea (*shai*). Nothing goes to waste in my kitchen.

MY VERY FIRST ORANGE CAKE
(Real orange loaf cake with fresh orange juice)

This is the simplest and most delicious melt-in-your-mouth orange cake, which cuts like butter and packs a zesty punch with fragrant orange flavours and citrusy goodness. It is so simple and irresistible that I bake it every weekend with my children.

In fact, this is the first cake I ever made. Taught to me by my very lovely Umi Qamar at the humble age of 11, I may have forgotten a few details in life but this I remember by heart – I can make it blindfolded and with one hand tied behind my back. It is a recipe where my heart takes full control of my brain, as with most of my recipes.

In 2023, I made this cake as a homage to Umi Qamar and all of those beautiful souls who are not with us anymore for whatever reason. I posted it on social media and it became the first ever reel for me that went viral, putting me on the world map of great social media. I haven't looked back since.

INGREDIENTS:

- Zest and juice of 2 juicy ripe oranges
- 220g (7¾oz/1 cup plus 2 tbsp) granulated sugar
- 3 large eggs
- 100ml (3½fl oz/scant ½ cup) double (heavy) cream
- 190g (6¾oz/1½ cups) cake flour (see tip overleaf)
- ½ tsp baking powder
- Pinch of salt
- 60ml (2fl oz/¼ cup) neutral oil (I prefer groundnut oil as it doesn't stain the bright colour of the cake, but vegetable can be used too, or melted butter), plus extra for greasing
- 1 tsp orange extract (optional)
- 20g (¾oz/1½ tbsp) unsalted butter, softened

For soaking and garnishing:

- 60–80ml (2–2½fl oz/¼–⅓ cup) freshly squeezed orange juice
- 1 tbsp granulated sugar (optional, if the oranges are really tart)
- 1 tbsp thick-cut marmalade (optional but works well, let the Paddington bear in you run free)
- ½ tbsp slivered pistachios or almonds

Serves 8–10

★V

Preheat the oven to 175°C (345°F), gas 3, and grease and line a 900g (2lb) loaf tin.

In a large bowl, rub together the orange zest and sugar to form a fragrant sugary sand.

Add the eggs and whisk together with an electric beater for 5–6 minutes, or until very pale and fluffy. Then, add the cream, whisking for another 2 minutes.

Sift in the cake flour and baking powder, and add the pinch of salt. Fold in gently.

Add the oil and orange extract, if using, then fold until well combined. Add 60ml (2fl oz/¼ cup) of the orange juice and give a gentle mix, then pour it into the prepared tin. Pipe the softened butter in a straight line down the middle of the cake – it gives a visually pleasing bakery-style look to the loaf cake.

Bake for 45–50 minutes until risen and golden and a skewer inserted into the cake comes out clean. Let it cool down for 10–15 minutes, then drizzle another 60–80ml (2–2½fl oz/¼–⅓ cup) fresh orange juice over the cake. If the oranges are not very sweet, stir the sugar into the juice first. Wrap the cake in cling film (plastic wrap) and let the soaked cake rest for 4–6 hours in the fridge.

Spread some marmalade over the top of the cake and decorate with slivered pistachios or almonds.

TIP: You can make your own cake flour by using the following ratio: For every 100g (3½oz) of plain (all-purpose) flour, add 10g (⅓oz) of cornflour (cornstarch) and sift twice. If you are a keen baker like me, make a big batch and store the cake flour in an airtight container for a couple of months.

SAUDI KELEEJA
(Cookie with an unusual filling)

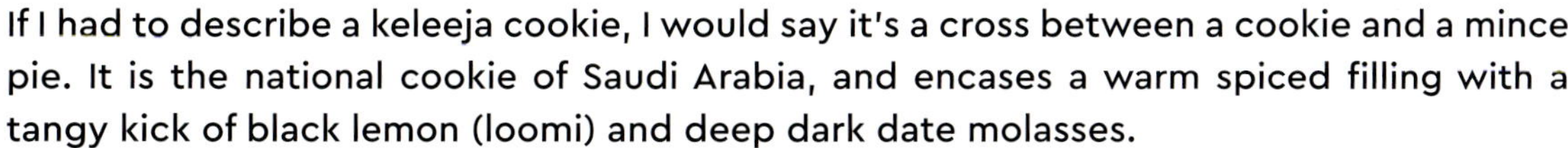

If I had to describe a keleeja cookie, I would say it's a cross between a cookie and a mince pie. It is the national cookie of Saudi Arabia, and encases a warm spiced filling with a tangy kick of black lemon (loomi) and deep dark date molasses.

Keleeja is not just a cookie, it is a whole Bedouin tradition in itself, native to Saudi Arabia. After her nuptials, the bride takes a tray full of these cookies with her when departing from her parents' house and stepping into her husband's house for the very first time.

The name "keleeja" is derived from the wooden mould used to make it, known as a "kellesha". This is a specific diamond-patterned mould, a bit like a ma'amoul mould, and is still in use to make these cookies. Ideally serve them with Saudi coffee, although my Italian friends love them with their espresso as well.

INGREDIENTS:

- 50g (1¾oz/¼ cup) caster (granulated) sugar
- 1 tsp dried active yeast
- 300ml (10½fl oz/1¼ cups) whole milk, warm
- 250g (9oz/1 cup plus 2 tbsp) unsalted butter, melted
- 450g (1lb/3½ cups) wholemeal flour
- 150g (5½oz) plain (all-purpose) flour, plus extra for dusting
- 1 tbsp ground green cardamom
- 1 tbsp ground ginger
- 1 tbsp ground sweet cinnamon
- 1½ tbsp ground dried black lemon (loomi)
- 200ml (7fl oz/scant 1 cup) date molasses (or 135g/4¾oz dark muscovado sugar)
- 1 large (US extra large) egg, beaten

Makes 8

★V

Dissolve the sugar and yeast in the warm milk and let it bloom until frothy, about 10 minutes.

Now, add the melted butter to the bloomed yeast mixture and mix well.

Place both flours in a wide bowl and make a well in the middle. Gradually add the milk mixture, using your hand to draw flour inwards and mix it with the liquid.

Knead thoroughly until a nice smooth dough begins to form – this will take about 5 minutes.

Bring the dough together in a ball shape, place it in the bowl, cover with cling film (plastic wrap) and let it rest for about an hour, until it has almost doubled in size.

In the meantime, prepare the filling by mixing the cardamom, ginger, cinnamon and black loomi with the date molasses or muscovado sugar in a bowl.

Preheat the oven to 180°C (350°F), gas 4, and line a baking tray with baking paper.

Dust the work surface with some plain flour. Roll out the dough into a log. Divide it into eight even portions, then roll each into a ball about the size of a walnut

Cover the balls with a tea towel and let them rest for another 10 minutes or so, until they have risen slightly and the gluten has relaxed a bit.

Flatten out a ball on the palm of your hand and add a spoonful of the filling in the middle. Bring the edges together and seal, then roll to reshape it into a ball between your hands. Repeat to fill all the cookies.

If you have an embossed patterned cookie mould or a Chinese cookie mould, press each ball against the mould firmly, then turn it upside down and tap it over the work surface to release the cookie.

Place the cookies onto the lined baking tray and brush with the beaten egg. Bake in the oven for around 20–25 minutes, or until golden brown. Take them out of the oven and let them cool completely.

These cookies can be stored for up to 2 months in an airtight container.

OM ALI GONE FRENCH
(An ode to the rich Egyptian history of the Mamluk Era)

Om Ali is more than just a dessert; it is a tale of royalty, rivalry and an enduring love for indulgence. A story of the rich Islamic history, told in layers of golden, buttery pastry, soaked in the warmth of rich milk and infused with the whispers of cinnamon and vanilla.

I vividly remember my very first taste of Om Ali at Sofitel luxury resort in Jeddah in the early 1990s. It was Eid al Fitr and Aba Jan took us for a buffet dine out. The first spoonful in and I was daydreaming. The crispy flaky pastry soaked in creamy spiced milk, embedded with a crunchy layer of toasted nuts, the gentle chew of plump sultanas, and the delicate notes of coconut, kissed by the slightly smoky depth of caramelized sugar, leaving behind memories of comfort and nostalgia. It was a joy to eat and I fell in love with it at the very first bite.

Served warm, Om Ali is not merely eaten; it is savoured. Its rich aroma fills the air like a warm motherly embrace, nostalgia and comfort that lingers long after the last spoonful is gone.

Oh, Om Ali, with every bite,

You turn the dark to golden light.

Traditionally, it's made with a thin, crispy flatbread-like pastry known as *rukaak* or *goulash*, but this is my easy hack; literally any sweet French pastry will work.

INGREDIENTS:

- Unsalted butter, softened, for greasing
- 450g (1lb) large croissants (about 12, or 24 small ones)
- 3–4 tbsp melted ghee
- 1 litre (35fl oz/4¼ cups) whole milk (high quality, with at least 5% fat, preferably Jersey cow or buffalo; I use Golden Top)
- A dash of vanilla extract
- ¼ tsp ground sweet cinnamon
- 150g (5½oz/¾ cup) soft brown sugar, plus extra for dusting
- 30ml (1fl oz) coconut cream
- 1 × 170g (6oz) can of ashta/qashta (Arab-style clotted cream) or clotted cream if you really can't find ashta.
- 75g (2½oz) toasted hazelnuts, halved or crushed, plus extra to garnish
- 75g (2½oz) toasted almond flakes, plus extra to garnish
- 25g (1oz) walnuts, crushed, plus a couple of walnut halves to garnish
- 25g (1oz) flaked or slivered pistachios, plus extra to garnish
- 50g (1¾oz) sultanas (golden raisins), plus extra to garnish
- 30g (1oz) desiccated (dried shredded) coconut
- 200g (7oz) clotted cream or ashta/qashta (see above)
- A few toasted coconut flakes, to garnish

Serves 6 generously

★V

Preheat the oven the to 180°C (350°F), gas 4, and grease six individual baking dishes or a large family-sized ovenproof dish with butter.

Cut the large croissants horizontally in half, then into 2.5cm (1-inch) chunks so that the inner white part of the croissants is exposed for maximum crunchiness. (If using small croissants, cut them down the middle vertically so that you have two ears from each of them.)

Line a baking tray with greaseproof paper and arrange the croissant pieces on the tray so that they are not overlapping each other and the inner sides of the croissants are facing up.

Drizzle the croissants with the melted ghee and place in the oven for about 5–6 minutes, or until they have browned and crisped up nicely – the crispier the better. Keep an eye on them to make sure they are not burning. Leave them to cool down completely, resisting the temptation to devour.

To prepare the creamy milk soak, put the milk, vanilla extract, cinnamon and sugar in a large saucepan on a high heat and bring it to a boil. Once it boils, remove it from the heat, and add the coconut cream and ashta.

Once cooled down, arrange half of the toasted croissants in the prepared baking dishes. Scatter over the nuts and sultanas, along with the desiccated coconut. Pour over enough of the milk so the pastry is just barely emerging from it. Press down gently.

Place the rest of the croissants on top of the soaked ones and pour over the remaining milk. Smother the whole dish with the 200g (7oz) clotted cream and sprinkle with brown sugar, to help caramelize the dish.

Set the grill (broiler) to low and place the Om Ali under it. Once the top layer is caramelized, bubbly and toasty, remove it. Garnish it with the extras and serve warm.

TIP: You can use any leftover pastries instead of croissants. I have made Om Ali with chocolate twists, pain au raisin, pain au chocolate, Danish pastries, apple turnovers, palmiers and plain baked puff pastry.

THE ICONIC KUNAFA CHOCOLATE BAR BASQUE CHEESECAKE

Kunafa, pistachio and chocolate have been consumed together in many ways and forms in the Middle East, long before this combo shot to fame in the West, when all of a sudden it started to appear everywhere. Here is my homage to the pistachio spread and kunafa I grew up eating in Saudi Arabia.

The deep, decadent richness of velvety, fudgy brownie effortlessly complements the nutty, buttery and very moreish pistachio notes of the Basque cheesecake, with a crunchy layer of toasted kataifi pastry and a slightly burnt, bitter top, offering layers of textures and a balance of flavours in every mouthful. A dessert straight out of heaven!

INGREDIENTS:

For the brownie base:

- 50g (1¾oz) milk chocolate (36% cocoa solids)
- 75g (2½oz) dark chocolate (53% cocoa solids)
- 80g (2¾oz/⅓ cup) unsalted butter, plus extra, softened, for greasing
- 2 large (US extra large) eggs
- 30g (1oz/2½ tbsp) caster (granulated) sugar
- 100g (3½oz/½ cup) light muscovado sugar or light brown sugar
- Fat pinch of sea salt
- ½ tsp vanilla extract
- 80g (2¾oz/⅔ cup less 1 tbsp) plain (all-purpose) flour
- 10g (⅓oz/1½ tbsp) cocoa powder, plus optional extra for dusting

For the kunafa filling:

- 20g (¾oz/1½ tbsp) unsalted butter, melted
- 75g (2½oz) shredded kataifi pastry
- 100g (3½oz) pistachio paste
- 15g (½oz/1 tbsp) tahini paste
- Dash of vanilla extract

For the pistachio cheesecake:

- 400g (14oz/1¾ cups) full-fat cream cheese
- 300g (10½oz) pistachio cream
- 3 large (US extra large) eggs
- 1 tsp vanilla bean paste or 1 tbsp vanilla extract
- 30g (1oz/3⅔ tbsp) cake flour (see tip, page 222), sifted
- 50g (1¾oz/¼ cup) caster (granulated) sugar
- 230ml (7¾fl oz/scant 1 cup) double (heavy) cream

For the crunchy shards (optional):

- 4 filo (phyllo) pastry sheets
- 60g (2oz/¼ cup) unsalted butter, melted
- 2 tbsp slivered green pistachios
- 50g (1¾oz) dark chocolate, melted

For the pistachio mascarpone cream topping:

- 100ml (3½oz/scant ½ cup) double (heavy) cream
- 30g (1oz/3½ tbsp) icing (confectioners') sugar
- 100g (3½oz/scant ½ cup) mascarpone cheese, chilled
- 50g (1¾oz) pistachio paste
- 1 tsp vanilla extract

Makes 1 cake, to serve 8–10

★V

Grease a 20cm (8-inch) springform cake tin with butter. Cut a square piece of baking paper and push it into the tin. Spread more butter on the inside of the baking paper. Set aside.

Melt the two chocolates and butter in the microwave or in a heatproof bowl set over a saucepan of simmering water. Once melted, set aside to cool a little.

In a large mixing bowl, beat together the eggs, caster sugar, muscovado sugar, salt and vanilla with an electric hand whisk or in a stand mixer for 4–5 minutes until pale.

Fold in the slightly cooled chocolate mixture with a spatula. Sift the plain flour and cocoa powder together, then add them to the bowl and fold in gently with the spatula.

Pour the brownie mix into the lined cake tin and freeze for 15 minutes.

Preheat the oven to 220°C (425°F), gas 7, on the "top and bottom" conventional setting.

To make the kunafa filling, melt the butter in a wide non-stick pan, then add the shredded kataifi pastry and sauté until it is evenly golden, stirring frequently. Let it cool down.

Once at room temperature, add the rest of the filling ingredients and mix well. Take the cake tin out of the freezer and spread the kataifi filling evenly on top, leaving a 1cm (½-inch) border around the sides. Put the tin in the fridge.

For the pistachio cheesecake layer, mix the cream cheese and pistachio cream together with an electric hand whisk. Add the eggs, one at a time, mixing well between each, then mix in the vanilla bean paste or extract.

Tip in the sifted flour and mix well, then add the sugar and double cream. Mix until silky smooth.

Take the cake tin out of the fridge and pour the cheesecake mixture through a sieve on top, ensuring that the kataifi isn't disturbed too much. Tap the cheesecake gently on the work surface to get rid of any large bubbles.

Bake in the oven for 25 minutes. Using the conventional oven setting ensures the top of the cheesecake burns ever so slightly. It should still be jiggly when you take it out the oven.

Let the cheesecake cool in the tin on a wire rack for 30 minutes, then cover and let it chill in the fridge for at least 4 hours, or overnight.

For the crunchy shards, if you are making them, preheat the oven to 200°C (400°F), gas 6. Brush each filo pastry sheet with the melted butter and layer them on top of each other on a baking tray. Fold the sheets in half lengthways, brush again with the butter and sprinkle over the slivered pistachios. Bake in the preheated oven until golden and crisp.

Remove from the oven and let it cool down a little before breaking into shards.

To make the cream topping, in a mixing bowl, whip the cream and icing sugar together until soft peaks form.

In a separate bowl, mix together the mascarpone cheese, pistachio paste and vanilla extract. Now fold the mascarpone mixture into the cream and whisk until soft peaks form. Do not overmix. Refrigerate until ready to assemble.

To serve, take the cake out of the tin. Pipe the creamy topping in small swirls. If adding the crunchy shards, dip their edges in the melted chocolate and then slightly push them into the topping so that they give a nice height. Alternatively, sprinkle with slivered pistachios and cocoa powder for a minimalistic look.

TIP: Do not leave the cheesecake out of the fridge for more than 10 minutes, or it will become too soft.

PINEAPPLE FRESH CREAM CAKE

(With my signature passionfruit and mango caramel sauce)

As French patisseries dawned on the Saudi bakery scene in the late 1980s, a lot of fresh cream cakes with the lightest genoise sponges imaginable started to appear in their displays. Of course, I was bound to fall in love with them. It was an *Alice in Wonderland* situation, where I kept on exploring one category after another and wanted to have a lifetime's supply of this glorious sunshine on a plate.

They were a pretty sight and I had my favourite flavour combo: pineapple, passionfruit and mango. A fresh cream cake soaked in pineapple juice and loaded with pineapple chunks, with a cherry on top, was the ultimate treat. This particular version evolved with the arrival of South Asian pastry chefs to the kingdom.

INGREDIENTS:

For the genoise sponge:

- Butter, for greasing
- 6 large (US extra large) eggs
- 200g (7oz/1 cup) granulated sugar
- 195g (6¾oz/1½ cups) cake flour (see tip, page 222)
- 5g (⅛oz) cornflour (cornstarch)
- ½ tsp baking powder
- 30ml (1fl oz/2 tbsp) warm milk
- 60ml (2fl oz/¼ cup) neutral oil
- 1 tsp vanilla extract

For the passionfruit and mango caramel drip:

- 50ml (1¾fl oz/3½ tbsp) passionfruit pulp (I use M&S passionfruit pulp)
- 50ml (1¾fl oz/3½ tbsp) mango purée (I use Boiron brand purée)
- 50g (1¾oz/¼ cup) white sugar

For the filling and topping:

- 600ml (21fl oz/2½ cups) double (heavy) cream
- 60g (2oz/7 tbsp) icing (confectioners') sugar
- ½ tsp vanilla extract
- 300ml (10½fl oz/1¼ cups) whipping cream
- 1 × 435g (15½oz) can of pineapple slices in juice (I use Del Monte Gold as it has a richer colour and taste), cut into equal-sized chunks, juice reserved (also reserve a couple of whole slices for the top)
- Cocktail cherries
- Tiny mint leaves

Makes 1 cake

★V

Preheat the oven to 180°C (350°F), gas 4. Grease two 20cm (8-inch) cake tins with butter and line with baking paper. You will need to make sure the tins you use for this have a solid base – not loose-based or springform – or the liquid may leak out.

Tip the eggs and sugar into a heatproof bowl and set it over a saucepan of simmering water. Whisk over the heat until the sugar is dissolved and the mixture feels slightly warm to the touch. If you live in a warm country, then skip the above step.

Now, remove the bowl from the heat and whisk the eggs with an electric hand whisk on the highest speed for 10 minutes, then whisk on a low speed for another 5 minutes.

Sift the cake flour, cornflour and baking powder together, then add the flour mixture to the eggs. Using a cut and fold motion, incorporate it with the help of a spatula, working quickly and with a very light hand so that you don't lose too much volume. Do not use an electric whisk for this.

Once the flour is well mixed in, add your milk, oil and vanilla extract and fold through quickly.

Divide the batter evenly between the two cake tins, then tap them gently on the work surface so that any large air bubbles can escape.

Place the cake tins on a large roasting tray. Pour boiling water into the baking tray until it reaches one-third the way up the cake tins.

Bake the cakes for 35–40 minutes, or until the cakes spring back to your touch.

Remove the cakes from the oven and let them cool for 5 minutes. Flip them over onto a wire rack and let them down completely with the tins still in place, then remove the tins and lining paper They will slightly lose their shape, but that is okay as they will get trimmed.

Once the cakes have cooled down, finely trim off the edges and trim away the brown top as thinly as you can so that the whole cake is pale. Slice each cake in half horizontally, so that you have four layers, and cover them with cling film (plastic wrap). They can be refrigerated for a couple of days at this stage.

Next, prepare the passionfruit and mango caramel. Combine the passionfruit pulp and mango purée in a bowl.

Put the sugar in a small saucepan and add 25ml (1fl oz/2 tbsp) water. Let the sugar melt and simmer until it reaches 165°C (329°F) – a sugar thermometer will be handy – and you see the colour of the sugar syrup turning slightly caramel golden in colour.

At this stage remove the hot caramel from the heat and add the fruit purée, but be careful as the caramel will spit. Mix well, then return to the heat and cook for a further few minutes until it reaches a light sauce consistency, let it cool down completely. This sauce will live happily in the fridge for up to a week – that is, if it lasts that long.

Now, whip the double cream with 45g (1½oz/ 5 tablespoons) of the icing sugar and the vanilla extract until fluffy firm peaks are formed. Whip the whipping cream with the remaining icing sugar to firm peaks, then set aside in the fridge.

To assemble the cake, place one layer of sponge onto a cake board or a serving plate and, using a pastry brush, dab the cake with pineapple juice from the tin.

Dollop some whipped double cream onto the sponge and evenly spread it into a 5mm (¼-inch) thick layer onto the cake, place some pineapple chunks in rounds, top up with another layer of double cream, covering the pineapple chunks, and repeat with the rest of the layers except the last one.

Now crumb coat the cake with the residual double cream by spreading it all over the cake, covering all of the sides thinly and evenly, with the help of a palate knife if possible. Let it rest in the fridge for at least 30 minutes – longer is better.

Once chilled, gently whip up the whipping cream again to incorporate air and make it fluffy, and use it to cover and decorate the cake. I coat the top and sides of the cake with the cream, then use a star nozzle (because that is one of only two nozzles I own) to pipe some fancy florets on top – but you can use any nozzle to make it look pretty. I usually scrape the sides of the cake with a toothed cake comb to give it the classic stripes, but you can just leave it as plain, as in the photo.

Place your reserved pineapple slices on top of the cake in a circle (or pile up chunks of pineapple if you prefer), then top the cake with cocktail cherries. I also add some tiny fresh mint tips to add colour – your call.

Drip the passionfruit caramel over or serve it on the side. I recommend doing both!

Below: My whole point of existence: my buzz balls and my life support, posing for darling Patricia for the pineapple cake shoot.

Me aged 12, at my birthday with my paternal grandparents and the pineapple cake.

Just in time for desserts

In another life, I would rather be born as a dessert then a human. Not to be a mere option in a long list of a menu but to be the most anticipated desire, ending a meal on a high note, satisfying every inch of soul. I always had a sweet tooth, and to pair my inclination towards sweet things further I fell in love with my husband who happened to have a savagely sweet tooth. But my love affair with desserts began, as in most of my stories, with Dad. Aba Jan had a passion for desserts like no one else in the family. He taught me to appreciate the local and seasonal produce, and when Saudi Arabia bloomed with locally grown varieties of pears, peaches, apricots, figs and others, so did our kitchen with all sorts of sweet concoctions.

In this chapter you will find a very diverse variety of desserts. From deeply traditional ones like Sh'ariyah (page 254) and Areeka Malakiya (page 241) to my very modern takes on Saudi classics like Hibiscus Poached Pears (page 247), Mastic Buttermilk Panna Cotta Topped with Debyaza (page 251) and Mishmish (page 245).

Let me briefly introduce you to one of the most loved traditional Saudi desserts, Areeka Malakiya. It is the luxurious and highly nutritious Saudi version of a humble British crumble. No Eid or celebration is complete without a dish of warm Areeka, adorned with loads of toppings.

Then comes Shariyah, or balaleet, an Arab counterpart of South Asian Sewaiyaan (sweet vermicelli cooked in a rich milky broth loaded with nuts). Egg or no egg on top, it's your choice. I like it with a dollop of clotted cream. Eid al Fitr is incomplete without it. In Middle Eastern and South Asian households, Ramadan and Eid celebrations require a bowl of sheer khurma (using milk, as below) or sh'ariyah (without milk). This particular version (page 254) hails from the Holy cities of Makkah and Madinah, where it is served reverently throughout the year and is a highlight of *ta'teema*, which is the Arabic word for a bridal shower.

Mishmish is my homage to one of the best apricots I have ever tasted and that too was in Saudi Arabia. I often make these stone-fruit dishes on hot, very muggy July/August days. I take the baking dish of these soft, caramelized, squishy cherubs and a dollop of labneh, with thin, hairy pieces of pashmak (Middle Eastern candy floss) running through the apricots and my hair at the same time. I sit cross-legged on my patio deck and devour the whole thing, licking the dish clean.

So what are you waiting for? Turn the page over, enjoy the ride to the land of my sweet dreams and explore my contemporary takes on some classics, which make some epic showstoppers to any feast.

QASHD AL-TAMR
(Warm and cosy date crumble)

One bite of *Qashd Al-Tamr*, your eyes closed, and for a moment you will completely forget where the world is heading. For a moment, just a tiny moment, you are lost in the deep, dark noirs of treacly flavour, as if the universe has stopped. Washed down with a fragrant and ever-so-slightly bitter Saudi coffee, qashd is soul food at its best: nourishing and comforting.

Even though this beautiful dessert belongs to the central region of Al-Qaseem, qashd is made lovingly throughout the Kingdom of Saudi Arabia. No celebration, like Eid or a wedding, is complete without it.

INGREDIENTS:

- 100g (3½oz) unsalted butter
- 60g (2oz) coarse wholemeal flour (or use oat flour for a gluten-free option)
- 75ml (2½fl oz) buttermilk
- 450g (1lb) pitted Khalas or Burni dates (these often come in a vacuum pack of 1kg/2¼lb and are usually pitted)
- 25g (1oz) shredded coconut, toasted
- Date molasses, to drizzle (optional, but enhances the decadence of the crumble)
- Clotted cream and Saudi coffee (see page 290), to serve

Serves 4–6

★V★GF

In a wide frying pan, melt the butter over a medium heat. As soon as the butter melts, add the flour and toast it for about 5–7 minutes until nutty and golden.

Pour in the buttermilk gradually, constantly stirring to avoid lumps. Cook for 15–20 minutes, stirring continuously until the mixture starts to crumble.

Add the dates and gently mix on a low heat until all the dates are coated in the crumble.

Serve warm in small serving bowls, drizzled with some date molasses, sprinkled with toasted coconut and with a small quenelle of clotted cream on top, and a Saudi qahwa (coffee) on the side.

AREEKA MALAKIYA
(The Royal Areeka: when crumble and trifle have a baby)

If I had to describe the national dessert of Saudi Arabia, it has to be Areeka Malakiya (or Royal Areeka, aka *ma'asoob*). It has a crunchy and flaky pastry base, layered with mashed and sliced banana, topped with chocolate chips, clotted cream, ghee, honey, nuts and cornflakes: is there anything left!

There are so many variations of this delicacy, you can add pretty much anything and everything that can go in a dessert. Locally, it is made with a traditional bread that is lightly fried in ghee, called *fateer*, similar to south Asian paratha. This is topped with minced dates and more ghee passed together through a mincer (but I have a way easier method I share here), then layered with lashings of banana, draped in a thick blanket of clotted cream. Glistening drizzles of Yemeni Sidr honey slip between the layers – its floral sweetness a perfect contrast to the earthy richness beneath – and a scattering of toasted cashews, slivered almonds, chopped dates and cornflakes add a satisfying crunch. Finally, a good helping of mature Cheddar for that salty umami lactic hit to cut through the sweetness. (Saudis use Kraft tinned orange cheese and call it "Cheddar jubna" – *jubna* is Arabic for cheese.)

A dessert as rich in history as it is in flavour, it is a tribute to the land's bounty – a delicate harmony of textures and tastes woven together like a Bedouin *khayma* (tent).

INGREDIENTS:

- 5 frozen parathas or 6 large all-butter croissants
- 125g (4½oz) unsalted butter or ghee
- 250g (9oz) medjool dates, pitted and chopped
- 1 tsp ground green cardamom
- 1 tsp coarsely ground fennel seeds
- ½ tsp nigella seeds
- 400g (14oz) clotted cream
- 1 × 410g (14½oz) can evaporated milk
- 1 × 397g (14oz) can sweetened condensed milk
- 4–6 large overly ripe bananas, sliced (more or less, as your preference)
- 100g (3½oz) yellow processed cheese or mature Cheddar cheese, grated
- 100g (3½oz) roasted cashews
- 100g (3½oz) caramelized pecans (or use any nut of your choice)
- 50g (1¾oz) milk chocolate chips (optional, but my lot love them)
- 100g (3½oz) cornflakes
- Honey, to drizzle
- Date molasses, to drizzle

Serves 6

★V

If using frozen parathas, cook them as per the packet instructions, then let them cool down completely.

Shred the parathas or croissants into small pieces, put them in a food processor and grind them to a very rough crumb. Just a couple of pulses are required here.

Put the butter in a wide frying pan and let it melt, then tip the crumb into the pan and toast on a low heat until very crisp and amber gold in colour. Let it cool down.

Put half of the dates in the food processor along with the ground cardamom and fennel and the toasted crumb and pulse a few times until it resembles coarse sea salt. Add the nigella seeds and mix in with a spoon.

In a bowl, mix together the clotted cream and half of the evaporated milk – this will loosen the cream up a bit.

Assemble the dessert in a large trifle bowl or serving dish. Spoon in one-third of the cream mixture first, spreading it out over the base, followed by one-third of the crumb mixture, a generous drizzle of condensed milk, a layer of sliced bananas, a sprinkle of cheese, a scattering of cashews, pecans, chocolate chips (if using), cornflakes and chopped dates, finishing with a drizzle of the remaining evaporated milk and some honey and date molasses.

Repeat the layers until you have used up all the ingredients.

Enjoy warm or at room temperature.

MISHMISH
(Roast apricots, whipped labneh, caramelized pistachios and candy floss)

A sunset-orange-coloured jewel of late summer, *mishmish* (the Arabic for apricots) are tiny rays of warm sunshine trapped in velvety skin, glowing with crimson gold warmth. Mid-July to the end of August was the time when you could find apricots in abundance, bursting with a bewitching sweet, honey-like fragrance tinged with a whisper of tartness. Their scent was like a secret told on the wind, pulling you towards them. They would be loaded on wooden carts or in the back of pickups along the roadside like a makeshift boot sale in the rural city of Jeddah. They were mostly grown in the southwestern region of Jizan and Taif, an enchanting green valley of the Hijaz region, between Makkah and Jeddah.

Upon returning from work, Aba Jan used to stop at these stalls to get some farm-fresh fruit almost every other day. Mama would make them into all sorts of jams, cordials and juices. She paired these ripe, but not so soft, woolly babies with many things for endless decadent possibilities.

This recipe is a depiction of my nostalgic memories. As I grew up, I inherited a love of experimentation from Aba Jan and came up with this very simple, comforting hug in a bowl. It is the taste of sun-kissed orchards, roars of father–daughter laughter on warm lazy afternoons, and the quiet promise of seasons turning.

INGREDIENTS:

- 250ml (9fl oz/1 cup) grape juice or non-alcoholic white wine (I use Shloer)
- 1 tsp lemon juice
- 30g (1oz/2½ tbsp) sugar
- ¼ tsp vanilla extract
- A few saffron strands bloomed on a small ice cube (see tip overleaf)
- 6 large fully ripe apricots, halved lengthways and stones removed

For the caramelized pistachios:

- 50g (1¾oz/¼ cup) white granulated sugar
- Pinch of sea salt
- Handful of unsalted green pistachios (about 50g/1¾oz)

For the whipped labneh:

- 100ml (3½fl oz/scant ½ cup) whipping cream or double (heavy) cream
- 120g (4¼oz) labneh or Greek-style yogurt, lightly whipped
- Turkish/Persian candy floss (cotton candy) (aka pashmak), to decorate

Serves 6

★V★GF

Preheat the oven to 170°C (325°F), gas 3, and line a baking sheet with baking paper.

Prepare a simple syrup. In a small saucepan, combine the grape juice, lemon juice, sugar, vanilla extract and bloomed saffron. Bring it to a boil, let the sugar dissolve, then turn off the heat and let it infuse for 5 minutes.

In the meantime, arrange the halved apricots, cut sides up, in a roasting tray. Drizzle the prepared syrup over them, allowing it to pool in the hollows where the stones were. Roast for about 20–25 minutes (depending on the ripeness and size of apricots) until jammy and very tender. Remove from the oven and let them cool down completely. (These can be cooked a day or two ahead of a party.) Reserve any juice as this will go in the labneh mix or to drizzle on top.

For the caramelized pistachios, heat the sugar with the salt in a small pan until it melts and just starts to turn a light golden colour. Be very watchful as caramel has a tendency to go dark very quickly and we don't want that.

Add the pistachios and, with a very brisk motion, using a metal spoon, coat the kernels entirely. Tip this hot caramel-coated mixture onto the lined baking sheet. Let it cool down and go hard, then remove from the baking tray and pound it to a coarse crumb in a pestle and mortar or put it in a food bag and use a rolling pin (or something heavy).

For the whipped labneh, whip the cream to soft peaks, then fold in the labneh or Greek yogurt, along with half of any roasted apricot juices.

To serve, spread a dollop of whipped labneh onto six dessert plates and place two halves of roasted apricot on top. Drizzle with any leftover apricot syrup, and sprinkle with the caramelized pistachio crumb. Finally, top each plate with pashmak and serve.

TIP: To bloom saffron in the authentic Persian way, place an ice cube in a very small bowl and sprinkle a pinch of saffron strands on top of the ice cube. As the ice melts, the saffron strands release a very distinctive deep orange colour along with their signature aroma. This can't be achieved by soaking saffron in hot water – this method just ruins the texture, aroma and colour of a very expensive ingredient, and we are left with a much-diluted dye which tastes of nothing. Once bloomed, this mixture can be bottled and stored in the fridge for up to a week.

HIBISCUS POACHED PEARS AND RICOTTA CREAM WITH CORNFLAKE BRITTLE

(*Karkade*, the Arabic for hibiscus, is used to make a much-loved summer drink also known as Karkade)

This recipe is very dear to me as it is an ode to all those bitter-sweet Saudi memories and flavours I grew up with. Summer holidays meant one thing: that it was time to explore the hidden gems of the kingdom. Far from Jeddah to the south, Jizan (also Jazan) is a heaven of fresh produce. It has one of the most stunning views, a lush green valley nestled between charcoal hills, with the most surreal star-studded sky – it's a place straight out of a fairytale. I spent many nights lying down on Aba Jan's Toyota Cressida's bonnet, star gazing with him, often dozing off and falling down, bruising myself.

Jizan's orchards burst into a festival of colour and life during early spring and late summer. Heavy with ruby-red pomegranates, mangoes blushing gold, fragrant ripe pears and nectar-dripping figs, fruit-laden trees bend in humbleness, as if they are making an offering to humankind. The air is thick with the perfume of citrus and honey, while the rustling leaves sing in harmony with the whispers of the Red Sea. Under the cool shade of ancient branches, time slows, and the land tells stories of abundance, passion and an eternal dance between earth and sky.

Witnessing my love and attachment to pears, my husband bought our home because it had two luscious pear trees.

Imagine a just-ripe Comice or Rocha pear, bathed in a deep crimson sea of hibiscus syrup, its delicate flesh blushing like twilight clouds soaked in the last kiss of the sun. The floral perfume of hibiscus clings to it, wrapping it in soft murmurs of tart, ruby-tinted nectar. As your spoon cuts through, the fruit surrenders effortlessly, releasing warmth and the essence of autumn's embrace.

Beside it, a cloud of whipped ricotta cream, luscious and airy, like the first snowfall settling over the orchard. It just melts against your tongue, balancing the pear's gentle tang with whispers of vanilla and floral hibiscus. Each bite is a romance of textures and flavours, a symphony of warmth, crispness, and smoothness, telling a story of autumn's departure and winter's anticipation. I want to cry now.

INGREDIENTS:

- 100g (3½oz/½ cup) golden caster or light brown sugar
- ½ vanilla pod or 1 tsp vanilla bean paste
- 2 tbsp dried hibiscus flower petals (more can be added to intensify flavour and colour)
- 6 medium-sized just-ripe pears (I use my home-grown Williams or Comice variety)
- 1 tbsp lemon juice
- 20g (¾oz) toasted crushed hazelnuts
- Edible flower petals, to decorate (optional)

For the crunchy nut cornflake brittle:

- 100g (3½oz/½ cup) light brown sugar
- 120g (4¼oz/½ cup) unsalted butter
- 150g (5½oz) plain cornflakes
- 30g (1oz) slivered almonds (optional)
- Sea salt

For the whipped ricotta cream:

- 300g (10½oz) ricotta (the best you can find)
- 75g (2½oz) icing (confectioners') sugar
- 150ml (5fl oz/scant ⅔ cup) whipping cream

Serves 6

★V

First, poach the pears. Ideally, this step should be done the night before serving to capture the full essence of hibiscus and pears. Prepare the hibiscus infused syrup by combining the sugar, vanilla pod, hibiscus dried flower petals and 150ml (5fl oz/scant ⅔ cup) water in a saucepan that's large enough to fit all the pears. Bring the liquid to a gentle boil on a low heat, let it simmer for 10 minutes on a very low heat, then take the pan off the heat and set aside so that the floral colour and flavour intensify.

In the meantime, peel the pears and soak them in a bowl of cold water with the lemon juice added (this prevents them going brown). If you are using large pears or you want them to cook in half the time, you can cut them in half lengthways and remove the core.

Now return the syrup to the heat, bring to a simmer, and plunge the pears into the syrup. Cover and cook gently for 12–15 minutes, depending on the size and ripeness of the pears, until a knife can be inserted through the flesh easily without much resistance. Remove the pan from heat and let the pears and syrup cool down completely before chilling them in the fridge overnight, or for at least 4–6 hours.

An hour before serving, take the saucepan out of the fridge, remove the pears and, over a medium heat, reduce the syrup down until it thickens to the consistency of honey. This will act as a very shiny and intense glaze. Let it cool down, before brushing the pears with the syrup.

To make the brittle, preheat the oven to 180°C (350°F), gas 4. Grease a small baking tray and line it with baking paper.

In a saucepan, combine the sugar, butter and a hefty pinch of sea salt. Cook for a couple of minutes on a medium heat until the butter has melted and the sugar

has dissolved. Bring it to a gentle boil and let it simmer for another 1–2 minutes, then take it off the heat.

Put the cornflakes in a bowl with the almonds, if using. Pour the hot sugar mixture onto the cornflakes and mix well until everything is well coated. Tip the mixture onto the prepared baking tray and spread out evenly. Bake for 12–15 minutes or until a rich golden brown.

Set aside and let it cool down completely before breaking it into pieces, which will give your dessert that irresistible snap. (Any leftovers can be stored in an airtight container for up to a week but I doubt it will last that long.)

For the whipped ricotta cream, beat the ricotta and sugar in a mixing bowl until completely smooth

In a separate bowl, whip the cream to firm peaks, then fold the cream through the ricotta mixture. Set aside in the fridge until ready to serve.

To serve, place a dollop of whipped ricotta cream (make a quenelle if you want to be fancy) onto each serving plate. Sprinkle with some toasted crushed hazelnuts and top it with a crunchy cornflake brittle shard – they give a lovely height to the dessert and add a beautiful texture.

Glaze the pears with the syrup and place one on each serving plate, then finish with some edible flower petals. Enjoy.

MASTIC BUTTERMILK PANNA COTTA TOPPED WITH DEBYAZA (Debyaza is a Saudi dried fruit compote made with apricots and dried fruits)

"O debyaza, make it beautiful, brighten up the Eid spread": words from a folk song often sung by the housewives of Makkah and Medina to mark the end of Ramadan and to begin the preparation of Eid al-Fitr feasting.

This whole set-up of a dessert is my modern take on a classic Hijazi dessert, debyaza – a Saudi compote made with apricots and dried fruits. To lighten it up and make it more fun, I have paired the richness of debyaza with a very light, perfumed, palate-cleansing panna cotta with the lactic tang of buttermilk. The addition of the dried cranberries is also my twist; they cut through the excessive sweetness. This has been an instant hit at my get-togethers, enjoyed with an unparalleled level of happiness and laughter breaking out in the background. What more can you ask from life other than these beautiful moments?

Debyaza can be served on its own or paired with panna cotta, as I have done in this recipe. It can be served warm or chilled. You can find apricot leather and dried brittle dates at any Middle Eastern, Asian or Arabian store.

INGREDIENTS:

For the mastic buttermilk panna cotta:

- 12g (⅓oz) gelatine powder
- 4 crystals of mastic resin
- 110g (3¾oz/heaped ½ cup) white granulated sugar, plus ½ tsp for the mastic
- 300ml (10½fl oz/1¼ cups) double (heavy) cream
- 1 tsp rose water or orange blossom water
- 600ml (21fl oz/2½ cups) buttermilk
- Oil, for greasing the ramekins

For the debyaza:

- 300g (10½oz) qamar-ad-din (apricot leather), chopped into small pieces
- 75g (2½oz) dried brittle dates or pitted fresh dates
- A pinch of ground green cardamom
- 2.5cm (1 inch) cinnamon stick
- 1 black clove
- 30g (1oz) ghee or virgin coconut oil
- 100g (3½oz) blanched almonds
- 50g (1¾oz) cashews
- 50g (1¾oz) hazelnuts
- 50g (1¾oz) pistachios
- 50g (1¾oz) pecans
- 100g (3½oz) dried apricots, halved
- 75g (2½oz) dried figs, halved
- 25g (1oz) sultanas (golden raisins) or raisins
- 25g (1oz) dried cranberries
- 150g (5½oz/1¾ cups) light brown sugar

Serves 6–8

★GF

Start by preparing the panna cotta. Soak the gelatine powder in 60ml (2fl oz/¼ cup) cold water.

Put the mastic and ½ teaspoon sugar in a pestle and mortar and grind together into a powder.

Pour the cream into a heavy-based saucepan and bring to a boil, then turn the heat down and mix in the sugar and powdered mastic vigorously until all dissolved. Take it off the heat and let it cool down ever so slightly (to around 80°C/176°F).

Once cooled, add the bloomed gelatine and the rose or orange blossom water and mix until thoroughly combined.

Put the buttermilk in a jug and place a sieve (fine-mesh strainer) over the top. Pour the cream mixture through the sieve onto the buttermilk and mix gently without incorporating any air bubbles. Pour into greased ramekins and leave in the fridge to set, preferably overnight.

For the debyaza, soak the apricot leather pieces in 750ml (26fl oz/3 cups) of water for at least 2 hours, or overnight. If using dried dates, soak these in water overnight too, in a separate bowl.

Once all of apricot leather pieces have softened and can be easily stirred into a mush, transfer to a saucepan (along with the soaking water), add the cardamom, cinnamon and clove and bring it to a boil. Let it simmer, stirring every now and then, until it thickens to a runny-honey-like consistency.

In a pan that is large enough to eventually hold everything, heat the ghee or coconut oil and fry all the nuts until lightly golden in colour.

Now add the soaked dried dates (if using), the dried apricot and fig halves and the sultanas and cranberries to the pan and fry for another minute on a low heat.

Transfer the apricot leather mixture to the pan with the nuts and dried fruit and add the light brown sugar. Stir well and bring it to a rolling boil, then let it simmer for 20–25 minutes until the sugar is completely dissolved and it thickens a bit. If using the fresh dates, add these right at the end so that they become just soft and warmed through without losing their shape. Turn off the heat and let it cool down a bit, then it's ready to serve.

To serve, dip the panna cotta moulds in warm water for a few seconds to make unmoulding easy, then loosen the edges and flip them onto serving dishes. Top the jiggly panna cotta with as much debyaza as you like and enjoy the beautiful and sublime mess on your plate.

SH'ARIYAH
(The Saudi version of Indian dum seviyan)

If you have a sweet tooth, you will be addicted to this no-fuss treat. It is a crowd-pleaser that is super quick to put together. Khoya are milk solids, easily found at Asian grocery stores, but you can substitute with plain *burfi* or clotted cream with a sprinkle of raw cane sugar.

INGREDIENTS:

For the saffron-infused sugar syrup:

- 200ml (7fl oz/scant 1 cup) milk (can be replaced with water for a lighter version or a non-dairy option like virgin coconut oil or plant-based butter)
- 200g (7oz/1 cup) white granulated sugar
- A few strands of saffron
- 4–6 green cardamom pods, lightly crushed
- A pinch of yellow or orange food colouring (optional)
- A few drops of rose water

For the sh'ariyah:

- 100g (3½oz/scant ½ cup) ghee
- 200g (7oz) thin vermicelli (seviyan), broken
- 40g (1½oz/¼ cup) almonds, chopped or slivered
- 40g (1½oz/¼ cup) cashews, chopped
- 35g (1¼oz/¼ cup) pistachios, chopped or sliced
- 40g (1½oz/¼ cup) raisins
- 20g (¾oz/¼ cup) coconut flakes
- 100g (3½oz) crumbled khoya
- Nuts of your choice, chopped or slivered, to garnish

Serves 6–8

★V

Prepare the saffron-infused syrup by combining all of the syrup ingredients with 200ml (7fl oz/scant 1 cup) water in a saucepan. Bring it to a boil, then let it simmer on a low heat for 5 minutes.

Meanwhile, in a wide frying pan, melt the ghee, then add the broken vermicelli. Toast for 3–4 minutes until golden in colour, then add the nuts, raisins and coconut flakes and sauté for another 1–2 minutes.

Pour in the hot sugar syrup, turn the heat up to high and cook for 1 minute while continuously stirring. Then sprinkle in the crumbled khoya and cover the pan with a lid, bring the heat down to very low and leave for 5 minutes or so.

Remove the lid and check if there is any liquid remaining. If so, cover and cook for a further 2 minutes.

Fluff the vermicelli to mix in the now softened khoya, then dish out into a serving bowl and garnish with nuts of your choice. Serve.

ICE ICE BABY

These four sorbets and the coffee and date ice cream are the essence of the glorious fresh produce of Saudi Arabia, thanks to the very firm government stance towards sustainability and the diverse multicultural workforce that implements the government's vision with a religious commitment.

Across the country's vast and varied landscapes, the earth gifts its bounty in a breathtaking spectrum of colours, floral fragrances and flavours.

In the southwestern regions of Asir, Baha and Najran, terraced farms cascade down misty slopes, where emerald-green coffee cherries glisten with morning dew, and figs ripen under the watchful gaze of ancient mountains. The crisp air carries the perfume of apricots, peaches and grapes, their sweetness kissed by the sun.

The steep hillsides of the southernmost Jazan region are home to many coffee plantations, including the 100-year-old coffee farm of Hassan Al Malky. The orchards overflow with mangoes so luscious they drip with nectar, while papayas and bananas dance in the gentle coastal breeze. The land hums with life, a vibrant embrace of tropical abundance.

In the heart of the Najd and Hijaz, wheat, other grains and the juiciest watermelons grow. Saudi Arabia is actually self-sufficient in watermelon production. In Madinah and the Makkah region, date palms stand like silent sentinels, their fruit amber, caramel and deep mahogany, brimming with the richness of being cared for well by devoted farmers who have looked after the trees like their own children. These are the jewels of the desert that hold the warmth of a thousand sunsets in every bite.

In the eastern province of Al Ahsa, Dammam and the Al Khobar region, where the Persian Gulf kisses the shore, baskets spill over with freshly harvested seafood, small crisp cucumbers and bright, sweet giant mulberries, their juices bursting with the very essence of summer.

Tabuk, situated in the northwestern region of KSA, is a land of vast lavender fields perfuming the air, a violet, fragrant tapestry woven into the land's golden embrace. At dusk, the sky blushes in shades of rose and amber, casting an ethereal glow over the endless purple expanse. Bees hum a lullaby, weaving between petals as if enchanted by the land's quiet symphony. Even the local honey produced there has a hue of violet, with a very distinctive floral lavender note to it.

From the mountains to the valleys, from the desert's heart to the whispering coast, Saudi Arabia's fresh produce is a story of diversity and resilience, of life flourishing against all odds, a testament to the land's unbreakable spirit and timeless beauty.

Aba Jan and I made all sorts of ice creams and sorbets using luscious fruit locally grown in Saudi Arabia. I would eat them by the bowlful at breakfast, something very typical of me. The fruits are still blooming in that part of the world, but Aba Jan is not there anymore, in the kitchen or in my life. But his out-of-nowhere flavour concoctions and my insane love for bananas are still there. I have included a handful of damn easy, memory-laden sorbet recipes for you to enjoy.

FOUR PALATE-CLEANSING SORBETS

Cucumber & Mint Skanjabeen/Lemooni Sorbet

INGREDIENTS:

- 250g (9oz/1¼ cups) granulated sugar
- 2 tbsp liquid glucose or light corn syrup
- 700g (1lb 9oz) cucumbers
- 30 leaves of fresh mint
- Zest and juice of 1 large lemon
- Zest and juice of 2 limes
- Sea salt crystals, to serve
- Tajin mix or sumac, to serve (optional, but highly recommended)

Makes 1 litre (35fl oz)

★V★DF★GF

In a saucepan, combine the sugar and glucose with 250ml (9fl oz/1 cup) water. Let the sugar dissolve on a medium heat without boiling it. Remove from the heat and let it cool down completely.

Roughly chop cucumbers, then add them to a food processor with the mint leaves and blend to a purée.

Line a sieve with a muslin cloth and place it over a bowl, then pass the minty cucumber purée through this set-up. Extract all of the gorgeous green juice by squeezing the cloth as much as you can.

Add the lemon and lime juice and zest to the cucumber juice, along with the cooled sugar syrup. Give it a mix and let it chill in the fridge for a couple of hours.

Once chilled, churn in an ice cream machine according to the manufacturer's instructions, then transfer to a freezable container to freeze for up to an hour before serving.

Sprinkle some sea salt crystals, along with some Tajin and/or sumac (that's my twist and it works wonders), on top before serving.

Store any leftovers in a freezer-friendly airtight container in the freezer.

Mulberry & Black Lime (Loomi) Sorbet

INGREDIENTS:

- 2 tbsp liquid glucose or light corn syrup
- 200g (7oz/1 cup) granulated sugar
- 1 dried black lime (loomi), freshly ground to a powder
- zest of 1 lime plus 1 tbsp lime juice
- 750g (1lb 10oz) fresh dark mulberries, washed (or use blackberries)

Makes 1 litre (35fl oz)
★V★DF★GF

In a medium-sized saucepan, combine 200ml (7fl oz/ scant 1 cup) water with the light corn syrup and sugar. Bring it to a boil until the sugar dissolves, then turn off the heat, add the ground loomi and let it infuse for 10–15 minutes.

Strain the syrup to remove any loomi pith, then return to a boil and let it simmer gently for another 3–4 minutes. Turn off the heat and let it cool a little, then add the lime zest and juice.

Meanwhile, put the mulberries in a blender and pour the syrup over them while it is still warm. Blend into a purée.

Pour the purée into a bowl, allow to cool, and let it chill in the fridge for an hour.

If you have an ice cream machine, transfer the purée to it and churn following the manufacturer's instructions. If the sorbet is a bit too soft to serve straight away, transfer it to a container and freeze for up to an hour before serving.

If you don't have an ice cream machine, pour the purée into a 5cm (2-inch) deep freezer-safe tray or a container lined with cling film (plastic wrap), cover and freeze for 4–6 hours or until completely frozen. Once frozen, cut the purée into roughly 4cm (1½-inch) cubes, and blend them on high speed until fluffy and smooth, with no big chunks. Transfer the blended sorbet to a freezer-safe container, cover with a lid and freeze until it is just firm – this will take up to an hour.

Scoop the sorbet into small bowls and serve.

Store any leftovers in a freezer-friendly airtight container in the freezer.

Peach & Lavender Sorbet

INGREDIENTS:

- 200g (7oz/1 cup) granulated sugar
- 3 small clusters of fresh edible lavender flowers or 1 tbsp dried culinary lavender
- 750g (1lb 10oz) very ripe peaches, cut into chunks
- Finely grated zest and juice of 2 large lemons

Makes 1 litre (35fl oz)
★V★DF★GF

Tip the sugar into a small saucepan, add 100ml (3½fl oz/scant ½ cup) water and bring it to a boil, swirling it around the pan until the sugar has dissolved and you have a shiny, thick sugar syrup.

Drop in the lavender flowers, cover and let the syrup cool down and infuse with the floral notes.

While the syrup is cooling down, put the peach chunks in a large bowl, add the lemon zest and juice and allow them to macerate.

Once the syrup is cool, pour it over the peaches, cover the bowl and let the whole lot infuse, ideally overnight in the fridge.

Blend everything together into a smooth purée and resist the temptation of face-planting the floral purée. Not yet. Pass the purée through a sieve, pressing down with a spoon to squeeze out every single drop of that infused nectar and discarding any unwanted bits of lavender and lemon.

If you have an ice cream machine, transfer the purée to it and churn following the manufacturer's instructions. If the sorbet is a bit too soft to serve straight away, transfer it to a container and freeze for up to an hour.

If you don't have an ice cream machine, pour the purée into a 5cm (2-inch) deep freezer-safe tray or a container lined with cling film (plastic wrap), cover, and freeze for 4–6 hours or until completely frozen. Once frozen, cut the purée into roughly 4cm (1½-inch) cubes, and blend them on high speed until fluffy and smooth, with no big chunks. Transfer the blended sorbet to a freezer-safe container, cover with a lid and freeze until it is just firm – this will take up to an hour.

Scoop the sorbet into small bowls and serve. Store any leftovers in an airtight container in the freezer.

Watermelon & Marjoram Sorbet

INGREDIENTS:

- 1 smallish watermelon (which yields around 750g/1lb 10oz of fruit after removing the outer skin)
- 100g (3½oz/½ cup) sugar (depending on the sweetness of the watermelon)
- 1 tbsp liquid glucose (optional, for a smoother consistency)
- 3 small sprigs of fresh marjoram or 1 tbsp dried marjoram
- Juice of 1 lemon
- Pinch of sea salt and freshly ground black pepper (optional)

Makes 1 litre (35fl oz)

★V★DF★GF

Cut the watermelon into chunks, removing the skin, pith and any large seeds as you go. Spread out on a freezer-safe baking tray and freeze until solid.

Meanwhile, prepare the sugar syrup by combining the sugar and glucose with 100ml (3½fl oz/scant ½ cup) water in a saucepan over a low-medium heat. Let the sugar dissolve, swirling the pan occasionally, for a few minutes until you have a thick shiny syrup.

Take the pan off the heat and let the syrup cool down slightly, then tip in the marjoram and cover. Let the syrup infuse or an hour, then strain the syrup through a fine sieve.

Once the watermelon chunks are solid, take them out of the freezer and leave to soften for 5 minutes – this helps them blend more easily.

Transfer the chunks to a high-powered blender and blend until smooth, adding the lemon juice and marjoram-infused sugar syrup, alternately little by little, until smooth.

The sorbet can be served straight away, scooped into small bowls and sprinkled with a little sea salt and black pepper, if you like. Or transfer to a freezer-proof container and store in the freezer. Allow to soften for a few minutes before serving.

DATE AND QAHWA SWIRL ICE CREAM

Qahwa is Saudi coffee made from very lightly roasted coffee beans. I love it, but it is an acquired taste, so in order to tick all the boxes for my very diverse group of foodie friends and family, I kind of winged it. And guess what ... it worked.

Now, whenever I make this quick-fix, no-churn ice cream for any get-together or summer picnic (or a Saudi-style Sundae Royale – see page 264), the crowd keeps coming back for seconds and thirds. It's that good and easy peasy. Trust me, if you love coffee, you've got to try it.

INGREDIENTS:

- 30g (1oz) instant coffee
- 1 tsp vanilla paste (optional)
- 150g (5½oz/1 cup) icing (confectioners') sugar
- 60ml (2fl oz/¼ cup) hot water
- 400g (14fl oz/1¾ cups) double (heavy) cream
- 150g (5½oz/scant ⅔ cup) condensed milk
- 1 tsp ground green cardamom
- 1 tbsp very lightly roasted ground coffee (optional but it gives that authentic Saudi taste)
- 50g (1¾oz) medjool dates, chopped
- 50ml (1¾fl oz/3½ tbsp) date molasses for swirling, plus extra for drizzling on top
- Sea salt, for sprinkling (optional)

Serves 6

★V★GF

In a large bowl, combine the instant coffee, vanilla (if using), icing sugar and hot water. Whisk with a balloon whisk or electric beater for 4–5 minutes until very light and airy.

In a separate bowl, whip the double cream until soft and just beginning to hold peaks. Gently fold in the condensed milk, cardamom and coffee grounds, if using.

Now, transfer the whipped cream mixture to the aerated coffee mixture in two batches, folding in gently but swiftly without knocking out too much air. Add the chopped dates and gently fold in.

Transfer one-third of the mixture to a freezable container, drizzle with one-third of the date molasses and feather it out lightly with a skewer so it is swirled through the cream mixture. Repeat twice more to use up all of the cream mixture and date molasses. Cover and freeze overnight.

Take the ice cream out of the freezer 5 minutes before serving. Scoop and drizzle with more date syrup and sprinkle with a few sea salt crystals, if you like. Enjoy!

SUNDAE ROYALE SAUDI STYLE
(Made with date and coffee ice cream with a salted date caramel sauce and crunchy nut cornflakes)

This recipe comes straight from my childhood and is currently an obsession with my children: they literally lick the sundae glasses clean!

Pairing banana with almost every dessert is a very typical Saudi thing. It has some religious reverence from the time of Prophet Muhammad (PBUH), and it is considered a highly nutritious fruit and a quintessential part of my children's diet these days.

Aba Jan used to buy a whole hand of ripe bananas and my mama lost count of how many bananas I ate in a day. The situation hasn't changed much with my children; even the assistants at my local greengrocers give me puzzled looks seeing the amount of bananas in my shopping trolley. It runs in the genes, I guess.

To navigate my attention away from hoarding bananas, Aba Jan often made me a very simple version of a banana split, just adding a couple of scoops of homemade ice cream to sliced bananas, with a drizzle of date syrup and sometimes a few walnuts on top.

This recipe is my current pimped-up, much-loved creation, with tart cherry compote to cut through the sweetness and a crunchy cornflake brittle to add texture. And to give it a very regal touch, I have layered it all up with some heady Middle Eastern notes – a pistachio paste drizzle and some walnuts. I have grown up now and have realized that it was not my stomach that was hungry; it was and always is my soul that seeks fulfilment.

INGREDIENTS:

For the cherry compote:

- 250g (9oz) frozen pitted cherries
- 1 tbsp granulated sugar
- Zest and juice of 1 lemon

For the salted date caramel sauce:

- 200g (7oz/1 cup) muscovado sugar
- 200ml (7fl oz/scant 1 cup) date molasses
- 100g (3½oz/7 tbsp) unsalted butter, cubed
- 150ml (5fl oz/scant ⅔ cup) double (heavy) cream
- A hefty pinch of sea salt

To assemble the sundae:

- 1 x recipe quantity Date and Qahwa Swirl Ice Cream (see page 263)
- 4 ripe bananas, sliced
- Crunchy nut cornflakes, to sprinkle
- Pistachio paste, warmed up to drizzling consistency
- Handful of walnuts or pecans, roughly chopped

Serves 4

★V

Prepare the cherry compote first as it will take time to cool down (it can be made up to 3 days in advance). Put the frozen cherries, sugar and lemon juice and zest in a small saucepan. Cook on a low heat with a lid partially covering the pan until the cherries are fully soft and plumped up and the whole mixture starts to look like a thick, chunky jam. It will take about 8–10 minutes. Remove from the heat and set aside.

Next comes the salted date caramel sauce. Put the sugar and date molasses in a saucepan and let it heat up on a low-medium heat until the sugar dissolves and the mixture starts to bubble up. Being careful as this is very hot, whisk in the butter cubes one by one, whisking constantly until all of them are melted into the mixture.

Add the cream and whisk constantly until incorporated. Bring the whole lot to a boil, then turn off the heat, add the salt and set aside.

Assembly time: place a small spoonful of cherry compote into each base of four large sundae glasses (see tip). Add a small scoop of ice cream and top with banana slices, then add a drizzle of salted caramel sauce and a few cornflakes. Repeat to layer up the glasses, then top with a drizzle of pistachio paste and a sprinkle of walnuts or pecans, if you like.

TIP: Any extra cherry compote and caramel sauce can be stored in the fridge and used to dollop over scones, cakes and cookies, or spread on thick toasted brioche slices with clotted cream... Let your imagination run wild.

If you don't have four sundae glasses, you can use four dessert bowls or assemble it all in one large serving bowl.

Cheers to drinks & all the hard work

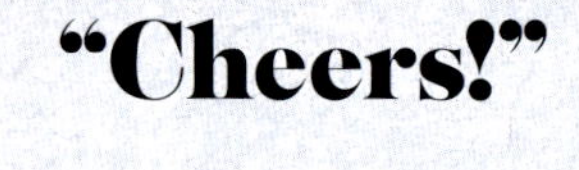

There is a reason why we say this, because drinks of all sorts exist for a reason. Be it a celebration, a morning routine, summer holidays, comforting a mother who has just given birth or to mark a rite of passage. We all need a liquid form of refreshment that soothes every corner of our body and soul at some point in our lives.

In this chapter, you will find an array of both traditional and modern Saudi drinks. A drink for the darkest time in your life. A drink for the hottest of days. A drink for the chilliest of winter nights. For the times you want to announce your achievements, to the times when you just want to forget and move on, or something in between. These drinks showcase the hidden and often unspoken gems of Saudi culture and tradition.

As a contemporary take on a greener, more modern and minimalistic approach, I have a Go Green smoothie (page 275). It will not help you rule the world or make it greener overnight, but it will definitely give you a feel-good mood.

Aseer Shammam (page 274) was a childhood favourite for me and many others who grew up in and around the coastal cities and towns of the Red Sea in the 1970s and 80s. Served in a transparent plastic bag with a straw passing through its tight knot, it was an after-school treat to enjoy while walking back home with friends under the scorching sun.

You will also find a winter warmer, Qahwa El-Loz (page 284). It is often given to new mums and used to beat the winter chills due to its high nutritional value. Once a favourite drink of the affluent only, Saudi white coffee (aka almond coffee) is the nation's heartthrob now. It is generously served at pretty much every celebration and occasion, particularly on the first day of Islamic New Year, as a symbol of happiness, prosperity and peace.

A beloved "beat the heat" kind of a drink for mango lovers is Araisi (page 272). It was often sold in those small transparent plastic bags in the 80s. But no longer, as we have become more civilized and started using disposable paper and plastic cups, taking the fun bit away of blowing up and popping the plastic bag after finishing the drink.

And then comes the Saudi Fruit Cocktail (page 278), one of the most classic drinks that you will find at every juice corner and in the chilled aisles of every grocery store in Saudi Arabia.

Go on. Make and share these delicious concoctions with your loved ones. Go out there, enjoy the stories and recreate the liquid magic in your kitchen.

HALEEB MANJO (AKA ARAISI)

(Saudi mango shake on another level)

I fondly remember that as soon as the Pakistani cargo of mangoes docked at Jeddah Islamic sea port in early May, almost every juice corner (drinks kiosks that are usually on corners) and café in the Hijaz region had their own variation of this mango shake on their menus. It was the star seller, and once you take your very first sip, you will realize why: it is simple and packed full of fresh mangoes. The ideal varieties to use are Pakistani or Indian mangoes, but avoid Brazilian ones.

Often loaded with nuts of your choice, and with diced mango and whipped cream on top, it is true happiness for a mango maniac like me. If you can't find Vimto (which is widely available) you can substitute it with mango purée or fruit coulis of your choice.

INGREDIENTS:

- 2 large fully ripe mangoes, diced and frozen, plus extra diced mango to serve
- 1 small banana, diced and frozen
- 250ml (9fl oz/1 cup) canned mango pulp
- 500ml (17fl oz/2 cups) chilled full-fat milk or any non-dairy alternative
- 250ml (9fl oz/1 cup) evaporated milk
- Handful of ice cubes, to blend
- Vimto concentrate (preferred), or ready-made mango syrup or coulis, to drizzle
- 6 scoops of vanilla or mango ice cream

For topping (optional):

- Squirty cream, whipped cream or ice cream
- Fresh raspberries, cherries or any finely diced fresh fruit
- Pistachio slivers and/or shredded coconut

Serves 6

★V★GF

In a blender, blitz the frozen diced mango, banana and mango pulp with the milk, evaporated milk and ice cubes.

In each of six serving glasses, drizzle Vimto or mango syrup/coulis around the insides of the glass to make a squiggly pattern.

Pour the milkshake into the glasses and top each with a scoop of ice-cream.

Squirt or pipe the whipped cream on top and garnish with the topping of your choice – raspberries, cherries, pistachio slivers, coconut, etc.

Add the mango dice and a final drizzle of Vimto and serve immediately.

ASEER SHAMMAM
(Cantaloupe melon celebration, a midsummer delight)

INGREDIENTS:
- ¼ small ripe cantaloupe melon, peeled, deseeded and cubed
- 2 tbsp honey or sugar (or your preferred sweetener)
- 150ml (5fl oz/scant ⅔ cup) coconut milk (or you can use coconut water or just plain water)
- 2–3 ice cubes, to blend
- Crushed ice, to serve
- Melon balls scooped out from the rest of the melon, to serve (optional)

Serves 1
*V*DF*GF

Put the melon, honey, coconut milk and ice cubes in a blender and blitz until smooth.

Put the crushed ice in a glass and pour the drink over. If desired, serve with a few melon balls on top for fun.

YEMENI LEMOONI
(Cousin to Brazilian lemonade)

Be prepared for that zap of limes, a refreshing minty kick, and a slightly sweet milky finish. This is a thirst-quencher on a hot day, or any day you need to zhuzh up your spirit.

INGREDIENTS:
- 6 limes, peeled, pith removed and halved
- Handful of fresh mint leaves
- 4 tbsp whole milk powder
- 140g (5oz/scant ¾ cup) granulated sugar
- 1 litre (35fl oz/4¼ cups) ice cold water
- Ice cubes, to serve

Serves 6
*V*GF

Place everything except the ice cubes in a blender and blend for 3–5 minutes until super smooth.

Sieve the drink if you prefer an extra-smooth, velvety texture.

Serve the lemooni in glasses over cubed ice.

GO GREEN
(A tribute to the Saudi flag and to Saudi's efforts to go green)

During my recent visit to Saudi Arabia, I was pleasantly surprised by the advancements that they have made as a nation in generating awareness on renewable energy, and their efforts to go green. At the same time, contemporary Saudi cooking and the modernization of their native flavours wowed me. This gleaming, green, super-charged smoothie is my take on a drink that I was served in a luxury hotel on the seafront in Jeddah. Boy, I still remember the addictive taste.

INGREDIENTS:

- 1 banana, sliced and frozen
- ½ small granny smith apple, cubed and frozen
- Juice of 1 lime
- 1 tbsp passionfruit purée (or pulp of a fresh passionfruit, without seeds)
- ½ small guava (preferably an Egyptian or south Asian variety)
- Small handful of baby spinach leaves (optional)
- 1½ tsp green spirulina powder
- 175ml (5½fl oz/¾ cup) coconut water, chilled
- About 1 tsp (or to taste) Yemeni Sidr honey or maple syrup

To serve:

- 1 scoop of mango sorbet (or see tip)
- 1 tsp toasted granola
- 1 tsp crushed roasted almonds
- 1 tbsp cherry compote (see page 266, or use store-bought)
- Edible flowers

Serves 1

★V★DF★GF

In a blender, blend together all the ingredients until smooth.

Put the mango sorbet at the bottom of a serving glass, then pour in the blended smoothie.

Top with the toasted granola, roasted almonds and cherry compote.

Garnish with edible flowers and serve.

TIP: If you don't have mango sorbet, you could also freeze mango purée, then blitz it quickly into a sorbet before use.

SAUDI CHAMPAGNE
(Yes, you read it right – but there is no alcohol in sight!)

Probably the only commonality between French champagne and Saudi "champagne" is the colour. Saudi champagne is a lovely satisfying drink, designed to beat the heat. It is heavily infused with fresh fruit and lots of mint, and built over plenty of ice.

Attractive, sassy and classy, this drink is a modern Saudi concoction that can be enjoyed throughout the year, but it is during Ramadan and outdoor summer parties when it is particularly enjoyable, for me at least!

This is a recipe for a party; it will serve many people, and it can be kept topped up with more lemonade and apple juice, when needed.

INGREDIENTS:

- 1 × 1kg (2¼lb) bag of ice cubes
- 1 red apple (Honeycrisp or Jazz work well), cored and sliced
- 1 Granny Smith apple, cored and sliced
- 1 ripe but firm yellow-flesh peach, sliced
- 1 Jaffa orange, sliced
- 1 unwaxed lemon, sliced
- 1 unwaxed lime, sliced
- Juice of 1 lime
- 1.5 litres (52fl oz/6 cups) clear apple juice
- A bunch of mint
- 660ml (22¼fl oz/2¾ cups) Sprite, or any clear fizzy lemonade

Makes 2.25 litres (2¼ quarts)

★V★DF★GF

Put the ice cubes in a large pitcher (mine is 5.5 litres/6 quarts) or a vessel with a tap attachment. Add all of the sliced fruit, lime juice, apple juice and mint, stir and let it sit for a few minutes. At this stage you can also leave it in the fridge to let the fruity flavours infuse.

Just before serving, top up with the lemonade, stir thoroughly and enjoy.

SAUDI FRUIT COCKTAIL
(Fruit punch to you and me)

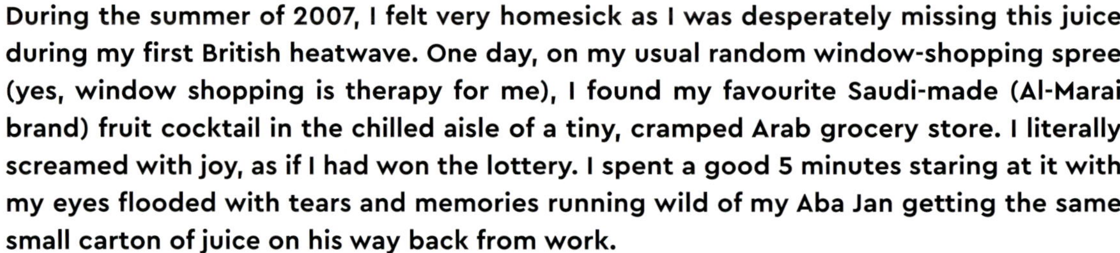

During the summer of 2007, I felt very homesick as I was desperately missing this juice during my first British heatwave. One day, on my usual random window-shopping spree (yes, window shopping is therapy for me), I found my favourite Saudi-made (Al-Marai brand) fruit cocktail in the chilled aisle of a tiny, cramped Arab grocery store. I literally screamed with joy, as if I had won the lottery. I spent a good 5 minutes staring at it with my eyes flooded with tears and memories running wild of my Aba Jan getting the same small carton of juice on his way back from work.

Finally, I gathered myself from an emotional meltdown, put my hand in my purse and found £1.63, which was thankfully enough. I bought it, came home, and enjoyed it to the very last drop, tipping the carton upside down and squeezing every precious bit of juice into my mouth in a way that satisfied my soul. I flipped the carton over and read the ingredients, thinking of recreating it at home. This is what I came up with; it's almost there, if I say so myself.

INGREDIENTS:

- 2 heaped tbsp canned mixed fruit cocktail in syrup, plus 2 tbsp syrup from the can
- 5–6 strawberries, hulled and frozen (store-bought frozen can be used)
- 2 raspberries (frozen or fresh)
- ½ small banana, sliced and frozen
- 1 small guava, peeled and cut into chunks
- 150ml (5fl oz/scant ⅔ cup) coconut water
- Dash of vanilla extract (optional)
- Crushed ice, to serve

Serves 1
★V★DF★GF

Blend everything together in a blender until smooth.

Put crushed ice in a glass (if you like super chilled, as I do), pour the smoothie over and serve.

الربيع
فواكه
مشكلة
نكتار
استمتع بالخيرات

SOUBYA
(A Saudi version of lemon and barley water)

Due to its cooling properties, soubya is very popular during the month of Ramadan. It can be made as a red or white variation, depending on whether you add hibiscus syrup. I tend to use the leftover hibiscus syrup from my poached pear recipe (see page 247).

Local to Makkah and Jeddah, soubya is a light, sweetened drink, just like a juicy ale, except it is not alcoholic. Because the key ingredients – barley, flour, sugar, raisins and water – used to make this blissful drink are similar to those used in beer brewing, it is often referred to as *halal nabeeth*, which translates literally into "halal wine". Soubya is not left long enough to produce the alcohol content in the beverage.

INGREDIENTS:

- 2 large brown pitta breads or ½ loaf wholemeal sourdough, torn into pieces
- 1 white dinner roll, torn into small pieces
- Pinch of dried yeast (not needed if using sourdough)
- 1 tbsp black raisins (or any raisins)
- 3–4 pitted dates
- 1½ tsp ground cardamom
- 1½ tsp ground sweet cinnamon
- 100g (3½oz) crushed pearl barley (see tip)
- A generous pinch of salt
- 150g (5½oz) sugar or honey (plus more to taste)
- 250ml (9fl oz/1 cup) hibiscus syrup (see page 247), if you are making the red version
- Ice cubes, to serve

Serves 6
★V★DF

Place all of the ingredients (except the hibiscus syrup and ice) in a plastic or glass container with a lid and add 1 litre (35fl oz/4¼ cups) water. Let the mixture infuse for 24–48 hours in a dark corner of your house – the longer you leave it to ferment, the stronger the taste will be.

Strain the liquid through a sieve lined with a muslin cloth, squeezing every single drop out of it. Discard the solids left in the cloth – or see my tip below. Dilute the liquid with water to your desired consistency and flavour, add the hibiscus syrup (if using), and adjust the sweetness. Serve the soubya in glasses over cubed ice.

TIP: Crushed pearl barley is readily available in Arab shops and online speciality stores, but if you can't find it, you can grind whole pearl barley in a coffee or spice grinder until coarsely crushed.

Rather than discarding them, you can make use of the fermented solids in the sieve. I usually spread them out on a baking tray, drizzle with a little olive oil and bake in an oven preheated to 120°C (250°F), gas 1, for 20 minutes, or until dried out, stirring a couple of times during cooking to break up any large lumps. Once cool, break into bite-sized crumbs. I use it as a crunchy topping on my breakfast yogurt instead of granola.

ZAA ZAA
(An avocado shake like no other)

Originating from Morocco, this silky smooth and creamy avocado milkshake is in a league of its own. It is a perfect thirst-quencher that will keep you full and satisfied for a while.

What's more, the way it is served – with strikingly bright layers of fruit – melts away the stubbornness of even the toughest, pickiest critics (children), so they at least give it a go. Before you know it, they have gulped it down.

INGREDIENTS:

- 2 large avocados, peeled, pitted and chilled
- 600ml (21fl oz/2½ cups) whole milk or any non-dairy alternative
- 4 tbsp caster (granulated) sugar or 5–6 medjool dates (adjust the sweetness to taste)
- 5 almonds
- 5 cashews
- 5 pistachios
- A drop or two of vanilla extract (optional)
- A handful of ice cubes

To serve (suggestions):

- Fruit
- Chopped or slivered nuts
- Sweet treats (such as squares of chocolate or chocolate flakes)

Serves 4

★V★DF★GF

Add all the shake ingredients to a blender and blend until smooth.

In tall serving glasses, build the drinks by placing your choice of fruit, nuts and chocolate at the bottom, then pour over the luscious milkshake.

Garnish with more fruit and nuts. Serve chilled.

QAHWA EL-LOZ
(Saudi almond coffee with no coffee beans in sight)

Nutritious, soul-warming, aromatic and comforting, this drink swiftly found its way to being my firm companion during the constantly cold and wet autumnal evenings when I arrived in the UK. This cosy drink washed away my homesickness blues and is now so loved by my clan that it has become a permanent winter resident at my home. It's a home-away-from-home kind of feeling.

INGREDIENTS:

- ½ tsp ground green cardamom
- 2 tbsp kewra (screwpine) water, rose water, or orange blossom water
- 1 litre (35fl oz/4¼ cups) whole milk
- 60g (2oz) rice flour
- 75g (2¾oz/heaped ½ cup) blanched almonds, slivered or roughly ground
- 50g (1¾oz/¼ cup) sugar

To serve:

- Ground cardamom
- Ground sweet cinnamon
- Cocoa powder (optional)
- Toasted almond flakes
- Tiny drizzle of honey (optional)

Serves 4–6

⋆V⋆GF

Soak the ground cardamom in the kewra water (or rose or orange blossom water) and set aside.

In a saucepan, whisk the milk, rice flour, almonds and sugar together, ensuring there are no lumps. Place the pan on a medium heat, stirring constantly until it comes to the boil – it will take about 5 minutes.

Lower the heat and let the milk simmer for another 5–7 minutes, stirring constantly. Once it reaches a thin custard consistency, turn off the heat. Add the soaked cardamom and stir thoroughly.

Pour the almond coffee into cups or mugs and garnish with a sprinkling of ground spices and cocoa powder, if wished. Top it up with a hefty amount of toasted almond flakes, drizzle with honey, if using, and serve hot.

THE SAUDI COFFEE CULTURE

القهوه خص و الشاى قص

Coffee with intention and tea with flow

(Arab proverb)

A light roast and a coffee that mirrors liquid gold. An elixir with spicy, floral and woody undertones, handcrafted for those who appreciate coffee and its origins. That's Saudi coffee in a nutshell.

Now, I could certainly write a whole book on Saudi coffee, but that is not the aim of this book, so without delving too much into history, let's talk Saudi coffee culture. Coffee (qahwa) has been an integral part of Saudi tradition dating back to old Silk Route trading, one of the priciest commodities to be exported by the Arab traders, and hence coffee was introduced to the world.

Bursting the historic bubble and moving on to the modern-day Saudi Arabia, the coffee and the artisanal café-culture scene gleaming with modern Instagrammable interiors is unparalleled. You will find some of the best coffees and concoctions in the world in Riyadh, the Royal capital and sparkling financial district of Saudi Arabia (sorry my Italian friends, the Saudis have got this).

Here is a brief introduction to the coffee baskets of Saudi Arabia. There are three main regions in the kingdom – Jazan, Aseer and Al Baha – that produce specialist coffee tree varieties, their roots going back to many centuries of local farming. These emerald-green landscapes are nestled in the most southern and southwestern plateaus of Saudi Arabia, closest to the historic coffee bean producers like Yemen and Ethiopia. These regions are also found within the "bean belt" of the equatorial zone between the two tropics of Cancer and Capricorn. Their climate, altitude and mineral-rich, fertile lands create the best conditions for high-quality coffee production.

Jazan

There is a majesty to the Jazan mountain range and the everlasting bounty of "pearling basket" harbour. Its diverse flora and fauna thrive in its deep forests and the quiet shores of the Farasan Islands (a marine sanctuary). Jazan is the largest coffee producer in the kingdom.

Nestled along the sapphire fringe of the Red Sea in Saudi Arabia's southwestern corner, the Jazan region unfolds like a Bedouin carpet, full of surprising artistry. Here, ancient mountains brood over fertile plains, and the salt-kissed air of the sea brushes against orchards bursting with coffee berries, mangoes, papayas and the rare Sidr honey.

Jazan is a place that hums with the rhythm of the heart, slow and gentle. Distant folk songs in the air as the fishermen return with their boats full of the catch at dawn, with the clink of coffee cups in palm tree-woven shaded courtyards, with the rustle of palm fronds swaying in a desert wind that smells faintly of cardamom and sea salt. It is home to the iconic red coral reefs, so rich they seem to breathe colour.

Aseer and its Famous Flower Men

The flower men of Aseer, a term coined by Thierry Mauger, refers to the local coffee picker men who often wear bright floral headpieces made up of dazzling yellow, ombre orange and sometimes vibrant maroon marigolds. Humming and singing traditional folklore, they wear a striped shirt like a humbug in a vast emerald-green landscape. They make their way through the coffee plantation to pick the bright-red ripe coffee berries, a well-curated topiary, a sight to behold.

There about 300 coffee farms in the Aseer region, mostly family-run, and they have been in the families for a few generations, each distinctive and proud in its own right.

Al Baha, the Garden of Hijaz

This is the land of Shadawi coffee beans. Apparently it's the most difficult variety to cultivate, according to the local producers, but it is well worth the agony as it is one of the best coffee varieties produced in Saudi Arabia.

Regional Roasts and the Making of Saudi Coffee

HIJAZ WESTERN REGION: This is the most revered region of Saudi Arabia, land of the two holiest sites for Muslims, Makkah (Mecca) and Medina. Located on the crossroads of the old Silk Route, this is a melting pot of diversity, and the coffee here says it all. It is a light golden to medium roast that is then brewed with hefty amounts of freshly pounded cardamom and floral mastic resin. Often accompanied by a selection of premium dates and Taawa (see page 66).

NORTHERN REGION: Mesopotamian influences play a key role in defining how locals prefer their coffee here. The roast is very dark, showcasing the bordering Jordanian culture. Brewed low and slow with either cardamom or saffron for a good half an hour, this is probably the longest brew anywhere in the kingdom.

SOUTHERN REGION: The heart of Saudi coffee growing. Bordering with Yemen, the luscious green region has miles upon miles of fruiting landscape and cooler weather. The coffee roast is lightest of all here, retaining a hint of green colour. It is infused with fiery ginger root, fennel seeds, cinnamon, sometimes cloves (usually during winter), saffron and cardamom.

EASTERN REGION: An ancient date palm oasis and once home to the great Dilmun Civilization, the easternmost part of Saudi Arabia connected the trade routes to Asia. Coffee here is roasted to a beige-brown medium roast that unlocks its nutty taste. It is usually infused with saffron and cardamom for 10–15 minutes. Served with the famous Khalas dates or, as I do, with Qashd al-Tamr (page 240).

NAJD CENTRAL REGION: As this is the royal seat, they love to indulge their guests in luxury, and that starts right at the doorstep with qahwa. The most glistening coloured coffee, medium-roast and heavily infused with cloves, cardamom and saffron, which are steeped for a few minutes rather than vigorously boiled. The end result is a smooth, aromatic, velvety coffee. It's warm, verdant and with a piercing golden colour. One whiff of it and your tiredness is gone.

The Etiquette of Serving Saudi Coffee

Despite the modernization of the country, a few traditions still remain the same, and serving qahwa is one of them. Its tools may have changed over time but the customs remain intact.

Qahwa is served in a very traditional pot with a particular crescent-shaped spout and appearance known as dallah and little bone china cups called finjan. Typically a dallah is made of silver, copper or brass, but other metals are now used as part of commercialization.

Then comes the art of pouring and serving the coffee. This is usually the responsibility of the youngest adult hosting in the room. Not out of servitude but as part of their training to host guests; it's a responsibility and honour for them.

The stacked-up little finjan cups are held in the right hand, which is a skill in its own right. Nowadays little caddies to hold these cups are also available, but holding them in hand is still preferable. The dallah brimming with coffee is held in the left hand.

The person holding the coffee approaches the guest (the eldest first) and without uttering a single word the server clinks the cups to the pot to grab the guest's attention. The server then pours in the coffee, filling up about a third of the finjan, and serves the guest. This is called a *hishma* pour. A bit more will send signals to the guest that he/she is not welcomed. The serving continues, and the server keeps on refilling the cups until the guest raises the cup and shakes it gently like a little bell, meaning "Thank you, I've had enough."

Enough on the coffee talk, let's make a nice dallah of coffee now...

SAUDI COFFEE
(Qahwa, or Gahwa)

In the Saudi dialect of Arabic, a Q is pronounced as a G. Every region and family has their preferred method for making coffee. This one is from the Hijaz Region, the coastal area on the mighty Red Sea. It's also my favourite – it's lighter, less acidic, fruitier and nuttier than other versions.

This coffee is best served with sweets, date cookies or fresh dates – or Qashd al-Tamr (see page 240).

INGREDIENTS:

- 6–8 strands of saffron (depending on the intensity you prefer)
- 35g (1¼oz) light to medium roasted coffee beans (I use Arabica or Ethiopian beans), coarsely ground
- 15g (½oz) freshly ground green cardamom
- ¼ tsp ground ginger
- 1–2 cloves (optional)

Makes 1 litre (35fl oz)
★V★DF★GF

In a heavy-based saucepan or electric dallah (specific Arab coffee pot with a long beak-like spout), boil 1 litre (35fl oz/4 cups) of water.

Once the water starts to boil, add the saffron and ground coffee together. Give it a good stir, cover and let the coffee brew on a low heat for 20–25 minutes, until the coffee grounds bloom and start to settle at the bottom.

Now add the cardamom, ginger and cloves (if using – I personally don't like them in my coffee) and let it brew for another 2–3 minutes on a low-medium heat, so that the spices infuse the coffee.

Sieve the coffee, pour it into a serving dallah and serve it in finjans (specific Arab cups for this coffee), filling only halfway up, or in standard espresso cups.

SHUKRAN
(Acknowledgement, a big thank you, an afterword)

I always thought that acknowledgements in books were kind of pointless: why are they even in the book? It is like preparing for an award speech without having won anything. And then I wrote this mammoth of a book. It just made me realise that how grateful I am to so many people who have contributed to my entire existence as well as this book.

You don't have to read it unless you are like me, someone who actually starts reading a book from back to front. Sounds crazy, I know.

This cookbook is a bit of a memoir revolving around Aba Jan (my beloved dad) who has moved to his eternal abode. My whole fairytale bubble is a lost world forever now. But I am so glad that I wrote down those beautiful memories of time well spent together. So thank you Aba Jan, for living in it with me – for us.

It took me six long years to write this book. Losing Aba Jan, having a rainbow baby who fell to sepsis but came back fighting strong, ploughing through a pandemic that brought the world to its knees, suffering from post-natal depression and panic attacks (as if there was a space for that in my life) – in between all of this chaos, I entered the realms of MasterChef UK, giving birth to my bundle of joy before putting an end to my birthing canal.

This book started its journey on my flight back to UK after Aba Jan's funeral. Little did I know I would end up writing in A&E hospital corridors, labour rooms, mosques, amidst grief, in fish markets, in a Premier Inn and during dark, long, lonely nights with a very poorly baby to nurse, checking if he is breathing. You don't write under such circumstances without a strong supporting village of talented people.

I wanted to set this book into the context of time and the longing of a land where I once lived, and to give Aba Jan the applaudable ending he deserved. The man who made me laugh in my bleak moments, who made me hug trees (yes, I am a tree hugger, particularly date palms). Both of us, grand prix fanatics. I never thought I would write my dad an ending, but here we are. I am glad I wrote about him and us here. I am glad there is somewhere where he is alive and will always be. I am glad you get to know him.

I don't suffer from post-natal depression anymore, nor do I have to count every single penny in my pocket to buy a small carton of Saudi fruit cocktail. I have a nice little house with a fruiting garden, bustling with all sorts of happy, chirpy noises and voices. And I have a garage that has been my very secret pantry. I buy fancy ingredients, some of which I don't even know, and cook every single day... well, almost!

Sometimes, I cook elaborate dinners out of the blue just to surprise my lot. Sometimes I wake up in the middle of night, make a nice mug of almond coffee (page 282) and sit on the doorstep of my house so as not to wake up anyone from their beauty sleep. I can't believe how blessed I am to be able to write these words in a way that resonates with so many of us and makes sense to us all.

Maybe you are going through a rough patch or struggling in life while reading this book. I just want to say to you: hold on, for the love of whoever you believe in, hold on tight. Everything that you fear will come to pass. Everything that I ever feared in my life or ran away from or never thought about, happened to me, but I survived and here I am. I have cried a lot, lost a lot, slept hungry a lot, and lived through a failed relationship and being made redundant. I am like you and everyone else, a mere mortal. I am grateful to be alive and happy.

I am writing it to you: to hang onto life because there is light at the end of the tunnel. Your struggles will pass. Hang on. There is always something worth living for.

I wanted to write this piece, because we often don't talk about mental health as we should. This for my children when I am no longer around. They will have my words for comfort and to take hard time by its horns and slay it.

So a heartfelt Shukran (thank you in Arabic) to all who have made this book possible.

SHUKRAN Aba Jan for being part of my life. Aba Jan, how could I ever thank you?

To my mother, we are good friends.

To Saima, you nestled me as an elder sister when I was a stranger in a country I now call home.

To my Saudi friends, neighbours (Abui, Umi Qamar, Bilqees, Osama, Nu and Salwa; may this book find you soon), fish mongers, street hawkers, restaurateurs, date and coffee farmers and everyone who has contributed to the making of this book.

To my beloved husband, a big shout-out for the invaluable help in all sorts of ways, for the expert advice, charring the toast, tasting endlessly with a poker face, driving me to places, bearing with my hormonal mood swings and babysitting our 3 buzz balls. You have lived up to your wedding vows. I love you.

To my very lovely agent and a friend, Darryl. For handling very gracefully all the troubles that I gave you.

To my amazing commissioning editor and editorial director, Ella Chappell, thank you for hearing me out and honouring my vision for The Red Sea. For bringing a dream team together for this project and to the wider team at Watkins.

For the beautiful book cover and the entire stunning book design, thank you Karen Smith. I know I have been a pain; for that I am ever so sorry.

To the lovely duo of food stylists, Polly and Susannah, your work shines through and thank you for cooking on the first hottest day of the year and rescuing that pineapple cake from melting away.

To Patricia Niven the Great, where do I even start? You have brought this book and my memories to life. Your peerless photography is magical. You are a creative genius.

And to all those who follow me on Instagram, Facebook and TikTok, without your continuing support this book would not have been possible. Thank you, thank you, thank you, lovely people.

Madeeha Qureshi, July 2025

INDEX

A

aish abou lahem (spiced lamb galette) 96–8, **97**
aish al jazar (carrot rice) 169–70, **171**
Al Baha 288
al ulawi soup 30–2, **31**
almond 104–5, 124–6, 168, 187, 227–8, 247–50, 251–4, 282
  hawaij spiced crunchy nuts **180**, 186
  Saudi almond coffee 284, **285**
amba **180**, 182
anchovy 17
apple 274, 276
apricot
  debyaza 251–3, **252**
  roast apricot, whipped labneh, caramelized pistachios and candy floss **244**, 245–6
areeka malakiya 241–2, **243**
Aseer 288
aseer shammam (cantaloupe melon celebration) **273–4**, 274
ashta/qashta 227–8
aubergine (eggplant) 173–4
  3H baked aubergine, fig and feta salad with orange-tahini dressing 86–8, **87**
  stuffed aubergine roll mops with garlicky labneh 54, **55**
  tahini aubergine and cauliflower tray bake **140**, 141–2, **142**
  a very relaxed aubergine fatteh 137–8, **139**
avocado shake 282, **283**

B

baleela **34**, 35–6
banana 241–2, 264–6, 272, 274, 278
batata harra, sweet potato 61
bay leaves 20
BBQ sauce, pomegranate 119–20, **121**
bean(s) 17, 76–9, 169–70, 173–4
  tuna and butter bean salad **83**, 85
  see also fava bean
beansprouts 76–9
beef
  farmouza **208**, 209–10
  Medinian buffs 26–8, **27**
  stuffed vine leaves cooked in beef trotter broth 106–9, **107**
  taawa keema 110–12, **111**
beetroot (pickled) **34**, 35–6
  funky pinky beetroot hummus **48**, 52, **52**
  whipped feta dip with pickled beetroot, dill and pistachios **56**, 57
black pepper 20
bread 15, 157–74, 280
  2 types of naan 160–1
  beehive bread 211–12, **213**
  fatoot 162–4, **163**
  pitta bread 137–8, 141–2, 166, **167**, 280
  Yemeni paratha flat bread 165
brittle, cornflake 247–50, **249**
buffs, Medinian 26–8, **27**
bulghur (cracked) wheat
  burghul pillav 113–14, **115**
  harees 128–30, **129**
  tabouleh **82**, 84
butter 15–16
  butter naan 160
  citrusy garlic 146–8, **147**
  garlic 161
butter bean (lima bean) 173–4
  tuna and butter bean salad **83**, 85
buttermilk mastic panna cotta topped with debyaza 251–3, **252**

C

cabbage 76–9
cakes 199–235
  orange **220**, 221–2
  pineapple fresh cream 232, **233–5**
canned produce 17
caramel
  passionfruit and mango caramel dip 232, **233–5**
  salted date caramel sauce 264–6, **265**
cardamom 20
carrot 33, 76–9, 99–100, 106–9, 124–6, 173–4
  carrot rice 169–70, **171**
  heritage carrot salad **74**, 75
cashew nut 104–5, 131–2, 168, 241–2, 251–3, 282
  hawaij spiced crunchy nuts **180**, 186
  sh'ariyah 254, **255**
cauliflower and aubergine tahini tray bake **140**, 141–2, **142**
Champagne, Saudi 276, **277**
chana dal 96–8
cheese 15
  areeka malakiya 241–2, **243**
  beehive bread 211–12, **213**

chilli-Cheddar crisp 33
muhammarah parcels 217–18, **219**
Yemen lahsa 62, **63**
see also cream cheese; feta; goat's cheese; halloumi
cheesecake, the iconic kunafa chocolate bar Basque cheesecake 229–30, **231**
cherry compote 264–6, **265**
chicken
al ulawi soup 30–2, **31**
mutabbaq **39**, 40
Moroccan harissa chicken with burghul pillav 113–14, **115**
Saudi coffee & hawaij sticky chicken wings with pomegranate BBQ sauce 119–20, **121**
Saudi kabsa 124–6, **127**
Saudi risotto with roast chicken 94, **116**, 117–18
taawa keema (chicken mince on a hot plate) 110–12, **111**
tandoori chicken tenders with hummus **48**, 51, **51**
chicken liver, kammouneh-infused grilled 41–2, **43**
chickpea(s)
baleela **34**, 35–6
chickpea sauce 137–8, **139**
hummus 18, 44–5, **48**, 50–1, **50–1**, 53, **53**
musabaha 37
ta'amiyyah 58–60, **59**
chilli 17, 19
chilli-Cheddar crisp 33
chilli-garlic oil 54, **55**
shatta (hot sauce) **181**, 195
chocolate
areeka malakiya 241–2, **243**
beehive bread 211–12, **213**
the iconic kunafa chocolate bar Basque cheesecake 229–30, **231**
cinnamon 20
citrus 17
citrusy garlic butter 146–8, **147**
see also orange
clotted cream 227–8, 241–2
coconut cream 227–8
coconut (desiccated) 227–8
coconut flakes 254
coconut milk 76–9, 274
coconut (shredded) 240
sassy coconut prawns **64**, 65
coconut water 274, 278
coffee
date and qahwa swirl ice cream 263, 264–6, **265**
etiquette 289
regional roasts 288–9
Saudi almond coffee 284, **285**
Saudi coffee (qahwa) 119–20, **121**, 286–9, 290
compote, cherry 264–6, **265**
condensed milk 241–2, 263, 264–6
condiments 177–97
cookies
ma'amoul tray bake **214**, 215–16
Saudi keleeja 223–4, **225**
coriander (cilantro)
dried 20
fresh 20, 40, 161, 173–4, 183, 192
cornflakes
areeka malakiya 241–2, 264–6
cornflake brittle 247–50, **249**
courgette (zucchini) 75, 99–100, 173–4
couscous, giant **172**, 173–4
crab meat 17
cranberry (dried) 104–5, 168, 251–3
cream 57, 221–2, 229–30, 264–6
crème pâtissière 205–6, **207**
date and qahwa swirl ice cream 263, 264–6, **265**
panna cotta 251–3, **252**
pineapple fresh cream cake 232, **233–5**
pistachio mascarpone cream 229–30, **231**
ricotta cream 247–50, **249**
saffron mascarpone cream 202–4, **203**
see also clotted cream
cream cheese 29
cheesecake 229–30, **231**
crème pâtissière 205–6, **207**
croissants
areeka malakiya 241–2, **243**
Om Ali gone French **226**, 227–8
crumble, date 240
cuckoo's crescent 202–4, **203**
cucumber 57, 75, 76–9, 89, 190
cucumber & mint skanjabeen/lemooni sorbet 258, **258**, **259**
pickles **34**, 35–6
cumin 20
black 19
cumin seed 196
curry
prawn curry 149
samak hamour 154

D
daqqus (Saudi salsa) **180**, 183
date(s) 18, 155, 215–16, 241–2, 251–3
date crumble 240
date and qahwa swirl ice cream 263, 264–6, **265**
pan-fried radicchio and date salad 80, **81**
salted date caramel sauce 264–6, **265**
debyaza 251–3, **252**
desserts 237–66
dipping sauces **64**, 65
dips
passionfruit and mango caramel 232, **233–5**
whipped feta **56**, 57
dressings
orange-tahini 86–8, **87**
shatta-tahini 80, **81**
vinaigrette 89

dried fruit 21
debyaza 251–3, **252**
see also specific dried fruit
drinks 269–90
dukkah *see* Madinian dukkah; Madinian dukkah oil

E
egg 15, 169–70
cakes **220**, 221–2, 232, **233–5**
cheesecake 229–30, **231**
cuckoo's crescent 202–4, **203**
gado-gado salad 76–9, **77**
Medinian buffs 26–8, **27**
mutabbaq **39**, 40
Saudi kabsa 124–6, **127**
washes/glazes 164, 212, **213**
Yemen lahsa 62, **63**
Eid 94, 202–4, **203**, **214**, 215–16, **226**, 227, 239–40, 251–3, **252**
emperor/coral trout fish, fried 152–3, **153**
evaporated milk 241–2, 272

F
falafel's big daddy 58–60, **59**
Farasan Islands 13
farmouza **208**, 209–10
fatoot 162–4, **163**
fatteh, aubergine 137–8, **139**
fava bean
ful iskandarani 134, **135**
hummus bil ful **48**, 49
my ful hasawi **135**, 136
ta'amiyyah 58–60, **59**
feta
3H baked aubergine, fig and feta salad 86–8, **87**
baladi salad with a twist 89
muhammarah parcels 217–18, **219**
whipped feta dip with pickled beetroot, dill and pistachios **56**, 57
fig 251–3
3H baked aubergine, fig and feta salad 86–8, **87**
Madinian dukkah & hot honey baked figs with goat's cheese 44, **45**
fish 17
fried emperor/coral trout fish 152–3, **153**
giant whole fried fish 94
pan-fried red mullet with crushed spicy potatoes & tahiniya sauce 150–1
samak hamour 154
tuna and butter bean salad **83**, 85
flour 16
freekeh 30–2, 128–30
fruit
cuckoo's crescent 202–4, **203**
rainbow tart 205–6, **207**
Saudi fruit cocktail **277**, 278, **279**
see also dried fruit; *specific fruit*
ful 2 ways 134–6, **135**
ful iskandarani 134, **135**
my ful hasawi **135**, 136

G
garlic 17
citrusy garlic butter 146–8, **147**
garlic butter 161
garlic naan 161
garlicky labneh 54, **55**
genoise sponge 232, **233–5**
ghee 16
gherkins 131–2
ginger 17–18, 106–9
glazes 164, 212, **213**
go green **273**, 274, **275**
goat's cheese with Madinian dukkah & hot honey baked figs 44, **45**
grains 17
Greek-style yogurt 15, 86–8, 123, 127, 166, 190
tahini yogurt 137–8, **139**
green bean 76–9, 169–70
guava 274, 278

H
haleeb manjo 272, **272–3**
halloumi cheese with Madinian dukkah oil and mint crisps (veg) 131–2, **133**
harees, my Silk Route 128–30, **129**
harissa
hot harissa honey 46, **47**, 86–8, **87**, **181**, 191
Moroccan harissa chicken with burghul pillav 113–14, **115**
hawaij spice blend **180**, 185
hawaij spiced crunchy nuts 80, **81**, **180**, 186
hawaij sticky chicken wings 119–20, **121**
hazelnut 227–8, 247–50
debyaza 251–3, **252**
Madinian dukkah **180**, 187
herbs 21
hibiscus 280
hibiscus poached pears and ricotta cream with cornflake brittle 247–50, **249**
honey 18
see also hot harissa honey
hooli (daikon radish) 75
hot harissa honey **181**, 191
3H baked aubergine, fig and feta salad with orange-tahini dressing 86–8, **87**
Madinian dukkah & hot honey baked figs with goat's cheese 44, **45**
hummus 18, 46–53
pitch black hummus 53, **53**
roasted red pepper hummus 50, **50**
tandoori chicken tenders with hummus 51, **51**
humr (hot tamarind dip) **180**, 188

I
ice cream
date and qahwa swirl 263, 264–6, **265**

haleeb manjo 272, **272–3**
sundae royale 264–6, **265**

J

jajeek **181**, 190
jam, watermelon pith 179, **181**, 197
Jazan 13, 287
Jeddah 12

K

kabsa, Saudi 93, 124–6, **127**
kammouneh **181**, 196
kammouneh-infused grilled chicken livers 41–2, **43**
kawareh wa kubeibat (stuffed vine leaves cooked in beef trotter broth) 106–9, **107**
kababs, Saudi lamb **122**, 123
keleeja, Saudi 223–4, **225**
khaliyat al nahal (beehive bread) 211–12, **213**
khoya 254
kitchen equipment 21
kunafa chocolate bar Basque cheesecake 229–30, **231**

L

labneh
garlicky 54, **55**
whipped **244**, 245–6
lahm al mandi 94, **102–3**, 104–5
lahsa, Yemen 62, **63**
lamb
al ulawi soup 30–2, **31**
farmouza **208**, 209–10
marqooq 94–5, 99–100, **101**
my Silk Route harees 128–30, **129**
roasted lamb with fragrant jewelled rice 94, **102–3**, 104–5
Saudi lamb kebabs over charcoal **122**, 123
spiced lamb galette 96–8, **97**
taawa keema (lamb mince on a hot plate) 110–12, **111**
lavender 20
peach & lavender sorbet **259**, 261, **261**
leek 96–8
lentil(s) (red) 33
lettuce 76–9, 89
lobster, grilled/broiled 146–8, **147**
loomi (dried lemon) 20, 29, 260

M

ma'amoul tray bake **214**, 215–16
mabshoor (Saudi lamb kebabs over charcoal) **122**, 123
Madinian dukkah **180**, 187
Madinian dukkah & hot honey baked figs with goat's cheese 44, **45**
Madinian dukkah oil 131–2, **133**
maftoul, roasted autumnal vegetable **172**, 173–4
mains 91–142
makarona bil laban 127
mandi 94, **102–3**, 104–5
mango
amba **180**, 182
haleeb manjo 272, **272–3**
passionfruit and mango caramel dip 232, **233–5**
marinades 119–20, **121**, 146–8, **147**
harissa 113–14, **115**
marqooq 94–5, 99–100, **101**
mascarpone cream
pistachio 229–30, **231**
saffron 202–4, **203**
mastic buttermilk panna cotta topped with debyaza 251–3, **252**
melon *see* aseer shammam; watermelon
meringue, cuckoo's crescent 202–4, **203**
milk 15
mint
cucumber & mint skanjabeen/lemooni sorbet 258, **258**, **259**
mint crisps 131–2, **133**
mishmish (roast apricot, whipped labneh, caramelized pistachios and candy floss) **244**, 245–6
mutabbaq 38, **39**, 40
mlawa (flat bread) 165
molasses 19
muhammara parcels 217–18, **219**
mulberry & black lime (loomi) sorbet **259**, 260, **260**
musabaha 37

N

naan
butter 160
garlic 161
nigella seed 19
nut(s) 21
hawaij spiced crunchy nuts 80, **81**, **180**, 186
see also specific nuts

O

oat(s) 30–2
oils 16–17
chilli-garlic 54, **55**
Madinian dukkah 131–2, **133**
olive oil 16–17
olive(s) 89
heritage tomato and olive salad 72, **73**
Om Ali gone French **226**, 227–8
onion 18
orange 75, 168, 276
my very first orange cake **220**, 221–2
orange-tahini dressing 86–8, **87**

P

panna cotta 251–3, **252**
pantries 14–21
paprika 19
parathas 241–2
Yemeni paratha flat bread 165
parsley 89
zhoug **181**, 192, **193**
parsley (flat-leaf) 26–8, 40, 84,

96–8, 146–8, 173–4
parsnip 173–4
passionfruit 274
passionfruit and mango caramel dip 232, **233–5**
pasta, makarona bil laban 127
pastry dishes
farmouza **208**, 209–10
mutabbaq **39**, 40
muhammarah parcels 217–18, **219**
rainbow tart 205–6, **207**
peach 276
peach & lavender sorbet **259**, 261, **261**
peanut
Madinian dukkah **180**, 187
Madinian dukkah oil 131–2, **133**
peanut sauce 76–9, **77**
pear, hibiscus poached pears and ricotta cream with cornflake brittle 247–50, **249**
pearl barley, Saudi lemon and barley water 280, **281**
pecan nut 241–2, 251–3, 264–6
hawaij spiced crunchy nuts **180**, 186
pepper (bell) 85, 89, 173–4, 217–18
roasted red pepper hummus **48**, 50, **50**
pickles **34**, 35–6, 131–2, **133**
pillav, burghul 113–14, **115**
pine nut 86–8, 104–5, 127, 137–8, 141–2, 168
pineapple fresh cream cake 201, 232, **233–5**
pistachio 227–8, 229–30, 264–6, 282
caramelized pistachios **244**, 245–6
debyaza 251–3, **252**
pistachio mascarpone cream 229–30, **231**
sh'ariyah 254, **255**
whipped feta dip with pickled beetroot, dill and pistachios **56**, 57
pitta bread 137–8, 141–2, 166, **167**, 280
pomegranate 19, 141–2
pomegranate BBQ sauce 119–20, **121**
potato 33, 76–9, 106–9
crushed spicy potatoes 150–1
prawn
grilled/broiled lobster and prawns 146–8, **147**
prawn curry 149
sassy coconut prawns **64**, 65
puff pastry dishes
farmouza **208**, 209–10
muhammarah parcels 217–18, **219**
pul biber 19
pumpkin 99–100, 173–4
pumpkin seed 173–4
hawaij spiced crunchy nuts **180**, 186
roasted and salted pumpkin seeds **181**, 194

Q

qahwa (Saudi coffee) 286–9, 290
qahwa & hawaij sticky chicken wings with pomegranate BBQ sauce 119–20, **121**
qahwa el-loz (Saudi almond coffee) 284, **285**
qashd al-tamr (date crumble) 240
quince preserve **180**, 189

R

radicchio, pan-fried radicchio and date salad with tahini and hawaij crunchy nuts 80, **81**
raisin(s) 104–5, 124–6, 168, 251–3, 254, 280
Ramadan 26–8, **27**, 30–2, **31**, 96–100, **97**, **101**, 134, **135**, 202, **208**, 209–10, **214**, 215–16, 239, 251–3, **252**, 276, **277**, 280, **281**
red mullet, pan-fried 150–1
Red Sea 11–13
rice 18, 157–74
basmati 18
carrot 169–70, **171**
fragrant jewelled **102–3**, 104–5
loaded jewelled 168, **168**
my Silk Route harees 128–30, **129**
risotto 18
Saudi kabsa 124–6, **127**
Saudi risotto with roast chicken 94, **116**, 117–18
sella basmati 18
stuffed vine leaves cooked in beef trotter broth 106–9, **107**
ricotta cream 247–50, **249**
risotto 18
Saudi risotto with roast chicken 94, **116**, 117–18
rocket 80, 86–8
roll mops, stuffed aubergine 54, **55**
rose water 20

S

saffron 19
saffron mascarpone cream 202–4, **203**
saffron-infused sugar syrup 254, **255**
Saudi coffee 290
salads 69–89
3H baked aubergine, fig and feta 86–8, **87**
baladi 89
gado-gado 76–9, **77**
heritage carrot **74**, 75
heritage tomato and olive 72, **73**
pan-fried radicchio and date 80, **81**
tabouleh **82**, 84
tuna and butter bean **83**, 85
saleeq (Saudi risotto with roast chicken) 94, **116**, 117–18
saloonat rubyan (prawn curry) 149

salsa, daqqus **180**, 183
salt 16
salted date caramel sauce 264–6, **265**
samak hamour 154
seafood 17, 143–54
seed(s) 21
see *also specific seeds*
semolina 215–16
shaoor/najal maghli (fried emperor/coral trout fish) 152–3, **153**
sh'ariyah 254, **255**
shatta (hot sauce) **181**, 195
shatta-tahini dressing 80, **81**
shorba adas with chilli-Cheddar crisp 33
small plates 23–66
sorbet
cucumber & mint skanjabeen/lemooni 258, **258**, **259**
mulberry & black lime **259**, 260, **260**
peach & lavender **259**, 261, **261**
watermelon & marjoram 262, **262**
soubya (Saudi lemon and barley water) 280, **281**
soups
al ulawi 30–2, **31**
shorba adas 33
spices 19–20
spinach 76–9, 274
spirulina 274
squash 173–4
sugar 16
sugar syrup, saffron-infused 254, **255**
sultana(s) 124–6, 227–8, 251–3
sumac 16
sundae royale Saudi style 264–6, **265**
sweet potato batata harra 61
sweetcorn 85
dirty BBQ corn with loomi and Madinian dukkah 29
syrup, saffron-infused sugar 254, **255**

T
ta'miyyah 58–60, **59**
taawa aka mandazi aka bakhumri 66, **67**
taawa keema (mince on a hot plate) 110–12, **111**
tabouleh 71
tabouleh with a Beirut touch **82**, 84
tahini 37, 45, 131–2, 229–30
orange-tahini dressing 86–8, **87**
shatta-tahini dressing 80, **81**
tahini aubergine and cauliflower tray bake **140**, 141–2, **142**
tahini sauce 96–8, **97**
tahini yogurt 137–8, **139**
tahiniya (tahini sauce) 150–1, **180**, 184
tamarind 20
hot tamarind dip **180**, 188
tart, rainbow 205–6, **207**
tofu/tempeh, gado-gado salad 76–9, **77**
tomato 30–2, 40, 62, 84, 89, 96–100, 106–9, 110–12, 124–6, 134, 137–8, 149, 169–70, 173–4, 190, 209–10
daqqus (Saudi salsa) **180**, 183
heritage tomato and olive salad 72, **73**
tuna 17
tuna and butter bean salad **83**, 85
turmeric 19–20

V
vegetables
frozen 18
see also specific vegetables
vermicelli, sh'ariyah 254, **255**
vinaigrette 89
vine leaves, stuffed vine leaves cooked in beef trotter broth 106–9, **107**
vinegar, drizzling **34**, 35–6

W
walnut 46, 217–18, 227–8, 264–6
hawaij spiced crunchy nuts **180**, 186
watercress 86–8
watermelon
watermelon & marjoram sorbet 262, **262**
watermelon pith jam 179, **181**, 197

Y
Yanbu 11
yogurt (natural) 15, 57, 154, 160, 161, 162–4, 166, 184
see also Greek-style yogurt

Z
zaa zaa (avocado shake) 282, **283**
za'atar 16
zhoug **181**, 192, **193**